BRINGING BACK
EDEN

Meditations of a Fly Fisher

ANTHONY
SURAGE

Contact author at:
suragea1@aol.com

ISBN-13: 978-1984129192
ISBN-10: 1984129198

Biblical quotations:
The Holy Bible, New International Version® NIV®
Copyright © 1973, 1978, 1984 by International Bible Society®
Used by permission. All rights reserved worldwide.

"The Tenth Elegy,"
translation copyright © 1982 by Stephen Mitchell; from
Selected Poetry of Rainer Maria Rilke by Rainer Maria Rilke,
translated by Stephen Mitchell.
Used by permission of Random House,
an imprint and division of Penguin Random House LLC.
All rights reserved.

Cover photo:
Cody Ensanian

Illustrations:
Sophia Surage

Cover and interior design:
The Publishing Pro, LLC,
Colorado Springs, Colorado

Dedication

To those who, while fishing ever ponder if Something more than a fish tugs on the line, and who contemplate the immensity and weight of what pulls.

Contents

I   Early Meanders on the Edge of Eden   **1**

II   Spiritual Longings
in the Expanses
of South Park, Colorado   **29**

III   Overcoming Divisions
and Understanding Connections   **65**

IV   The Call   **107**

V   The Pause   **127**

VI   Thousands upon Thousands of Casts   **143**

VII   Moving Out of Convention   **151**

VIII   Shallow Fishing: Going Deeper   **167**

IX   Perhaps There Persists   **179**

X   A Sense of Place, a Habitus   **193**

XI   Daring to Exist?   **215**

XII   Definitively Defeated   **225**

XIII   A Word Spoken In the Vast Silent Spaces   **233**

XIV   Finally Emerging   **247**

I

Early Meanders on the Edge of Eden

❧

A Creek with No Name

For the longest time, I did not know the source of the small creek that flowed into my pond. I did not even know its name. I learned only recently that it is Pearl Creek. It tumbles down from somewhere in the hills of northern New Jersey and through my hometown of West Paterson. Eons ago, when these hills were uplifted mountains and the water ran cold, there might have been brook trout in the creek; not anymore.

The creek meanders through a small valley and then drops down into a ravine behind my childhood home and into the large and dirty Passaic River. I walked to school along this river and sometimes imagined what it was like one hundred years ago. Today, the Passaic is a carp river. It is too warm and dirty to hold trout. Even the bass are gone. This was an unlikely place for a fly fisher of trout to be born.

"Something" of Soul and of Spirit at the Pond

In a small valley at the upper reaches of Pearl Creek, someone at some unknown time created a small earthen dam. The result was a ten-acre lake, which is what I came to call "the pond." This fertile water would teach me not only the art of fly-fishing but *Something* of the depth in my soul that would remain with me for the rest of my life. It is this Something, which I first experienced forty-five years ago and continue to experience through fly-fishing, that I address in this book.

I write as a disillusioned Christian, yet one who believes by faith that I was born of spirit. I believe that my true birth started here at this pond, where gentle breezes first blew down into the valley across my pensive face, rippled on the surface of the pond, and stirred Something in my heart.

"The wind blows wherever it pleases. You hear its
sound, but you cannot tell where it comes from
or where it is going. So it is with everyone born of
Spirit."—John 3:8

Rolf Jacobsen in a poem titled "The Guardian Angel" describes how an angel, without our awareness remains close to our heart. If someone or Something I did not perceive ever walked beside me, it would have happened here the first time.

The pond plays a pivotal role in my story. Norman Maclean in *A River Runs Through It*, spoke of the sound of water being pivotal in his life story. For me, it was perhaps the sight of water and all the searching I did below the surface of the waters I would fish. Perhaps at the pond, the sight of those waters, it was then that my own story began.

Here, at the waters of the pond, Something I could not understand touched my heart and stayed with me throughout the meanders of my life. Beginnings are mysterious places. I wonder why was I born in a certain place and time and how the meanders of a creek affected my life.

In the years to come, I took the biblical story of Eden lost and overlaid it upon my own life story. Throughout my life, I have gained a growing sense that my little story joins with this bigger biblical story, as a small creek joins a larger river. Where they joined and formed a new meander, I felt Something deep within my heart that I would never forget.

Life At the Edge of the Pond

Every day after school, I made a deliberate turn off my neighborhood street onto a trail that took me to the valley of the pond. In doing so, I was consciously veering off and avoiding the kids on the block, preferring to stand alone on the edge of the pond, contemplating its waters. The firm grassy banks of the pond provided me a place of stability. I learned to live and stand on an edge, deeply pondering the water of both the pond and my soul. The quietness of the pond has never left.

At the edge of the pond, I learned to see things differently. I learned to look at life through the lens of the pond. Through that lens, I could see sharper images and to a new depth. Thanks to the pond, I saw life differently even as I struggled to know where I belonged. I wondered to what extent I belonged with groups of people. Somehow, in part because of the pond, I was able to withhold giving my peer group authority over me. My peers and I did not validate each other. I often fished alone, preferring the solitude. I moved at my own pace. I would stand on that edge and wait, hoping that God might meet me there. I am not sure He ever did.

Nevertheless, I learned to wait at the edge of the pond. I would stand alone, even if unsteadily and uncertainly. Edges are not easy places for a boy to stand, trying to figure out where he belongs, especially in the damp winds under a low, gray, and dismal New Jersey sky.

Fire in the Soul: A Flickering Wick

My middle-school years, when I had no peer group, were somewhat difficult. However, this did not extinguish the "flickering wick" of my soul (Isaiah 42:3). It remained lit through the art of fly-fishing. Something burned just enough to sustain me. I ached for a new life that I could barely glimpse from a distance. If I learned to trust my own intuition and stand in the uncertain winds of life, it was here at the pond.

Fly-fishing at the pond allowed me, perhaps by accident, to find Something inside. Pablo Neruda in a poem titled "La Poeisa" spoke of the need to work out the intense fire within the soul. William Butler Yeats spoke of the need to go to the woods because of an inner fire.

I had to make sense of the intense feelings within. I had to take my own path, even though I often felt confused. I took the solitary path to the forest of my soul, using my developing intuition and my love of fly-fishing to decipher the burning fire.

I developed a strong sense of intuition by standing both on the outside edge of my peer group and on the edge of the pond seeking fish. I learned what and who could flame or damper that fire within. I could stand on the banks of the pond, gazing into the waters, feeling alone and disconnected yet lost in the intense mystery of my own solitude. In those moments of loneliness, I noticed I felt strangely connected to Something from beyond but, at the same time, from deeply within.

The Boy with the Golden Fingertips: Peering Below the Surface Waters

What did I perceive when I stood alone on the edge of the pond gazing down into the water? Did I only see fish? Could I see beyond myself? Did I see beyond my forlorn face reflected on the surface? What glimpses of God did I perceive below the surface of the waters? While gazing into those waters, I sometimes went somewhere else. It was wonderful. Perhaps the valley of the pond was what the Celts call a "thin place," a vulnerable place where "Something" could reach me.

Old stories helped me understand. In the old tale of Iron John, a young boy peers into a deep pool of water; a sacred spring. Down deep into that pool, he sees fish of golden hue. The boy has a childhood wound that manifests itself in his finger. After he dips his wounded finger in the clear cold water, he pulls it out and sees his finger has turned gold. The gold will not come off. We might say that his wound is now a sacred wound, and his life will never be the same.

What is the gold I sometimes find associated with my wounds? Could this gold come from my former glory, a time when I remember a world more radiant and whole? William Wordsworth suggested in his poem, "Ode: Intimations of Mortality from Recollections of Early Childhood," that we forgot where we came from when we were born into this world.

Captured in the fleeting images of my distant memory, I am

at times still able to return. Sometimes, perhaps more so as a child,
I got fleeting glimpses of that glorious place. As the sun was setting
and I cast across the waters, I saw shafts of golden light in the sky
and flecks of gold spraying out from my looping fly lines. I, like the
boy in the Iron John story, became aware of my golden fingertips.

I did not know this was happening at the time. Largely without my knowing, I found something gold in the pond waters that I
fished. It took time for me to realize that when I caught a fish and
reached down to unhook it, I was dipping my wounds in these healing waters. When I cast my line across the pond, I was casting off all
my uneasiness and anxieties. As I cast repeatedly, the fly line slid in
between my fingertips peeling off water droplets. Before falling, some
of those droplets lingered on my fingers and became a part of me. I
have remembered this all of my life. Somehow, on the edge of that
pond, I found goldenness, a peculiar otherness, Something I knew I
would never find in full and yet would remain.

Even as a child, I was aware of my golden fingertips when
I cast over the surface of the pond. I felt the rhythm of the cast
synchronizing with my internal rhythms. Forgotten places awakened deep inside me. This awakening was both wonderfully soothing
and yet, at times, overwhelming. Was I remembering Eden, my first
home?

Were these graceful rhythms of casting at the pond a reminder of where I had come from, where I might be going, and how life
could be? Was this sense of feeling golden, however faint, a light
that illumined a path for me to follow and that revealed to me that
there was more to my life than I could ever understand? Was I being
changed, both from what lay behind me and from what lay ahead?

I felt more goldenness on my fingertips when I learned to
hand tie flies. Then I could cast them and watch them sink slowly
below the surface to the places where fish were on the prowl. How

golden I felt, as a child without much power over all that I feared, to be able to craft my own flies and catch fish on them! This sense of goldenness, however scant and fleeting, allowed me to peer deeper into the waters of life and of my own soul. It empowered me to search for the source of all light, grace, fire, rhythm, and beauty. These slight sensations, which were in some sense infinitely heavy, foretold of a Beloved hidden in the beautiful places I would fish.

I wish young children today had what I had, an art and a craft that enabled me to perceive my own goldenness. Rather than connecting with their peer group, in person or via the internet, they would do better with a pond experience of their own that is far removed from the drama and noise of mainstream culture. How disappointing it will be when children realize that the drama they find on their touch screens does not touch their souls.

Type of Eden: The Pond as an Oasis For my Soul

This small New Jersey valley of my childhood and the waters of the pond were an oasis for my soul. It was the garden of my youth. The surrounding hillsides of dense green foliage were protective walls that kept city noise and childhood fears away. I felt enclosed, somewhat safe and secure in the womb of the forest.

Yet the pond and the surrounding forest provided more than protection. The pond provided me with solace and a small oasis that helped preserve the light-green places in my heart. I found relief from the anxieties I encountered as a young boy trying to grow up and find my place of belonging. The pond had its own cadence, which was a strange but wonderful contrast to the fast-paced urban life around me. I felt drawn to the otherness of the pond. While fishing, I felt the dense blanket of hickory and oak wrap gently around me. The forest kept the demands of culture and my peer group from penetrating and influencing my soul. Then I was free to explore the mysterious otherness of the pond and the mystery of my own life.

On the edge of the pond, I received an alternative education that I learned to treasure far more than school. In my five decades I have never had a learning experience comparable to teaching myself to fly-fish at the pond. I cannot imagine how life would have turned out for me if I had never learned to stand so patiently on the banks of the pond. The image of a boy walking on the banks of the pond casting to fish is still with me today, lives inside me, and forms the foundation of my story.

Choosing My Own Pace:
Going to the Wood to Live Deliberately

While I fished, the neighborhood kids rushed to grow up. I fell behind in some sense, even as something inside me grew. Emily Dickinson spoke of letting birds pass her by; she would wait and let late summer bring a fuller tune. Thoreau also spoke of following one's own pace and a different drummer.

I think I did hear a different drummer; a beat from far over the hills and mountains, and was able to, as Thoreau proclaimed, to live with deeper intentions. For the rest of my life, I have listened to that far off drummer even as I wrestled with many questions.

Was that far-off drummer Something revealing my path home? Was it my choice to be alone and follow that path? Did I choose my own pace in order to separate from my peer group, or did they choose not to be with me? Did I just run away from my social anxieties and retreat to the pond? Perhaps, my fears came from deep inside, where anxieties piled upon insecurities. Regardless of the reasons, I developed a deep sense of being alone while I wondered where I truly belonged.

Why did I tend to see so many vast distances that I could not span? Why was I haunted by basic questions: Who am I? Where do I belong? Is God here? Is God anywhere? What is the meaning of my life? I did not know how to answer these questions. I did not even know if these were the questions I should be asking. When I shared these feelings with others, they often were surprised to hear my struggle because, as a child and adult, I was not seen as a misfit. I was a good student and athlete. People often remarked that I was attractive and came from a good family.

When I look back, I wonder if I chose a solitary path for the simple reason that it felt better to be alone. By avoiding the discomforts of social anxiety, was I finding peace in my own solitude? However, in that avoidance did I unconsciously learn to love my inner solitude and associate those intense feelings with the God within my soul. In essence, was I beginning to feel closer to God by being alone and knowing myself better?

At such a young age, my choice to be alone probably had little to do with trying to follow what was right. I doubt that I was thinking about trying to preserve the nobility of my inner soul. If anything, the cultural norm was to be a part of the peer group. Something else was stirring below the surface, deep down in my heart.

As a young angler, I knew that sometimes, when there is nothing happening at the surface, Something down deep stirs, tugs, and swirls. As a fly-fisher, I learned that these sensations are worth paying attention to; they could mean the presence of a big fish. I wonder how many of my fellow anglers have followed their hunches, made a cast, and felt a powerful fish take the fly and leap out of the water?

Did I as a child sense that I could be sustained by whatever I could perceive below the surface waters of the pond? Did I know there was more to life and my loneliness, more that lay just under the reflection of my face? At the pond, I was just beginning to be able to experience a different rhythm that was soothing and in tune with my soul. Perhaps I was able to hear Something worth following. Did I vaguely hope that God, whoever God might be, would meet me at the edge of my loneliness?

When I look back and ask myself if I took the right or wrong path, I realize the complexities of the issues. I cannot easily answer my questions. Perhaps my choice to fish alone was a way of moving beyond, transcending ideas of what was right or wrong for me or for society.

Regardless of right or wrong, I was moving beyond the edges in pursuit of my longing. I was moving out to the meadow of the pond, hoping to meet love and perhaps the Eden I felt I had lost.

A Call to Wilderness

When I fish the wilds of nature today, I often reflect back to the pond and ponder the difficult existential questions of life. I contemplate how the Bible describes God using wilderness to speak to and teach the people of Israel.

> Therefore I am now going to allure her; I will lead
> her into the wilderness and speak tenderly to her.
> Hosea 2:14

I probably first heard the faint whisper of God's tenderness toward me at the little wilderness of the pond.

It think it took God only one springtime at the pond to win me over; I could have been smitten by just one gentle breeze against my face, the smell of sweet grass and clover in early morning, or the sight of silver bass chasing dragonflies. Or was it one bass tugging on the line after I watched it chase one of my hand-tied flies. With all this wonder and beauty, I had to acknowledge in the secret places of my heart that it came from Something beyond me, and I longed to know the source.

Wonder and beauty was enough to woo me, yet I was then and continue to be without complete understanding. Can I still respond although I remain so ignorant? Can I choose to believe that I really heard a tender voice in some wild form?

A voice, if I choose to believe it, led a fearful boy to a small path through the forest, into a valley, and to the edge of a small lake where he discovered some sense of his place in the world.

The Concrete World of the Pond

I have no way of verifying that I have been called by Something. I know that my pond was and still is a real place of water, earth, muck, moss, lily pads, dragon flies, and fish. I have stood on the stable banks of the pond and cast. The banks gave the pond concrete, distinct boundaries, contained its waters; they also helped me develop inner boundaries that contained my racing thoughts and anxieties. The banks of the pond and the surrounding forest held me together, provided me with limits, and gave me stability. This stability allowed me to at least begin to consider what was spiritual; the idea of being called.

Beyond the valley and the pond, there were neighborhoods, suburbs, and cities with millions of people whom I did not know and who did not know me. The masses of people were overwhelming to me. In time I imagined that there was Something else beyond those masses of people in suburbia, perhaps a place where I might belong. However, as a child I did not spend much time focusing on the chaos in those places. The pond was the special place where I could focus on the present moment. I could focus on what I could see and hold in my hands. I could focus on the silvery fish moving through the waters. When I caught one of those bass and held it in my hands, perhaps Something held me.

Then and now, I have been blessed to live in a real world that I can concretely feel, smell, and see, even as I try to understand the mysterious meanings of my existence. How could I ever even begin to understand spiritual things if I did not first understand earthly things? (John 3:12). When I was a child, it was enough for me to glimpse the fish that swam along the edges of the pond, cast to them, and then feel the tug at the end of my line. In the coming years, I would try to understand the deeper mysteries both beyond and within my own life. However, as a child it was sufficient to grasp in my hands the fish I caught. In fact, it was these tactile sensations that gave me my first glimpses of God.

Regardless of where I find myself in life, finding my way to a pond or a river with a fly rod in hand keeps my spirit alive. Whether I am looking heavenward for the greater things to come, living in the quiet of the present moment, or unraveling inside, I need to plant my feet firmly on the banks of a lake or on the bottom of a river and cast into the waters with hope. It is a blessing beyond belief. It is a most profound human, emotional, intellectual, and spiritual achievement.

Then again, maybe I need to redefine true achievement and occupation. Emily Dickinson considered it her occupation to gather paradise by spreading her narrow hands. Perhaps I too can find Something of Eden and this is my real occupation.

As a fly fisher, I can expand my casts outward over the waters I fish, and, in that process, I can open my heart to gather Something of paradise found in the natural world. Too often I live with narrow hands, failing to take in the life and beauty all around me. I also often fail to widen my narrow hands to accept people who are different or make different choices than I. In essence, in my own narrowness, I fail to love.

How blessed I was as a boy to be able to walk to the pond and stand upon its banks, to feel sunlight on my face, to wade into those waters and have my feet sink in the muck. How enlivening to look into those waters and find fish lurking along the bottom. How wonderful to feel and smell the earth. How luminous for a boy to be able to cast again and again in search of spotted, silvery fish.

How could I ever have learned such profound things from inside a school or church building or from books and computers? There was no limit to what I could learn by walking the edges of the pond, standing on its banks, and feeling the cool waters around my ankles as I studied my quarry. How grounding simply to walk, taking in this small world (yet infinitely large) of water, earth, sun, and life. What an incredible preparation for me to discover this whole other world, a world of wonder and awe and that could not only ground me but lift me in soaring contemplation.

There were discoveries. I felt each curve of the valley and pond. I learned intimately that the pond had three distinct coves, all with big fish, coves that would reach into my soul.

There was a cove with a prominent overhanging tree. Here I would cast white marabou streamers and popping bugs to a 24-inch bass hiding in the shade. It lived under that tree, and I came so close to landing it. This elusive fish and its sheltering tree are etched into my memory. Those images gave me a sense of familiarity when I fished near other trees in other places.

As the years past, I would become acquainted with other trees along the river of life. There was the tree of life in the garden. There was the reference to how an individual who meditates

on God's word is like a tree firmly planted by the waters (Psalm 1:3).
I developed a sense of the archetypal tree that would remain with
me and allow me to seek deeper nourishment below the surface level
of life. At times in life, I would miss this tree, ache for it, and in the
silence of my heart call out to her, wondering where she had gone. A
smaller cove had weed beds and a firm, inviting grass bank with trees
set back just enough for me to cast. Here I learned to discipline my
back cast. Many bass prowled the waters in this cove. Here is where
I learned to fish edges as I learned to cast to the open pockets and
strip flies along the edges of the weed beds. Dragonflies would land
on the weed beds and lay their eggs. Bass would leap out of the water
after them. I was amazed at how fluttering wings hovering over the
water could draw up big bass from below, exploding out of the water.

The last cove contained the inlet of Pearl Creek, which provided the source of water for the pond. I never explored and bush-
whacked up this creek to find its origin. Was there a bubbling spring?
I do not know. However, as a child it was enough for me to stay at
the pond and learn to entice the heavy bass that would congregate
in the inlet area. I would be satisfied to feel the fly line slip through
my fingertips as a heavy bass pulled out line. Perhaps now, if only, in
my imagination, I might take that journey up the creek to find the
source. Perhaps if I do so, I might find the true source of my life that
always seems to loom in the far off distant hillsides.

One side of the pond had a small sand beach and white
wooden docks built out over the water. Big bass hid under the docks
in the shadows. I learned to cast and retrieve my streamers along the
edge of the docks so that the bass would dart up to strike. Behind the
beach were some storage buildings that contained tubes and rafts
and different types of swimming equipment for the kids who came to
summer camp. These storage buildings, of no interest at first, came
to have significance to me.

Summer Camp and Distant Clamor at the Pond

The pond served as a summer day camp for kids. Parents dropped their kids off at the pond and then commuted to work in New York City. I quickly learned there was a drastic contrast between the pond and the hectic life of New York City. When I was several years older, I used to climb a small mountain and view the New York City skyline. The lights of cars, trucks, and suburbs overwhelmed me. Who was I among the millions of flickering lights?

To me, New York City was the definition of rat race. The rats scurried down highways and byways, merged into tollbooths, squeezed through tunnels and over bridges—all rushing to make a living. I was not a part of that world and never would be. In one of his songs, Bruce Springsteen called it a "death trap" and a "suicide rap." By the time, I officially joined the work force I was gone to the mountains of Colorado.

At camp, the kids, who were mostly my age at the time, swam in the beach and dock area, creating an uproar that I could hear from the far side of the pond. Even when I fished the cove on the far side of the pond, the clamor annoyed me. I would move away from the noise. Some people would call the hum of the voices a type of white noise. True, I could not decipher the words, but the hum was not benevolent. At best, I felt detached from the crowd of kids. They were in their world, and I was in mine. They were in my way like a noisy mob interfering with the quiet place inside my soul. However, in my loneliness I wondered if any of them thought and felt like me. So in some sense, although estranged from them, I was curious about them even as I fished in my own world.

I now wonder if any of those kids, even just one, ever glanced across the pond and, with curiosity, noticed the movements I was making with my fly rod. Did anyone ever notice how the fly line was looping through the air? Did anyone ever see the big bass take the fly and bend the rod? Was I, in part, casting for *them*?

Did any one of them ever look across the surface of the water and, even for a moment, leave the hum of the crowd, and share a moment of fishing with me. Maybe there was one child who found herself alone in that crowd, who for a moment glanced toward me and, without my knowing, entered my world under the shade of an overhanging tree. At times, I remember her.

I wonder if that same golden-haired girl ever wandered into the forest, and listened to the Something heard under the hum of dragonfly wings, songbirds, and rustling leaves. Did she ever prefer to be away from the clamor and to be in the quiet of the woods where she might experience, if only for a moment, a deeper sense of her own belonging? Did she ever contemplate some deeper meaning of her life as she lay on the cool, mossy forest floor under the shade of a tree and listened to the silent song of the forest? Did she, with me, hear the same song?

Because I mostly fished in the early morning before the crowds arrived, I don't think I ever saw the girl with the golden hair again. If I had seen her, I probably would have tried to possess her as part of the garden, my Eden, along with the fish and the trees. Yet she always remained at the edges of my imagination. In the coming years, I saw glimpses of her in the canyons and meadows that I would explore and fish, but she remained elusive, the one that got away.

The more I fished the pond, the more possessive I grew of the pond and the solitude it offered me. I belonged more to the pond than to my school and the adults in the rat race.

However, as much as I loved the pond, I would learn that it was not mine.

The Grounds Keeper:
An Unlikely Guardian of Eden

A groundskeeper watched over the pond and the valley. He was a guardian of sorts, protecting the pond and the storage buildings from vandalism, particularly in the off-season. I mainly remember him in the spring, getting things ready and cleaned up before the stampede of kids arriving for summer camp. I knew this man would pose a problem; he would not allow anyone to fish the pond.

He was a scary man to me. He seemed wired and on edge. I only know now how complicated life can be as I grow older. Perhaps he stressed about bills to pay or had anxiety about his job and family. Some of the locals said he had had a nervous breakdown and went crazy. I did not really know what that meant, but I wondered at how so much could go wrong in a man's life. This frightened me.

Fearfully and Magically Drawn to Eden

During my first attempts to fish the pond, I hiked up the trail, over the hill, and into the valley to fish the backside cove that curved into the woods. Here, if needed, I could quickly retreat to the forest. Each time, I fished this area until the groundskeeper saw me and started yelling, cussing, and waving his arms. Then I ran back through the woods and down the trail. He was a frightful troll guarding some unknown treasure, one I would not know the value of until decades later.

In spite of him, I was drawn to the pond, much as children in fairy tales are drawn to certain parts of a forest or a remote castle. In looking back, I am surprised I even had the courage to approach the pond. After all, this was private property guarded by a frightful man, and I was a timid kid. I do not know why I was so bold. I often wonder if an angel was in my midst urging me to follow. I have since learned that angels reside on the edges. Was my pond such a place?

I never saw or heard an angel, not in an obvious way. I only sensed I was safe and that somehow this pond was *meant* for me to fish. In some sense, the pond belonged to me, and I to the pond.

Because of an angel (the angel I did not see or hear), did I sense that everything was going to turn out all right? Or was it just my attitude toward the groundskeeper. I have come to believe that the attitude of my heart, which I express outward to others, affects the manner in which others respond to me. Even now, as a middle-age man, when I find myself hoping for a graceful response from others, I know I must begin with myself. If anything is going to change, it must begin with my own heart.

When I find myself growing more and more cynical, I think back to the pond and try to emulate the manner in which I walked the banks of the pond, when life seemed to respond more graciously to me. It is not easy. When I look back and see myself walking those banks, I can remember a quiet power, authority, and openness, along with a radiance that I no longer possess. I understand why William Wordsworth spoke of a loss of radiance as we age.

Sensing Beyond and Underneath the Clamor of Life

When I first approached the edge of the pond and peered into the waters, I felt as though I had walked into an enchanted land. Schools of perch flashing through the water appeared magically golden. At times, a largemouth bass came up from the depths chasing the school. These bass were amazing specimens—silver, deep bodied, and fourteen to twenty inches long. Some were even larger. Even as a kid, I knew this pond had to be unusual to produce such large fish. However, it was much more. Slowly, I was learning that this pond was not ordinary in any sense.

There was Something else drowned out by the clamor coming from the kids swimming at the docks. Underneath the huge bass chasing the golden fish, under the humming of dragonflies, and under the comfort of the green forest, there was Something else. Underneath everything was a different sound that I could not hear but could sense in some other manner. Was it a poem or a softly playing song I never heard before? Where was it coming from? Although I did not have the words, I had the sense that this was a sacred and magical place. I felt a little like Dorothy in Oz, I had the feeling that I was not in New Jersey anymore.

It was as if I was remembering something; perhaps the lost Eden of the past.

My eyes did not see only through the layers of the gray sky and the surface of the water but through the layers of my heart.

As I fished, I slowly became more and more aware of a presence that was under the hum of the dragonfly wings and the voices around me. I could feel longings deep inside me, aching to connect, not with the friends I left behind but with this other world. This other world was both beyond me and within my midst, a place where I might belong.

Oddly enough, it did not matter that I was trespassing. I felt neither guilt nor shame. Today, I think that trespassing to fish this pond was a sacred trespass, one of the most holy acts of disobedience I would ever initiate. This precise act of disobedience would transform my life.

Beyond Convention

Spurred on by this deep inner longing and the mystery of the pond, I kept coming back even though I was sneaking in and trespassing. Being respectful of authority and the property of others was something my parents instilled in me. I was an "A" student, (A's in conduct always). I was never in trouble, and I would follow the rules. Mostly.

However, following the rule of staying away from the pond went against Something deep inside me. This became an important life lesson; it was one of the first times I would follow my inner intuition over convention. My choice to follow the path to the pond gave me a sense of power and freedom that I never had before. It opened up a whole other spiritual world. Over the years, this power and freedom emerged in certain situations and helped me make difficult choices. I learned to follow my heart rather than the conventions and ways of others.

My choice to enter the valley of the pond reminds me of a poem by Robert Frost titled "Stopping by Woods on a Snowy Evening," in which the narrator follows his own heart, daring to enter a wood on a snowy night, the darkest evening of the year. He, too, was trespassing. Even his horse tries to warn him that path was frightening. Even so, he too enters the forest thinking or sensing that whatever is in the woods, for him is worth the risk. He ventures into the unknown, assuming the owner will not see him. I, too, like the narrator in the poem, assumed the caretaker would not see me. I had thought that, by this time, I would blend in with the trees and become a part of the valley. I was wrong.

Caught and Yet Calm

The caretaker of the pond did see me. Once again, he yelled at me. However, there was something different. There was a mysterious pause, and I sensed in that pause something of significance to me. Somehow, I *knew* that he had changed his mind in some way. This would not be the first time that my intuition of what someone meant was clearer than his or her actual words. He yelled again—and again. There *was* something different in his voice. His arm motions were different and less frantic. I could not hear his exact words, but I did "hear" intuitively that he wanted to talk to me. He yelled again, and this time I could hear his words, "No, wait, don't run away! I want to talk to you." I found myself walking to him, fly rod in hand, strangely calm.

As I stood before him, close up, he still appeared somewhat jittery and wired. I let him speak, and the words he spoke were profound. He asked, "You like to fish here, right?"

I nodded my head.

"I know you are a good kid and not doing any vandalism to these buildings," he said. "You are not like some of these teenagers who keep breaking in here to steal stuff. They make me so mad. Tell you what, I'll let you fish here, but I want you to let me know if you ever hear or see anyone who vandalizes the property."

I should have said, "It's a deal," but I do not remember ever agreeing to keep my end of the bargain. In fact, I do not remember saying anything at all, not even "yes." This wasn't odd on my part. I learned early on that adults should do most of the talking while I remained silent and listened. As I listened, I could "hear" that he wanted me to fish.

Somehow, I knew that it was enough for him that I would not vandalize the place. I never did try to find out who was doing the vandalism. I was not interested in this exchange of services. I only knew I wanted to fish, and that is what I did.

The Keys

In looking back at these events, I wonder how the groundskee-per knew I only wanted to fish and I was not interested in vandalism. Was he the intuitive one? When I fished the far side of the pond and he yelled to me, I was at least a couple hundred yards away from him. He could not have seen the expression on my face. I doubt he thought I could really find out who was doing the vandalism. As I think about this again, I am perplexed that he even bothered to call to me. I now wonder if someone or Something touched a tender place in his heart. Could an angel have spoken to him? Did he need healing in some way and need to know that some kids were not destructive? Maybe I was the only quiet kid he ever met. Did he need to be gracious to someone instead of cynical and angry, and did that gracious act of allowing me to fish heal something in him? I do not know. Back then, when I was a child, all I knew was that he gave me the keys to fish the pond.

How mysterious that such a person, ghastly in some respects, would give me access to the lake. He gave me the key to the gate. He was a peculiar blessing for me. His appearance and mannerisms kept others out, which resulted in me having the lake all to myself. This man opened the door to a treasure and a paradise that was all mine. I had my own private pond to fish. I was alone in the quiet of my Eden.

Just as I learned to sight fish below the surface, I would dis-cover I was not alone.

The Beginning of Sight Fishing

I fished and fished. I taught myself to cast, to tie my own white marabou streamers with a silver tinsel body, and to sight cast to large bass lurking in the coves. I learned to walk the edge of the pond while at the same time false casting, keeping the fly out of the grass, brush, and trees behind me. Then at the opportune moment, I was able to lay the fly out in front of large fish on the lurk. This ability to walk, stalk, sight fish, and false cast required a highly developed skill set. It felt like a dream—and still feels like a dream even as I write—to watch a large fish follow the fly and then suck it in. At other times, I watched the twitch of the floating line and knew a fish had taken the fly below the surface. How amazing it was to lift the rod and feel the shake of the fish's head and the pulsating power of a large fish hooked! Yes, I still see and feel it all as an adult when I fish the South Platte.

Over the next few years, my skills at sight fishing developed to a high level. The ability to sight fish has stayed with me and dominates my approach to fly-fishing and in guiding others. I hunt, stalk, and then lay the fly in front of a specific fish. I am always on the move, never passive, looking below the surface. I often see a fish when others see none. At times, I feel as though I can see *everything*, but I know that is not the case.

Much eludes me, even now; including angelic forms.

Unresolved: Was There an Angel?

I wonder how I would have responded if, while fishing the pond, an angel had come out of the woods to talk with me. Although I never actually saw or heard an angel, I can still see one in my mind, sometimes in the form of an older man or woman. Even today I wish an older man or woman had said these words to me, "Anthony, someday, everything is going to be okay. I know you are lonely. I know you feel out of place. I have been watching you for a long time now. Someday, you will use the same fly-fishing skills that you are learning now to help both kids and adults catch fish and find their way in life. You are going to be a father, a guide, a teacher, a counselor for others."

Of course, if an angel had appeared, I doubt I would have believed it. Yet, a fly-fishing guide is exactly what I became. After college, I ventured out to Colorado and became a teacher, a guide, and later a counselor. I had the opportunity to teach, counsel, and guide many young people, my own two daughters, and many adults on the river. I experienced many changes both in public education and fly-fishing Colorado's waters. Today, I make my living entirely as a fly-fishing guide and still am trying to unravel the mystery of my life. I still wonder what is beneath the waters I fish and what lies under the rocks of the rivers I wade. I still wonder if and how an angel can lead me to a place of deeper belonging.

If this sounds like a dream come true, I guess it is, at least in part. Yet I still struggle, which is difficult for others to understand. Inner Division remains. It is difficult for me to be completely honest and to admit the disconnect I still feel so often and the longing for Eden.

Looking Underneath the Clichés

In order to unravel these mysteries, I still look deeply at the art of fly-fishing and its impact on my life. Fly-fishing is a way, at least for some of us, to learn of God in a way that going to church cannot. Was Christ the angel who both appeared and did not appear, who spoke but did not speak to me at the pond? Could God speak to a boy through a pond and its fish? If an angel spoke, then what did the angel say?

I am not much moved by what churches have to offer. Much of their teaching seems superficial, nothing more than clichés. I desire to go deeper, below the bedrock of the rivers I fish and far below the language of evangelicals. Church left me spiritually, emotionally, and intellectually immature, feeling like a still-born mayfly unable to emerge. At the same time, I wish to move like a river under and around the rock-hard walls of atheists and cynics, who claim to be absolutely sure that there is no God and that an angel could never have called on me.

I make no effort to hide my own doubts and vulnerability. Much remains unresolved. I use language such as "perhaps," and "It is my hope." I use the language of poetry. I speak in paradoxes, perhaps believing that when and where I doubt the most are the areas where I believe most deeply. I believe the time has come for me to embrace my uncertainties, to question my absolutes, and to look more deeply at what Jesus truly said. I have to consider my own lack of transformation. I do not want to claim that I "know Jesus" or that I have been "found" (Matthew 25:35-40) while there is much evidence to the contrary.

I prefer to become desperately lost. I need to feel my true ignorance. Rather than claim to walk in the light, perhaps it is time for me to walk in darkness. T.S. Eliot once equated darkness with the light. Saint John of the Cross spoke of the darkness being more revealing than the rising sun. I will peer into the waters and look deeply through the darkness. I will speak of glimpses I experienced in my own life story. If I speak of what I see, I will reveal only what "I see dimly as through a dark glass." (I Cor Ch.13:12). I am like the mayfly nymphs crawling under the dark stones and dark waters, waiting to emerge into the light. However, before I can emerge in transformation, I have to learn to navigate in the darkness.

If you are resolved on the major issues, the existential questions, and the musings of your spiritual journey, you might disapprove of my language. If you have relied upon the church or a preacher to shine a big spotlight on the mystery of your life, you may want to consider shutting off that light. However, at the same time, you may find yourself surprised at how deeply pierced I am by the big story of the Bible, the teachings of Jesus, and the garden in Eden. In fact, my whole life has been an attempt to get back to Eden and a more intimate communion with Something.

Edges: Spanning the Distances

As a child, I learned to cast comfortably from the edge of both my pond and my social environment. As I write, I return to similar edges and then am able to speak from a place quite familiar to me. Having survived fishing at the pond, I am at least somewhat able now to tell my story, without concerning myself with solely pleasing others.

If my goal is *not* to please others, I can speak from the edge of the mainstream culture, and even my own fly-fishing business (as I have become leery of the fly-fishing industry, the impact of crowds on natural systems, and how those crowds change the individual, spiritual experience of those fishing on the river). To stand on an edge, at least somewhat reserved, is how I do not completely embrace practices that do harm to the fish and natural systems. It is my observation that the mainstream culture promotes entitlement and immediate gratification to not only catch as many fish as possible (and the largest) but also to obtain one experience after another.

I speak from the edges of nature as found along the banks of the rivers and lakes I fish. I speak as a layperson from the edge of the church, never completely belonging to the church institution and at the same time never completely belonging to the secular world. The edge is where I exist, like a nymph clinging to the edge of a stone on the bottom of a river, trying not to concern myself with doctrines that might give me a superficial sense of belonging to the church— nor with beliefs, scientific or philosophical, that might bond me to the secular world.

I will speak of vast distances, a sense of not belonging, even as I also at times, experience glorious connections to creation and a network of friends and family with whom I have fished over the years. Even now, the longing is still deep within me, to truly belong and to span the empty spaces. As a child, I imagined making one great cast, one sweeping arc, that would span pond and valley. As a child though, I could not span the distances with my cast. Even the small New Jersey valley of my youth contained vast distances that I would again and again revisit and try to span within my heart.

I like metaphors found in poetry. Metaphor means, "to carry across." When I speak of longing to span the distances with a single cast across the pond or the river, I embody metaphor. I project my deepest longing onto the vast sky and the landscapes I fish. As Rainer Rilke suggests, I experience a lingering homesickness or deep aching for God. This homesickness is unshakeable and compels me to search for a greater place of belonging.

I will revisit my experiences at the pond and how those experiences matured on the South Platte River during the past thirty-two years. In that process, I will return to a deep inner loneliness. From that loneliness, I will project my deepest longing on to the vast sky. I hope to display a vast image across the horizon. It should tell something of not just my story but perhaps a part of your story as you ache for Something. I will try to boldly project across the glorious, glowing sky, my longing to see what I seek face to face, hoping He will see my message portrayed in the midst of the burning colors in the sky.

When I consider my deepest longings to be reunited to the

vast creation, God, others, and myself, what better place to explore
and experience the vastness of God than in the vast plain of South
Park, Colorado, home of the South Platte River. I will cast into
the immeasurable loneliness and perhaps God will meet me in that
place.

II

Spiritual Longings
in the Expanses
of South Park, Colorado

❧❧

The Vastness of South Park

When I first moved to Colorado, it was South Park and the Dream Stream section of the South Platte River that had the greatest impact on me, both geographically and spiritually. In the Fall of 1983, I drove west over Wilkerson Pass for my first time and dropped  into the huge valley. Immediately, my eyes and certainly some part of my soul followed the meandering South Platte River through the grasses wavering in the wind. Surrounded by vast meadows and skies, I could not comprehend the vastness of the place.

I was from New Jersey. I had never experienced such horizons. Something about the vast distances and the big sky tugged at my heart. The rational part of me understood that God made the earth and that He stretched out the heavens, but seeing and fishing in such vastness was Something else. The outer landscape matched Something in my inner landscape.

Ironically, the vastness of South Park brought me back to the small valley and pond where I first learned to fly-fish in my youth. While the pond I fished as a child was quite small, and I felt safely enclosed in the hillsides of trees, there were vast distances within my soul. Did I think I could just walk away from the inner distances of my youth? When I walk in South Park today, those vast distances outside still touch lonely distances deep inside me. However, as I walk the banks of the river, I still find comfort in being able to see the dark forms moving below the surface, just as I did when I walked along the New Jersey pond.

Whenever I fish under the vast sky of South Park, I try to entice the dark elusive forms and at the same time edge toward a mystery I do not understand. I often see the fish quite clearly and embrace the challenge of making the skillful casts needed to catch them. At the same time, the tasks of knowing my own soul, where I belong, and who God is elude me.

South Park continues to be a breathtaking, magnificent, and stirring place to contemplate such mysteries. The vastness helps. South Park provides room enough for my deepest questions to breathe and stretch out into the heavens. Today, I consciously look forward to meeting what might lay both beyond and within, even within the river I fish. It is large enough to hold the questions of the past, while I cast forward beyond the present.

Looking Back At the Pond

As I fly fish in South Park, I often think back to the pond of northern New Jersey. I remember a small land often blanketed by a low gray sky. I remember how I tied my own flies, taught myself to cast, walked the pond while false casting, and stalked bass in the shallows. The pond, although small, was my world, and a wonderful world it was. It was a world within my reach. I brought that world with me to South Park.

While fly-fishing in South Park, I often think back to how the pond offered me solace from the social anxieties I was experiencing. I retreated to the pond, which was a world all its own. I never quite resolved my childhood anxieties, but the forest around the pond enclosed me and comforted me. I fished largely alone on the edge of my pond and my peer group. Even now, as I walk the meandering river in the immense valley of South Park, I am not quite sure where I belong.

At the pond, I did not know how to connect with my peers, but I did learn to connect to fish. Stalking and hooking fish stirred something deep inside me. The connection with the pond and the fish eased the disconnection I often felt inside when with others. I survived though, and I think I grew spiritually from having to live somewhat detached from the mainstream culture. In some sense the time I spent on an edge, possibly with the help of an angel, allowed me (or forced me) to remain true to what I believe and who I am. Perhaps most important I would forever consider the possibility that God *met* me at such edges.

No angel came to greet me—or at least not one that I could hear, see, or feel. Nevertheless, Something happened, and I still reach out to one. Did God reach for me? Did God speak to me or allow me to feel a presence?

While the pond and the valley were small enough to enclose and comfort me, South Park overwhelmed me with its immensity. In doing so, it pushed me back to the beginning of my life when I was a child trying to span some great distance.

How could I ever cast across the vastness and powerful winds of South Park?

Inner and Outer Distances

As an adult in Colorado, while fishing on the vast plain of South Park, I found myself revisiting the inner distances I once experienced at the pond. As I walked the vast treeless meadow, the ridges and hills seemed to rise as wrinkles in the land. The horizontal expanse is surrounded by snow-covered mountains looming in the distances. The main fishing drainage is the Middle Fork of the South Platte, which meanders its way through this valley marked by Spinney Mountain Reservoir and then four miles downstream to Eleven Mile Canyon Reservoir. The Dream Stream is the section between these two reservoirs and is the home to large trout.

When I walk through the immense valley of South Park, there is Something about the openness of the land and sky that causes me to feel small, insignificant, and intimidated. I look up at the lonely ridges and imagine myself trying to spend just one night alone in a tent. I always have the uneasy sense that emotionally and spiritually I could not survive the encounter. I could never put my finger on what it was that I felt or why I thought I could not endure the experience. Would the vastness of this place swallow me up? It was not the fear of wild animals or lightning or criminals; it was just the feeling of insignificance brought on by the sense of intense loneliness that pulled on me. The vastness of the place, the horizontal distances, always seemed to bring to the surface some inner loneliness and vulnerability.

When I fish in South Park, I feel exposed. It is a difficult place to hide. I think of an eagle swooping down and carrying me off that plain. I am clearly visible like a trout in clear shallow water. This sense of vulnerability brings me back emotionally and spiritually to the pond. I have a similar intense loneliness and a yearning to hide—and yet at the same time I want to be seen, found, and perhaps carried away.

Did Something back at the pond find me and take hold of me? Did Something catch me? Did I want Something to take me away? Perhaps, even now, some part of me longs for God to carry me off like an eagle to some far-off country, Eden perhaps. If not God, then perhaps a man, a woman, a stranger, could at least know my name.

South Park is where I remember the loneliness I felt as a child when I fished the pond, except the memory intensifies and gives birth to deeper longings of my soul. As I stand casting to large fish lurking under the bank, I am stirred, poised for a strong pull, and at the same time, braced against the winds of South Park. Dark clouds are looming over the continental divide.

The Longing Stirred In the Vastness

When I fish South Park, my longings inside stir. This immense valley could easily swallow up my home state of New Jersey, never mind my valley and pond. In some sense the pond was swallowed up as the remnants of my story went swirling down the South Platte, cascading into Eleven Mile and Cheesman Canyons, where my efforts to get fish to rise always stirred up old bits of my story. The memories are still there, spanning the distance between then and now. I felt distances as a child, still do, and wonder what those distances might mean today.

Perhaps nothing is ever lost. There was the cast I could not complete. There were people I could not reach and those who could not reach me. I could not even find myself. Yet, there always was a connection of sorts to some *other*. I felt then and still feel parts of my own life story overlapping with some bigger story from long ago. If this was not a connection, then at least there was the longing for this connection. The longings remained and continued to intensify into adulthood. I wanted to know beyond all else who is the true author of my life. Who am I? Who is the author? To whom do I belong? Where is Eden? The author is the most elusive one, whom I am seeking in the vast distances of the beautiful places I fish.

I believe my yearnings are ultimately for God, my home, and my true self. I find this challenging. I feel God's elusiveness in the stark beauty of South Park and project my longing for lost love, as poets have done, out toward the landscape. I look out at the curving landscape, interrupted now and then by a rocky crag and the meandering river. I long to be there; closer still, hoping to become a part of it; belonging. I want to lie down in the grassy depression resting in one of the earth's gentle curves and to awaken to the sounds of the river and rising fish.

God is the one who eludes me and the one I long for in the distances. Yet in nature, I sometimes feel I can reach out and touch God or sense the presence of a lost love or a place I barely remember. I think that if I can touch only one of the elusive fish, I might finally belong.

Each time I fish in South Park and consider my place of belonging or ask who I really am, I touch that vast meadow in a deeper way. When I look for elusive slender forms moving below the surface, the wonders seize my heart. I am filled with mysterious longing.

I see this longing for reunion in the pairing of rainbow trout in the spring and brown trout in the fall when they migrate out of Eleven Mile Reservoir and into the South Platte's Dream Stream. I see this longing in many souls on Earth who ache for love in another person. I see this lovesick longing in many love poems, including the prose found in the Song of Solomon, similar to how I feel this longing for Eden. It is as though the landscape itself, expresses this love, as the spring flowers bloom, and I long to hear a loving voice among the ripples on the river and the blowing of the wind. I long to see her image walking along the curving river. However, when I look across the land, she is gone.

As an adult, I am thankful for places such as South Park, where the winds ripple the grasses and the stream meanders gracefully, almost seductively. I feel wooed to be aware in both my past and present of the deep longings in the vast inner landscape of my heart. I am uncertain about spanning these vast distances, yet I still reach forward with each cast. I still reach out.

Conceivably, these vast distances are where I long for God to be. This intense longing is a projection of the God I believe in. My own wishful thinking forms part of this projection. Yet because I am made in God's image, I also reflect and project outward certain aspects of God's true being. The part of the projection that is of me, that stems from my own baggage, does not invalidate the integrity of the longing I cast into the skies. While casting under the endless skies of South Park, I glimpse a part of God's image that is both me and not me.

When I am in a vast place like South Park, I think of how Jesus taught his disciples to pray, starting with, "Our Father Who are in heaven." Jesus asked them to look up into the vast skies of heaven and speak to God. When I follow this simple and yet profound teaching, how can I not feel how far away God is in heaven?

This is particularly so when I look up through the immense skies of a place like South Park? "As far as the heavens are above the earth, so great is his love to those that fear him" (Psalms103:11). Here lies the paradox. Within the vast distances of South Park—not to mention the rest of creation—there is also a vast love. The vast distances that separate me from the true object of my desire also bind me. God is faraway and yet at the same time infinitely close, around me and within me.

This is the paradox of my faith. I can feel vastly far away from God and, at the same time, mysteriously close to God. I am just barely able to understand that if God's love spans these great distances, then this is a vast love indeed. As high as heaven is above the earth is how high his ways are from mine (Isaiah 55:9). I can perceive these vast distances and know deeply both of my ignorance and of his vast love. His love fills both the geographic distances and the inner spaces of my ignorance. I call out from my emptiness into those vast skies to my father who art in heaven.

My ignorance and lack of resolve creates the inner space in which God might enter. A reverent period of doubting, feeling humility, and questioning can create the opening, stripped bare of premature convictions.

Inner Plain Stripped Bare

The vastness tugs at me and hints at Something and my need for Something. It takes the vast distances of South Park, its expanse of the land and sky, to touch and remind me of the inner distances of my soul. Every time I fish the river and walk its meanders, I feel Something stir inside me. I understand this as my own inner plain, stripped of pretense and laid bare before God.

Perhaps this Something that stirs inside me is an invitation to let go of my acquired walls and false identities that protect the fragile ego that defines me.

With my inner landscape stripped bare like the plains of South Park, I can begin to understand who I truly am and understand that, in my inner most being, I am a lost soul hoping to find my home in God. If I want to spiritually journey deeply along the meanders of life, I have to face the fragile egos I have constructed along the way (that I use in order to superficially belong) and admit my longing for true belonging. This task is difficult, at times frightening, and takes courage.

It is dangerous to feel deeply, to be honest and vulnerable to my deepest desires. My deepest longings are to connect with and belong to creation. I have a sense that I will not endure the intensity of my desires. I either have to block them out entirely, something I am never able to completely do, or allow the desire to teach me what I really desire in life. Most often, I would rather not feel these intensities. Perhaps these are the times when I am "just fishing."

My true desire to belong is of such an intensity that I am tempted to protect myself by wearing masks. At times, my fly-fishing waders, boots, vest, and fly rod serve as a mask, but such masks never completely cover the inner problem. No matter how accomplished I become as an angler I can never quite sustain the perfect drift on the narrow seam line; the drift needed to bring the fish to rise, take the fly, and remain connected to me and all that I truly long for. Where is the narrow seam line? Where is this eternal place of connection that remains for me? It takes courage for me to admit that I cannot sustain the drift or more often, sustain myself in life and to admit the lack of connection I often feel.

Deep Longings for Homecoming

What is this longing to be true to who I am? At the same time, what is this longing to belong? Why do I possess an intense longing to be accepted and not separated from God? What is this landscape of my soul that refuses superficial connections and instead desires acceptance of my true self.

The wide expanse of the sky and land of South Park, the South Platte River meandering in between, and the howling winds intensify Something in my soul. I am there now, in the moment. The outer distances of sky and land pull on the inner distances of my soul. The vast empty place inside me is like a vast sky, stretching my heart toward heaven as I long for some place where I truly belong. Just as I walked the banks of the pond as a kid and the meanders of the South Platte River as an adult, I wander along the distances of my soul. I am hoping to find my home, even as I fear that the vast distances within might annihilate me. When I follow the meandering river, *home* is just around the next bend. In that bend, a huge brown trout might be lurking deep in the undercut bank. I release my cast to the exact place; the brown takes the fly and surges down river, and Something deep inside me awakens. I can only let the fish run, taking out more line. I follow. I pray, "Do not break me off," as the fish plunges deep. All around me becomes silent. I throw away logic and safety, and I struggle over logs and rocks, plunging into deep water in a dazed pursuit. Interwoven with my desire for this fish to not break off is a reverent awareness that my life is in need of healing. Deep down, I am pursuing Eden.

My fear that the fish might break off (or that I might be cut off) comes from being aware of my tendency to break my commitments. How do I endure being outside of Eden? How can I endure being connected to this fish and then suddenly be cut off? For a moment, it seems easier to give up and break off this connection myself. At least then I would be in control. However, each time I hook a large fish, underneath my fears I sense a new hope to once again follow the fish down the river and not to despair.

So I proceed. It does not matter how many times I have failed or how many fish I have lost. I chase the fish down river. Fly-fishing provides this new hope in spite if my failures.

Where Do I Belong? The Cast I Could Not Complete

My complex response to the question of where I belong is a dominant theme in my life. I wrestle with the unique experience of loving the natural world through fly-fishing while feeling out of place. Christ himself must have felt out of place.

> "Foxes have dens and birds have nests, but the Son
> of Man has no place to lay his head."—Luke 9:58

I am connected to this world, particularly to the places I fish, and yet I wander these same lands in search of Eden. Is there something inherently Christ-like about fly-fishing in wild places in hopes of spanning the vast distances I feel? Is this part of why I fished as a child? Is this why as an adult I am drawn to the vast places like South Park? Is this why I sometimes think I can bridge the gulf with one spectacular cast?

As a child I could not span the distances; I was too young—physically, emotionally, psychologically, and spiritually—to cast across the pond. My childhood pond was too vast. Of course, I could not cast across that pond. Not literally. But I could not do so symbolically either. No cast could bring back to me everything and everyone I longed to be part of my world. No cast could encompass it all: sky, family, friends, God, tree, water, mountain, fowl, and fish. Everything I wanted was out of reach, even with my fly rod. My heart ached too much, even though my longing reflected my true desire. I just could not find fulfillment and a place in this world.

If not understood, the growing awareness of a desire remaining unfulfilled leads to a type of madness, which occurred in my life from time to time. The reality of my life did not compare well with my longings. Even now, it is maddening for me to remember my Eden of the past while living in my present reality. How can the memories of my soul, developed from my childhood glimpses of Eden, not be at odds with my present circumstances of life? The latter seems so dim in comparison.

This makes me think of Don Quixote and insist that it is irrational for me to accept my life only for what it is instead of for what it *could* be. How could I ignore the glorious images and places I have been and have seen and experienced? Deep down, I want more than the human condition and circumstances of life can give. Like Quixote, I would rather pursue the Eden of my imagination, see giant monsters where there are windmills, or wander further and further up a meadow stream in hope of finding a pure pool where the river and its fish will speak to me.

When I was a child, fly-fishing provided me some relief from this strange existential madness. While I could not cast across the pond and fulfill my greatest longing, the pond had small coves that *were* within my reach. I could cast across to those coves to reach feeding bass, and *those* casts and *those* fish were of immense significance to me. While much would elude me, I learned that *some* things in life were attainable. Moreover, art and practice would improve my chances. I could reach *some* fish, hold them in my hands, and in some sense steady my life by them. I developed a slight sense of belonging because of the fish that I could reach even as some great "other" held me on the edge of Eden.

When I dare to ask where I belong and to whom I belong, I sense that I am approaching an edge. If I cross over that edge, it feels as though I am wandering on a vast plain without signposts. I can only ask for the courage to continue. It is my only prayer. As I slowly follow the meanders of the river, trying to perceive where fish might lie, sometimes there is Something else that I vaguely sense. I follow Something on the wind, even if I am wandering alone, confused.

The vast plain of South Park and its meandering Dream Stream has been and continues to be a place of deep contemplation where I can ask, "What is this that I feel?" The vast emptiness of this meadow dissipates all but the most stubborn of delusions. To fish in the expanses of South Park involves a return to a certain barren, empty, loneliness where the love I find, even in error and in my imagination, is a love that remains.

I stagger, I wander, and I make mistakes as I follow the river where my past life, my hopes for the future, and the life I am now living merge on the edges of Eden.

Merging Rivers

The merging of my childhood experiences at the pond with my adult experiences on the Dream Stream reveals a deeper longing of wanting God to sweep me up into his heart. Then I would be truly home. In my mind, the Dream Stream, meanders through the Eleven Mile and Cheesman Canyons all the way to the little creek that fed into the little pond I fished in that small valley in northern New Jersey. Perhaps Norman Maclean was right when he implied all things come together like a river.

I cannot ignore the boy I was back at the pond. At times, I

was lonely, fearful, and lost. At other times, I was the strong one, with keen eyes and golden fingertips, able to live from my soul. At times, I felt a peculiar joy. Back at the pond, perhaps in my soul I was able to sense the river I would someday fish.

When I look back, I still wonder if through nature God helped me, at least in small ways, to live from my soul. Did an angel whisper to me? Eventually, the boy I was, all of him, for better or for worse, would move downstream and merge into the man I am today, standing on the plain of South Park casting to elusive forms below the surface. And that river flowing beside me, and perhaps inside me, brings me a peculiar joy.

I cannot ignore the convergence and reoccurrence of common themes in my life. I remember the pond and my ache to belong, even as I now feel a similar ache while I fish in the vastness of South Park. As I fish, I am forever looking for a stretch of meadow and water I can call home. I cannot shake off the strange homesickness I felt as a child. I cannot ignore who I was at the pond, nor the man I am today when I stand casting on the plain of South Park; some of my casts reach rising fish, others collapse in the head winds, and still others snag the brush behind me, a reminder of my past.

While at the pond, I found rest in the rhythms of nature. I caught glimpses of divine beauty in between long periods of emptiness and loneliness. The path over the ridge and down to the lake took me away from my peer group. In the silence of waiting for a fish to strike, I received no validation for the time I was spending at the pond. I received no awards, verbal confirmation, or encouragement. There were no photographs. No one even hinted that fishing at the pond might be a good experience for me or that someday I might become a fishing guide. In the most obvious sense, no angel came to greet me, either at the pond or in the stark beauty of South Park. Nevertheless, today I reach out for Something while I walk the meanders of the Dream Stream.

It is not easy to keep asking the deep questions: Who am I? Where is God? Where do I belong? I ache for a fulfillment that seems impossible. Yet I learned as a child that there is Something in the emptiness of not catching fish. Something in that emptiness sustained me then and sustains me even now. Something in the emptiness fed me. I was learning what Jesus taught, "Man shall not live on bread alone" (Matthew 4:4), and "rivers of living water will flow" (John 7:38).

At times, I am willing to approach these vulnerable sensitive questions when I cross over to Wilkerson Pass onto the vast plain of South Park to look for large trout. While I fish, I consider what I had hoped for at the pond and how that hope might merge with my deepest longings today.

I give myself permission to let the search begin; I am willing to deal with the vast distances, both now and from my childhood. I enter this wide expanse with longing and hope for what might lie underneath: a treasure that far exceeds the distances, the loneliness, and the waiting.

Treasure Hidden

Even in this lonely landscape, I sense there is a spiritual treasure, just as I sensed there was treasure hidden at the pond I fished as a child. Could there be Something hidden in a field, for which I would sell all I have to possess? (Matthew 12:34). Perhaps the kingdom of God is hidden in a vast meadow that I walk or under the rocks of the rivers I fish.

I learn from the parable of the treasure hidden in the field that the man, after getting a glimpse of the treasure, is willing to pay any price. The man sees Something of such great value that he sells all that he has to purchase what is a worthless field in the eyes of the world. The man has the eyes to see the treasure, while others walk past.

As a fly fisher, I am able sometimes to glimpse treasure in the fish I seek. This treasure haunts me in my soul. I rearrange my life, my schedule, and my finances, based on what I can perceive when I walk along rivers in meadows and lonely canyons. I might sell all that I have for the sake of the treasure, even if I do not fully understand its true value.

The treasure is far more than having a passion for fly-fishing, far more than catching fish, and far more than enjoying an outdoor pastime in God's creation. Of course, there is value in enjoying a healthy hobby, but there is more. Fly-fishing provides me with a way out of the chaos of the realm of this world. Fly-fishing separates me from a culture that enslaves me to its values. Fly-fishing opens me to a whole other world.

As a child I stumbled upon treasure at the pond and then again, as an adult, when I stood on the banks of the South Platte River in South Park. The price I paid at the pond, perhaps not intentionally, was in standing alone on the edge of my peer group. Having paid the price, I was free from a value system that wasn't mine. I found my own rhythm. By fishing in solitude, I learned to cast in cadence with my soul. Somehow I was able to experience a profound separation and a mysterious connection at the same time. These are treasures, but there is more.

Thanks to my experience as a child at the pond, I am better able as an adult to withstand the pressures of a large and demanding culture. It insists that I belong to it even as my true soul belongs elsewhere. To the mainstream culture, catching fish only to release them makes no sense. However, because of the treasure I have found, I am now able to stand on the banks of the river looking for the elusive forms. I can stalk and cast, sometimes hooking and catching the beautiful creatures, only to release them back into the wild. In symbolic ways, fly-fishing is a re-jection of the mainstream culture and its values. It is a useless endeavor. Yet it touches a deeper aspect of what my soul seeks.

I now walk the banks of the South Platte, knowing there is no other place I would rather be. I experience a freedom and power beyond description. I remember feeling a similar power when I stood on the banks of the New Jersey pond, knowing I did not want to be part of the social cliques at school. The pond freed me from worrying about how I could belong to my peer group. Possessing this freedom and power is worth everything I own. I was becoming a young man with nothing to lose. Today I am an older man with nothing to lose. This is a powerful position.

While fishing, I do not think about making money or gain-ing stature. For a brief moment, I transcend a culture with its brutal demands. Jesus was emphatically clear that in order for me to possess the treasure of the Kingdom of God, I would have to give up every-thing. When Jesus told the rich man, "There is one thing you lack, go sell everything"(Mark 10:21), it was not so much a command to become poor as a call to become free. Jesus wanted the man to un-derstand the passions and intentions of his own heart; he challenged him to consider what was holding him back from pursuing his life in God.

Perhaps this is why Jesus told us that we are to go in our own room alone and pray; he knew how vulnerable the average person is to the prevailing culture and the pressures to conform. Fly-fishing gives me the freedom to remember my deepest and noblest inten-tions.

South Park is the sacred place where I do not think about the practicalities of life and what is required of me. When fishing alone in South Park, I can be intentional about my life rather than being driven by the demands of a culture gone mad. I can ignore those demands, at least for brief time, to focus on my looping casts. Sometimes they linger in an immense sky. As the fly lands and a fish rises, there is this connecting.

Each time I fly-fish, I choose to stand on an edge of the mainstream culture, hoping that God might meet me there. What greater treasure is there to glimpse the God hidden in the forms of nature?

Where Do I Take Someone to Find God?

Where do I take someone who wants to perceive God? Do I take them to church? Thirty-five years ago, I enjoyed taking people to certain churches to hear someone preach. Such churches had a charismatic speaker who delivered a meaningful message. Often, my friends did hear a good sermon. However, I have learned that listening to a charismatic speaker is not the same as glimpsing the invisible God as revealed in the creation. In nature, (which includes people), I have a chance to participate in that revelation *outside* of any individual or institutional agendas.

While fly-fishing I interact directly with nature. I touch, feel, and wrestle with it. When I hook a fish, I feel the tug of life on the end of my line. When God revealed Himself to Job, He confronted him from the whirlwind, the wilds of nature, and then asked him question after question about the natural world. And when Job got tangled in argument with his friends, he finally told them to speak to the animals, the fish, and the earth.

> "But ask the animals, they will teach you, or the
> birds in the sky, they will tell you; or speak to the
> earth, and it will teach you, or let the fish in the sea
> inform you."—Job 12:7-8

I bear witness to the power of God to speak through nature. I have learned to ask the fish of the river and the birds of the air to speak to me about God. I would rather be working the South Platte River, looking for big trout, than sitting in a church pew, where I am more inclined to be confused by politics, power, and business. Give me instead the God of the whirlwind, powerful and pure. Perhaps that God will bring me to Eden.

When I want to take someone to a place where they can experience something of the holiness and vastness of God, I take them to South Park. The skies, the vast meadows, and the fish will not ask me for money. They will not ask me to belong. The natural world will not bribe me into becoming a club member.

In spring I can experience the faithfulness of God in the return of the waters from the mountains and the hatch of the blue-winged olives and trico mayflies. I can feel Something of God when a large brown trout takes my streamer fly and surges downstream. Then I feel the pulsation of life in the rod. Rather than taking someone to church, I would take him or her to my first teacher, God in nature. I would take this person to natural places that revealed the word of God long before there were printed bibles and church bulletins. In the flowing waters within the vast natural landscape of South Park, the Word of God in nature concurs with the Word of God written on my heart (Jeremiah 31:33; Romans 2:15).

Of course, sometimes I understand that when I feel lazy, I find it easier to go to church, where I can supposedly hear the Word of God in warmth and comfort. The preachers will gladly provide their answers to the mysteries of life, their profound insights neatly outlined, and I can just sit. While there are times when I may prefer this kind of an arrangement, I know deep down, this is not my style of fishing for truth. I prefer not to be told what to think.

In this kind of a service, people remain largely passive. Listening to what amounts to a lecture is quite different from seeing and feeling God in his creation, alive and wild. In nature where I fish, God is in charge, and I have to problem solve and think. Far too many church services follow an outlined itinerary controlled by human agendas. Such services are vastly different from how I have experienced God, both as a boy at the pond and as an adult in the vast plain of South Park.

In South Park, I fish both by myself and with another, usually a client. In either case, I try to learn where and what the fish are eating. In the silence and in my ignorance, the fish might ignore me for hours. I listen to the silence and perceive the lack of response in the fish, forever trying to decipher God's true voice. I then might discern God's voice in the sweeping winds, the ripple on the water. Don't misunderstand me. Usually, this doesn't happen. Sometimes, I don't have a clue.

Most likely, I will not have some grand spiritual experience, nor will I find the secret fly that works. This is different from a church service, where the preacher tries to provide a simple formula or principle for living your life. Fishing is not so simple. I don't get— or give—simple instructions. I may never find the right fly. However, I might glance across the river and see a stranger who needs my help. This can be easy to miss, just as I might miss the subtle rise from a fish interested in my fly.

As I fish or share a meal with a stranger, I may look up at the vast skies and ask the difficult questions: Who am I? Do I belong here? Where are you God? Am I loved? Who is my mother, brother, sister? (Matthew 12:48). Who is my neighbor? (Luke 10:29).

Only God can answer these questions for me. No one can tell me; not the preacher, not the people who might sit next to me in church, not my family, not those of a fly fishing club.

When Pilate asked Jesus if he was a king, Jesus responds saying,

"Is that your own idea," Jesus asked, "or did others
talk to you about me?"— John 18:33-34

From this text it seems Jesus is particularly interested in knowing the true motive behind Pilate's convictions and if he arrived at those convictions on his own initiative. I am often more passionate about the things that have little to do with the heart of God. In spite of my strong views to the contrary, I have a tendency to conform to the patterns and beliefs of those around me more readily than the heart of God. I often believe something because someone told me what to believe. I would do better to ask the animals and the fish for the word of God.

The scriptures tell me that God's faithfulness toward me is visible in how high the heavens are above the earth (Psalms 103:11). This is difficult for me. As a child, I found distances overwhelming and frightening. There is a paradox here. In order to experience God's loving-kindness, I am supposed to feel the vast distances between Him and me. While I am in a church building, it is doubly hard for me to grasp this paradox. The walk to obtain a hot cup of coffee from the church lobby is not far enough to allow me to experience the vast distances that are supposed to be an indication of his love. The preacher's words are too close to his employment contract, the expectations of a board and church members, and perhaps his or her wallet. In contrast, I experience this paradox more often on the river, a place where the distances are obvious and vast, a place where I belong and do not belong.

The words of scripture say that the creation is singing and praising the creator. On the South Platte, I have fished during countless trico hatches, when millions of tiny trico mayflies flutter and glisten in the air above the river. They are flying all around me. I cannot say I ever heard a sound from one of them. However, I believe by faith they are singing and praising in the silence. The "sounds," of their singing and praising, while beyond my senses, invite me to join. I have never easily conformed, but I do get caught up in this magnificent event. I almost have no choice.

Give me instead the God of the wild whirlwind that spoke to Job. Give me God speaking through the power of nature in all its purity; through the tiny trico mayflies, the howling winds, and the wild geese overhead. I do not want to hear pleas for money to pay the church mortgage or for new church pews or renovations. I do not want to hear about new membership classes. I do not want to hear altar calls that have more to do with increasing business than building the Kingdom of God.

Just give me two or three gathered in his name, huddled on the river and bracing against each other while the strong wind does not permit us to cast. We have no choice but to take a break, lean against each other, and sit on the bank. Give me just two or three lonely souls finding comfort from each other, sharing a hot drink, breaking bread, and protecting each other from the wind.

What If I Had Never Fished the Pond?

I would have been a completely different person if I had never stumbled upon the pond hidden in a small valley in northern New Jersey. What if I had stumbled upon the pond but never experienced fly-fishing on the edge of the pond? What if I had walked away from the pond only to follow the crowd? Suppose I had betrayed my solitude, never gazed deeply into those waters, and never allowed the otherness of that place to mesmerize me. What if I had never made those first solitary casts to the fish I could see. Suppose I had not been able to bring any of those fish into my vision, instead taking in only the groups of people I met.

If I never experienced the pond, I doubt I would have the depth of soul to experience both the intense beauty and the vast distances of Eleven Mile and Cheesman Canyons and the Dream Stream. I would have experienced life differently, more shallowly. If I had fly-fished at all, my experiences would be limited to counting fish and talking about the latest new fly patterns and gear.

I do not think I would have developed the weight of soul to withstand the winds of life. I do not think I would be able experience the edges that would beckon me to a place where I truly belonged. If I had never experienced the pond, and felt the loneliness of being on the *outside*, I would not have able to see the edges that God would ask me to explore again.

I might have become an educator and a guide, but I doubt if I would have had anything to say, or teach, or share in depth. As an educator, I would have followed the curriculum, something I have never able to do, thanks to the pond. As a fly fisher, I would have become a propped up fly-fishing guide, bragging about how many fish my clients catch but never considering the deeper meanings of life and the river.

If I had never stood on the banks of the pond, at the edge of the mainstream culture, I would have become a member of a church. If I became a member too easily, by merely following customs of the group, I might never have known my true motive for joining. Was my motive to belong somewhere? By conforming to the pattern of the crowd, I might have *thought* I was responding to my longing for Eden.

My speculation here is based on some experience. Trying to

find my true path has tired me out at times. I have given in and sat among other group members and became like everyone else for a time. Deep inside, I have always known there is more to true belonging. Sooner rather than later, I heard everyone parroting the same old clichés. I thought I could fit in. All I had to do was conform and learn the language. Every club has its own language. Certainly, this is true of the Christian church, but its language has lost its vitality for me and is in need of redemption. Still, I sometimes become quite comfortable with it, satisfied with a superficial sense of belonging. Eventually though, I find myself aching for Eden.

For me, church institutions are not places where it is safe to doubt, struggle, and ask questions. This is terribly boring. Many church members think they must always have all the answers. They shy away from asking or responding to the tough questions. I find it difficult to speak the truth in such places, especially when I am a member of the club.

Jesus was not a member of the club. I do not see him as part of a system, group, or an institution. He walked an edge that was most often counter-cultural. Despised, rejected, and abandoned, he never belonged. When a man approached Jesus and declared, "I will follow you wherever you go," Jesus replied with a metaphor found in nature saying that each animal had his home but he himself had no place to rest.

I have ponds and rivers to fish, but where do I belong?

A Small God

I wonder how my spiritual perspective would have been different if I was never willing to feel my own smallness in the vast distances where I longed for God. Would my perception of God be different? If I never felt the longing for God to fill the emptiness of those vast places, then my view of God would have been quite small. Would my God have been so small that I would not even had need for Him? Would my ache for God, instead of covering the breadth of South Park, only be as wide as my manicured front yard, the desk in my office, a church pew, or the width of my TV? But that's not how it was for me. The vast emptiness of the physical places where I fished, which is where I hoped God would come into my heart, outlined the vastness of God. Even those were expanding lines that I could never touch. Ironically, C.S. Lewis in *The Four Loves*, spoke of being able to feel God, when and where we do *not* feel his presence. This is a complex paradox where I learn to experience something of God in the gaps.

Faith does not *fill* these gaps, but rather the gaps sustain the longing for the filling of those distances. Perhaps this is what it means to practice the absence of God. Fly-fishing in these vast spaces, casting in the wind, helps me remain and practice his absence. If God is absent, then at least he might exist.

Rather than playing around with small fish in small places, and a small god under my control, I would rather cast my longings into the vast expanse of where God *might* be or *ought* to be. I am forever hoping for Him to be in the wide spaces shaped by the last rays of the setting sun. South Park, where I cast into emptiness, is a stirring place for me to contemplate what I long for most.

A Disenchanted World?

As a child, when I made even one cast across the pond, I longed to know that God was with me. I wished to know that an angel had led me to the pond and gave me the eyes to see even just one fish below the surface of the waters. Even now, I like to think that, even for a few moments, I walked in the enchanted world of

Eden. Did I once hear the sounds of that enchanted place? Today, as a mature adult, I hope so. This has become my poetic message of fly-fishing. Yet how could anyone hear me in a society so disenchanted, so devoid of enchantment? How could anyone hear me?

Emily Dickinson spent much of her life observing nature and had a particular fascination with robins. She observed them singing and asked, "Wherefore sing?" She wanted to know to whom they were singing and if anyone heard. She concluded that no one was listening to the robins sing and perhaps she implied that no one was listening to her own voice. Emily answered her own question through the robin, implying that the robin sang because it is his own business to sing. To Emily, apparently, it is the robin's business to sing, even if nobody hears. Perhaps, while fishing, I can do the same—even if nobody hears. I fish, away from mainstream culture. Who sees me? Who hears me? I fish. It is what I do.

However, I have to ask myself if an angel ever heard my ache for belonging while I fished the pond. Did *anyone* hear my sad song? Was I alone? Did it concern God when I made a choice to fish the pond? Did God commend me when I walked the path to the pond and started to cast from its banks looking for fish? Did I miss Something? Emily asks this same question regarding the robin's song, and her own poetry. She considers the possibility that an angel listened and applauded her.

Jesus spoke of God's care for even one sparrow. I hope that an angel listened and applauded my steps as I walked to the pond. I hope that God applauded when I caught even one fish, even though no one else noticed. This longing for God to applaud me just once is the enchanting world I wish to live in, even if it does not exist. This is the hope I cast onto the waters I fish.

I can choose to believe that God was and is with me, that He hears me when I cast into the vast distances of South Park. Do

I have to be absolutely certain that Something walked with me to the pond and helped me make a cast? Do I have to know for sure that He is with me now as I walk the meanders of the South Platte? Perhaps it is enough; it is Something to hope by faith. If I insist that God must bow down to my every whim, that He must be Something I can control and hold in my hands, then genuine faith is lost.

I remain ignorant of what drives me to hope—just as I long for the dark forms on the bottom of the river to be fish and not rocks. I cast without certainty, yet I am in awe of the possibilities.

In spite of the treasures I may have found as a child at the pond and as an adult along the South Platte River, I remain largely an ignorant man. After seeing glimpses of beauty found in the creation, how could I understand anything with concrete certainty? I am either too dazed, or too rational, to decipher a world that still seems enchanted to me.

The society I live in is largely rational—and disenchanted. Even fly-fishing can become an exact science. The same can be said of faith, which too often relies on rote formulas. In the case of fly-fishing, I sometimes demand fish in the net in order to call my trip a success. In my drive for results, I can forget to pay attention to the mysterious and deeper meanings. There is not much room in my world of rational thought for hunches, intuitions, and angelic visitations. My world can become disenchanted, rationalized, computerized, and sterilized. It is only about the concrete, only about the facts. Sadly, it is often only about me and my rational explanations and attempts at catching fish. But how do I explain the fish that bites, against all odds and logic, seemingly out of nowhere?

Fortunately, I cannot long ignore the deeper hope in my soul that creation is teaching me. Something pulls on my soul from below the surface of the waters. I still anticipate the slight tug from below the surface of the waters and hope it might be a giant trout that took my fly for reasons that had nothing to do with my skill. I still imagine catching a fish that will teach me and declare something of the mystery of God, as it says in Job 12:7-8. I still imagine an enchanting fish granting me a wish as in the old tale of "The Fisherman and his Wife." I still imagine catching the "salmon of knowledge" that will teach me great wisdom and poetry.

While I lament the loss of the enchanted Eden of my youth, I still remember what lies hidden and forgotten by most of society. The poet Rilke spoke of field-madonna's and children who dream by the springs, being open to the sky and stars.

In this modern fast-paced world, I am not very good at sitting by lonely springs, singing like a child in the sun, and wondering wide-eyed to the stars. Like many children and adults, I too often am staring at an electronic gadget awaiting an incoming message.

If only I could get out of my rational mind for just a moment. If I see one fish rise to take my fly, and realize how beyond my understanding is that one fish, I can recover my sense of enchantment. While fishing, I often second-guess myself about what I have just seen or felt. "There is no way that was a fish!" Or, "Did a fish just take my fly?" I worry about this. If I cannot accurately perceive these physical sensations with any degree of certainty, how can I discern spiritual sensations that might come my way? How can I know who I am, where I came from, where I truly belong? How can I know where I am going, who God is, or if an angel touched my hand? How can I know if an angel whispered something to me? As it is, I am dazed even when I may catch fish after fish. I don't understand. What does it matter if I gain all the fish of the river and cannot find out where my soul belongs?

Perhaps by faith, by accepting God as Creator, I can believe God is in and beyond these vast open spaces. I can believe God has bridged these wide open spaces, even as Something has healed the inner distances in my soul. If this is true, if healing is taking place, then there seems to be Something spiritual and enchanting about the beautiful places I fish.

Admitting the Vast Distances

I cannot deny the vast distances in my life. Without them, I cannot long for the healing I need in my life.

Without the distances, I have no need for the Christ who promises to bridge the distances. Without those distances, my religious practice becomes superficial. If my Christianity becomes a shallow pretense, there can be no real spiritual experience. I will live my life looking for the wrong kind of experience. C.S. Lewis suggests that it is a mistake to think that our faith is going to eliminate our fears and sense of disconnection. He goes on to say that when individuals give up their faith because they sense how indifferent nature is to humanity, they may be having their first real spiritual experience.

Admitting that these distances exist, that I am alone, and that nature is indifferent toward me has been critical for me. Sometimes I experience Something so wonderful, majestic, and beautiful that, instead of feeling more connected, I feel incredibly alone. It's because I feel the indifference of nature toward me. I envy fish for the way they move, feed, and belong to the river. Their beauty has nothing to do with me. They do not swim to impress me or connect to me, no matter how intensely I long to understand them. Nevertheless, even in this irony, the fish teach me.

If my faith is authentic, the feeling of not belonging and the feeling of my own insignificance must intensify before lessening. These feelings are my genuine spiritual experience! How can

I boast of my own significance in the face of beauty that swims away from me? How can I stand naked before the wholeness of nature that is so beautifully clothed? Fly-fishing in South Park, where howling winds throw my casts back into my face, is a bewildering place. But it is also a place of great enlightenment. If I can truly feel the distances, experience the indifference of nature, and reach out with each cast toward the beauty I cannot possess, I am moved to God.

God made the world with such sprawling distances in the skies, plains, valleys, and mountains to overwhelm me. Often the overwhelming beauty of nature stirs a desire in me of such intensity that I feel uncomfortable. I want to possess this beauty, but the fact that I cannot do so forces me to admit my lack of control. What I cannot fully control frightens me. Intense beauty, as found in nature, frightens me.

When I was teaching, I often watched an adolescent boy who had a crush on a certain girl but who clearly could not comprehend the beauty that stood before him. The boy, possessed by mysterious feelings, simply did not know what to do. He stood dazed and terrified. Finally, in an impulsive frantic moment, the boy would chase the girl, tease her, call her names, or even throw rocks at her. Obviously, such strategies are a form of defense. The beauty that stands before him terrifies him. To that young boy, beauty initiates fear. And so it is for the rest of us.

I can think back to my own adolescence when I had my first crush on a girl. I recognized her beauty. I was both in awe and terror at the same time. I can picture her now. I recall the pure innocence of her smile, the sunlight on her face and golden hair, and the light reflecting off the leaves of the oak tree behind her. The experience was so powerful that the oak tree by itself almost consumed me. I was barely able to keep standing.

As an adult, I have had comparable experiences when confronted with the beauty of nature. I have stood before such beauty in awe and terror. In my ignorance, I did not know how to interpret what I saw. I could not sustain my gaze. I turned my face away. If I was fly-fishing, I cast my flies *at* the fish, hoping to capture it or scare it off. With either outcome, I would gain a slight sense of control. However, deep down I knew I was not in control. How could I control something so beautiful?

The beauty of creation is forever before me, expanding outward, forever out of my reach. It always is just beyond my grasp. The thirty-inch fish rises on the far bank that I cannot reach and, with my first cast, disappears into the darker and deeper waters. I feel separated and unable to close in on what I desire. I cannot admit that I want more than being able to capture the beauty. No matter how proficient I become at fly-fishing, I want more than being able to capture the fish in my net and grasp the fish in my hands.

Wanting More than Beauty

Sometimes, when I am fishing in South Park, I find myself almost wanting to eat the beauty around me. It is a strange sensation, I'll admit. I ache for what I see to be inside me. I yearn to be a part of the creation. It is not enough for me observe such beauty from my car window. I can't do it. Fly-fishing gets me out my car onto the banks of the river. From there I can wade into the waters deeper and deeper, venturing closer and closer to the fish. When I do this, I am trying to become a part of the river. It is never enough. Even when I catch the fish. I never arrive at my destination. I want more. I cannot quite understand this. Sometimes, I feel ashamed of myself for aching so deeply, and forever wanting more. I tell myself that this strange desire points to the God I cannot reach, control, capture, describe—or let alone. By acknowledging this, I hope I can let the fish be or at, the very least, not clutch the rod so tightly. C.S. Lewis spoke of wanting something beyond merely seeing the beauty of the natural world. He suggested we long to become part of everything.

I also want Something beyond beauty and want to belong and to become part of all that is around me.

I am well aware of this. When I fish the South Park landscape, I don't want just to fix my eyes upon the river or its fish. I want to be in it, part of it. I ache to become one with nature, with an intensity that I have often been too afraid to admit. I want to become the boulder that allows the fish to feel safe lying next to me. I want to become the submerged log that hides a large rainbow trout. I want to be part of that bubbling world that looks out on the anglers casting their lines and speaking with muffled sounds.

When I lose a big fish, I tend to mumble such things as, "It was the one that got away," or, "I was going to let it go anyway." When I walk away, I become aware that I am merely trying to console myself for losing what I can never have. Deep down, I am well aware of the intensity with which I wanted to hold the fish in my hands. I can only pretend for so long.

Pretending I Do Not Want More

The longings of my heart feel dangerous at times. Can I survive the intensity? I have learned to avoid looking too deeply in my heart. I often deny how much I want to belong to the overwhelming beauty around me. I shut down. I look the other way. I rush through life, not pausing to feel the intensity of my true longing.

When I stalk big fish, I might say to myself, "I just want to *see* a big fish and that will be enough." I am lying to myself. It is not enough to *see*. If I actually hook a big fish and battle it, I might say,

"I don't care if it gets off; it is enough to hook it." I am fooling myself. I want more. I want to *catch* the fish, but catching it is not enough. Mounting a fish on a wall does not help. Taking a photo and posting it on the internet does not help.

I refuse to "consider the lily of the field" as Jesus instructed. He used a strong word here. To *consider* something means to think about it, to ponder it, to tease out the deeper meaning. If I could bend down to *consider* just one Indian paintbrush flower on the vast meadow of South Park, I might learn Something. How often do I stop to consider the flowers in South Park? How often do I bend down to look for the insects that are crawling over and under the rocks? Do I ever take the time to admire the tiny trout I hooked before I revive it in the currents of the river?

In many decades past, men in sport coats and women in their summer dresses took the train up through South Park to look at the vast spring meadow in bloom. Times have changed. Can you imagine folks today traveling to South Park on a train to consider a flower. Could I, the fly fisher, travel all the way to the Dream Stream to consider one flower in bloom?

I do not make the time to consider anything often enough. Rather than taking time to consider, I try to tune out the beauty of nature. It is a defense. I am afraid of feeling too much. I am not completely successful in doing so. Sometimes, the vast beauty will leak through the chinks in my armor and stir me, even if I catch nothing. A trico or caddis hatch on the river could catch me unawares. A single mayfly emerging off the water could overwhelm me. In that experience, I myself might begin to emerge.

If I took off my armor, one orange flower blooming in the meadow would be enough to overwhelm me. I might lie down in the meadow next to the flower and allow a gentle breeze to flutter its colorful bracts against my face. Even this would not be enough.

As I stand dazed and overwhelmed by the beauty, it is easy to get confused and my wires crossed. I possess powerful surges of energy and passion. If I do not know the source of all of the beauty, I might get my longings all mixed up. I might fixate on the one flower, the one fish, the field madonna, or the woman in the summer dress. Then, the beauty around me will become a collection of idols. Then it would fade. The fish will vanish before my eyes. If I turn to the woman in the summer dress, she will vanish. The one flower I consider will wilt. Then I too will fade away in the sunset.

Heaping My Idols

Instead of acknowledging God as Creator and one who can bind all things together, I tend to heap my idols into the distances, thinking they might fill the vast spaces and build a bridge to span the abyss. I heap idols into the vast meadows and deep canyons of South Park. With my unexamined heart, I often fail to acknowledge the distances that separate me from the true source of beauty and from my true self.

In my ignorance, I use my fly rod, flies, and fly-fishing skills in an attempt to control the beauty around me. In my immense arrogance, I think I am the greatest fly fisher in the world. I think that all things, and certainly the fish, are under my control. I match the hatch. I perfect my casting skills. I cast my flies onto the river, thinking I can control what threatens to overwhelm me by capturing a fish. However, I never capture enough fish. Always one eludes me. I am not as powerful and skillful as I thought.

What I am truly looking for eludes me. How many fish must I catch to learn that Something remains just out of reach? All the idols I have heaped into South Park have done nothing to relieve me of loneliness and powerlessness. All my idols are not enough to build a bridge I am able to cross. No bridge is ever long enough. When I fish, I see tangled broken leaders and hooks dangling from bushes along the river. I see flies broken off in the mouths of fish. I see my failures. In spite of my best efforts, there are never enough fish caught to satisfy me completely. I keep saying, "One more cast; one more fish."

I am proud of being a fly fisher, but what I call a passion can really be a compulsion. Is there a way out of this madness? Can I give up my desperation to belong and become one with the beauty all around? I have tried acknowledging I am not in Eden. My best day of fishing might end with the realization that I have reached the door into Eden—and it is locked.

C.S. Lewis speaks of feeling like a stranger with a deep longing to bridge some chasm and of being on the outside of some door. To him this is our inconsolable secret. We persist, often without knowing it, to get past a door, and to span some gulf.

Understanding this secret gives me a new understanding into my dilemma. While fly-fishing in creation, I often feel like a stranger longing to be united and hoping to bridge some chasm. I think as I fly-fish, without always knowing it, I am projecting, reaching, casting out, trying to reunite with Something. I am still standing on that edge, outside some door, looking in. I may see a pond, a river, a church building, a great storm, or an astounding hatch that has brought the fish to the surface to feed.

I stand apart. God and Eden are there, and I am here. The door, perhaps only slightly open.

The Hope in Fly-fishing

While fly-fishing in beautiful vast places, I hope that the longings of my soul are not a neurotic fancy but an accurate reflection of the human condition. Can I as a follower of Christ, one who often feels like a stranger in a strange land, reach out my hand, hoping an angel will grasp it? Can I continue knocking on a door, hoping for it to swing open, finally to find God meeting me? Can I continue to cast in the beautiful creation, with trust, even as I sense that the beauty around me is indifferent toward me? Can I participate in creation, while living in the tension of not being certain where I belong or if I belong, and not demanding that creation (and its fish) be under my control? Can I long for God without demanding anything of God? Can I remain in the paradox, living in a kind of contentment and gratefulness while I long for what eludes me?

Fly-fishing in the great expanses of South Park has helped me embrace this paradox and live in the tension of unanswered questions. When I fly-fish in South Park, the surrounding vastness invites me to examine the expanses within my heart. As I approach the chasm in my heart, I sense I cannot cross the divide under my own power. I look for the door. I look for an opening in the vast skies.

III

Overcoming Divisions
and Understanding Connections

❧❧

Connecting Memories

I now see myself in South Park both as a boy and as a man, knocking on some door and with an outstretched hand, waiting for Something to meet me, which many of us call God. As I step back and look at myself, I see a young man hoping to make some bold connection that is as elusive as the fish he seeks. I see someone who is trying  to emerge into his true place of belonging. He casts his hopes and longings into the wind as he wanders the banks of the South Platte. He casts over the waters, looking and searching the depths, and waiting for a fish to rise or tug the line. This reflects some deeper inner connection he once knew or, with anticipation, might know. Every moment, perhaps the next step or cast, could be an opening to Eden. He gazes deeply into the currents, searching for the dark elusive forms. The fish he hooks touch an ache in his soul.

Each time he hooks a fish he feels, however brief, a connection to everything around him. He feels it personally and deeply as Something reminiscent of Eden. Yet these fish grant only temporary, slight sensations. After each initial strike or rise, the sensation subsides and his soul wanders. As he fights each fish, he often looks around at the vast skies above as though searching for something. He may even look around to others, those he fishes with or complete strangers, wondering if they notice him; as though their acknowledgement could justify his existence. Deep down, he knows it is neither their validation nor the fish itself that he seeks. If nothing else, he wants to know if there are others who experience life in a similar manner.

He has learned to change flies frequently and make other adjustments in his presentation to better his chances of hooking fish. He takes a slight step forward, backwards, or to the side—and then makes each cast. His whole body, not just his legs and arms, remember the similar slight adjustments he made long ago. He thinks back to the pond, how he taught himself to cast, how he made endless corrections to keep the line out of the grass and trees behind him. He remembers the slight changes in position, timing, and angles required to place the fly in front of the approaching bass. He now makes similar adjustments as he fishes the South Platte, but it is far more complex, thanks to the intricate currents of this river. He recalls how he was able to spot the fish, perfectly place the fly, and watch the fish take the fly.

He thinks back further to playing catch with his father in the backyard. To catch a pop fly, he learned to maneuver his body into position. He remembers in his body the slight adjustments. He had to position his feet and extend his arm at the right time and the right distance to make precise contact with the ball. His father's face lit up with each catch. He remembers a different face when he missed the ball; it was not a face of disapproval or scorn, just different.

He recalls how his father taught him to change slightly his batting stance when he faced a skilled fastball pitcher. His father would say, "Open up your stance. Slightly shift your left foot and body, so you can get the bat around quicker." The boy thinks back to a game. It was a late inning; after making that slight adjustment with his feet and body, he settled in, then tagged a 0-2 fastball for a three-run triple to deep left center.

The boy is now a man. As he fishes his dream stream, his heart settles on one powerful memory that dominates his being and can still be seen in his stride and approach to the river.

A competition played a pivotal role in connecting him beyond family and friends to everything in his world. It was an arranged confrontation, a wrestling match with the best wrestler in the state. At the time, he had the feeling that nothing could prevent this event, just as he now senses certain drifts where a fish will take the fly and a battle will occur. He could not walk away from his wrestling opponent, as much as he wanted to, anymore than an angler who hooks a powerful fish can break the line and retreat from the river. The angler fights to the end, even with only a remote hope of victory. This one experience would link the events of his life into a pattern and form a key component of his life story.

After this match, he would strive not only with fish but also with men and, at times, even with God. He would be able to identify with Jacob, striving with the angel and hoping for a blessing. He would understand that he was trying to overcome some deep division within himself.

Wrestling with God: From the Pond to the Mat

I brought to high school the memories of playing baseball and fishing at the pond. These experiences helped me prepare for the long hours of training needed to become a state champion wrestler. I chose this path, at least in part, as a defense mechanism against my fears and social isolation. The choice to train was a distraction; a way of emotionally surviving, perhaps similar to my choice to fish at the pond years earlier. Fear, distance, and a peculiar desperation motivated me and pushed me to the edge. I trained like a madman. I do not blame anyone for my anxiousness or fears. I cannot discern any defining event of my childhood that left me so fearful, anxious, and disconnected. Perhaps I was just a sensitive young man trying to find my way and make sense of the existential condition of life.

I shared earlier that there were times when I climbed a small mountain behind the pond that gave me a view of the New York City skyline and urban New Jersey. As the sky darkened, I would view millions of lights from houses and from cars traveling the Garden State Parkway, the New Jersey Turnpike, and hundreds of highways and byways. Thinking of the millions of people whom I did not know was quite overwhelming. Sometimes, because of this existential angst, I looked out and foolishly wondered what it would be like to be the best wrestler among all the millions of lights and people. I reasoned that if some of them could know me, I would not feel so lost and insignificant.

My experience at the pond had laid the foundation for this spiritual experience. It gave me the discipline to stand on the edge of the mainstream culture. This was an edge where I could train undistracted for long hours, often alone. I often denied my social life. This discipline enabled me to pursue the goal of becoming a state champion, and it went on for several years. I ran in the darkness and cold. I trained in my basement morning and night, lifting weights and practicing wrestling moves and techniques on a mat I had obtained.

During free periods at school, I went to the gym and practiced on a mat. I was on the edge of the social mainstream there as well, running the shadowy, flights of stairs on the outer edge of the school cafeteria where my peers mingled. The crowds in the cafeteria and the hum of their conversations reminded me of the noise of the kids swimming at the beach area of the pond. Their sound was close by yet far away from me. As at the pond, I chose this solitude and in some sense craved it. At night, I often ran the streets in the darkness on the edge of town. I found myself hoping that God might meet me at these edges, even though I did not know what this might mean.

There was something quite desperate in my hope, but the desperation sustained and drove me. I sometimes feel that same lonely desperation, even now, as I stand on the banks of the South Platte casting to elusive fish under the vast skies, trying to understand the meaning of my life and the world around me. Even now as a man struggling to live a life of faith, I often feel a quiet desperation, longing for something that feels both far away and yet mysteriously close. I carry within my solitude both the distances and the feeling that I am on the verge of meeting Something I barely sense.

The Road Less Traveled

As a child, my choice to follow a lonely path that led to the pond gave me the courage to follow a narrow path in high school. The 1970s were a wild time in northern New Jersey. I remember kids walking around school stoned out of their minds. There were huge wild parties. Many of my peers thought I was an oddity.

"How come you never drink?"

"Why don't you smoke?"

"You don't know what you are missing."

I did not know how to answer their questions; I did not know what was taking place inside me and why I felt it was so wrong to conform. Conformity felt like a deep inner betrayal. Did I have a hope, however remote, that if I stood alone, God would meet me on the edge? Did I think I had to pay a price to have an angel meet me? I do not know if an angel ever greeted me, but I did meet unique people with whom I formed deep and meaningful friendships. I learned that angels sometimes appear in human form.

These high-school friendships provided me with wonderful connections and relative stability. My friends came into my life seemingly from nowhere, similar to how a fish unexpectedly rises from the depths out of a narrow seam line to take a fly. These friends were God sent. One friend in particular, Marty, who was a year older, took me under his wing. He invited me to read the Bible. He spoke to me often of his faith and was certainly on the "road less traveled." We had wonderful deep conversations about life, the scriptures, and the vast distances in space among the millions of stars.

He was also a wrestler. We joined with other like-minded wrestlers who followed their own dreams and wrestled with their faith. We trained together. We ate together and had wonderful late-night talks at all-night diners in northern New Jersey. We never got in trouble, partied, or did drugs of any kind. We had great times together and felt we were different from the mainstream. I was on a narrow edge again, but at least I had some company! These relationships helped me develop my wrestling skills to a very high level.

The Match: 1978 N.J State Wrestling Championships

For the rest of my life this one match would haunt me. Some-how, this angelic-like, mysterious match transcended normal life and was not easily explainable. It was as though a river carried me to this exact place and moment in time; the moment beckoned and dared me to engage and claim as my own.

It was the last match of my senior year and the last match of my high-school wrestling career. The intense training, the learning to stand on the edge of the mainstream, both at the pond and in my high-school social life, the desperate longing to connect to Some-thing led me to this one match, the finals of the New Jersey High-School Wrestling Championships. This one contest would test all my limits physically, psychologically, and spiritually. It would dwarf all my other athletic competitions and would leave me always won-dering if Something had intervened.

On paper I could not win this match. I had lost to my op-ponent three times before. He was the T-Rex of the high-school wrestling world, feared by everyone, the winner of the state cham-pionship the previous year. He was undefeated for two years. Our paths crossed from time to time. I watched him at summer tourna-ments and in wrestling rooms throughout northern New Jersey. I shuddered when I saw him in a match. He later made the United States Olympic Greco-Roman wrestling team, far surpassing my own wrestling achievements. Most *knew* I did not have a chance.

Right before the match the camera zoomed in on my face, and it looked like I was going to cry. The narrator listed my opponent's accomplishments and then concluded with the awkward comment, "This should be interesting." This was the announcer's polite way of implying I was to be the victim of an embarrassing slaughter.

Throughout the season leading up to this match, my opponent had been in the spotlight at every match. Everyone knew who he was, and the crowds came to watch a show. His style was aggressive and dramatic. His moves were spectacular, and he won by large margins. The crowds would woo. For his competition, he was intimidating to watch. I remember watching him, trembling and feeling a bit sick in my core.

I also was undefeated, but my style was conservative and unnoticed by the wrestling community. I had never been in the spotlight. It was as though I remained in my dimly lit basement where I trained, hidden in the margins. After my opening victory in the state tournament, a news reporter, apparently not impressed with my style, approached me saying, "You didn't show too much out there. Is that going to be enough to beat the returning champion?"

I simply replied, "I don't know. This is just my style." Perhaps because I did not take the bait, the conversation ended with him walking away, shaking his head. I was already disillusioned with the integrity of media.

I thought of the first two Rocky movies, which came out during my wrestling years. I could not resist identifying with the unknown underdog. I was hidden, like Rocky training in the meat locker. When I look back, I wonder if I chose to hide in obscurity because of my fears. At the same time, I wonder if my hiding gave me some greater hope without my knowing it? At times, I felt as though I was following a script, the pattern of a story mysteriously living inside me, just waiting to emerge.

Although I was underrated as a wrestler, I had a few strengths that were difficult for anyone to fully know and understand. Dad had taught me how to practice; the skills I learned were with me in all my training and all my matches. From the beginning, I learned how to make adjustments by catching pop flies in the backyard and by casting to fish at the pond. Moreover, I had learned to translate these skills to wrestling. I could make the needed adjustments in my technique to accomplish a move or to defend myself from my opponent's attacks. I practiced certain moves repeatedly, thousands upon thousands of repetitions and with great intensity, similar to how I wore a groove in the top guide of my fly rod from casting repeatedly at the pond. I lifted heavy weights and had become incredibly strong. While I was not as sophisticated as my opponent, I had learned several powerful moves extremely well. My defense was nearly impenetrable; it was almost impossible to score on me. In fact, no one had scored a single takedown against me during my senior year. But no one noticed. Even harder to notice, I was desperate to make a connection. I was willing to endure any pain to achieve Something that was just within reach and yet infinitely far away. What was I seeking? Was it God or an angel or Eden? Was it my father and mother? Was it my friends I could not reach? Was it that one grand, sweeping cast across the pond, trying to bring back unto myself all that I longed for? This longing was a deep swirling current in my soul that could not be tamed.

The Final Minute

Wrestling competition has given me some of the most intense experiences of my life. I still occasionally wake up in the middle of the night caught in a nightmare, agonizing in the heat of a wrestling competition. The Greek word for contest is *agon*, from which we get the word *agony*. A close match that comes down to the wire can be sheer agony, and this was what I was about to encounter.

During the first five minutes of the championship match, we exchanged points back and forth; every point hard-earned. He was an explosive wrestler capable of scoring big points quickly, but I had been able to keep him at bay. With one minute left on the clock, I struggled out of his grasp for a one-point escape, giving me a precarious one-point lead.

With both of us on our feet, we squared off, toe to toe. He was getting frantic, intent on executing the two-point takedown that would win the match and reclaim his title. As the clock was winding down, I was barely holding off his attacks. Spectators started speculating about a possible upset, "Could this be? Who is this Anthony Surage? Surely, the returning champion will find a way. He has not lost in two years."

My opponent then made a series of attacks, lunging at me and driving me backwards and out of bounds. The referee, in accordance with the rules of wrestling, warned me for stalling. He did so in a robotic fashion, signaling the stalling call with his arms, one in the air with his hand in a tight fist and the other pointed right at me, pronouncing his judgment. I never looked at the referee to acknowledge the call. I knew the call was coming. I felt it in my body and what it meant. If I just played defense and backed up, my opponent would earn a point, tie the match, and bring it into overtime. I knew I would be unlikely to win in overtime. It was now or never. I had to act and stake my claim.

The clock stopped when my opponent and I went out of bounds. My opponent was bouncing up and down in the inner circle, waiting for me to return, hoping to overwhelm and conquer me with one last power surge. For him, this must have been a nightmare. I did not buy into his energy. I strolled back to the circle for the final countdown, calm and seemingly indifferent to him. I might as well have been walking the banks of the pond.

I had entered a dream world of my own, a place of strange silence. I was in a flow, as if I were taking that path down to the pond. I felt safe, enclosed in the forest. How wonderful to belong on its banks, detached from fear, the trees protecting me from my social anxieties. Even the caretaker was no longer blocking the way back to Eden. I no longer saw, felt, or feared my opponent.

Now I am totally in the present. I have no consciousness, thoughts, or game plan. I feel neither fear of nor exhilaration in anticipation of what could happen. I have no awareness that I am on the verge of winning or losing, the most significant athletic competition of my life. I stand on the banks of the pond with my feet firmly planted, waiting to make a claim for my life and the connection I long for.

Arriving at the inner circle, I reach my foot across to the tape, my body coiled, ready to do what it needs to do. As I place my foot on the tape, the referee blows the whistle, but I hear nothing. I have no recollection of choosing either an offensive or a defensive maneuver, yet I make a choice. Just as he lunges for me, I launch the single-leg attack I had practiced so often, gliding under his attack and taking hold of his leg. My timing is perfect, our movements merge. I am in deep with my arms wrapped tightly around his leg. If he is T-Rex, I am Triceratops, where the best offense is the best defense; the intensity of his attack allows me to dig deeper. I tighten my arms and pull his leg in. He counters. I hang on as he flattens me out, slashing at me, trying to get behind me to score. I squirm to my knees. Now I have only his foot. I slip down and am grasping only his toes. Still I have enough control to prevent the takedown. He squirms, cross-faces me and struggles, trying to break free like a ten-pound rainbow struggling to break free from a size 24 fly on 6X tippet.

As in fly-fishing, sometimes a miracle happens and the hook and the leader hold fast. I hold on and in the final seconds before the match ends, I awaken. Tears fill my eyes, and in an instant, all sound is back as a shock wave assaulting my senses. He cannot score.

I have won 4-3. People are cheering. I stand victorious and throwing my arm in the air, dazed, and uncertain of what just happened.

During the final countdown, my father had worked his way out of the seats, to and then under the barricade rope, and to the edge of the mat. As the final buzzer sounded, he ran onto the mat and picked me up. He held onto me, unwilling to let me go. Time stood still. Locked in this loving embrace, I know what eternity feels like. I am connected to everything; if there is a God, I feel his presence.

To this day, I wonder if an angel had reached for me. Did I reenter Eden? Did Eden come back to me, just for a moment? Secular psychologists might argue that I had a peak experience, a moment of self-actualization, or a special bonding between a father and a son. However, I know I experienced Something more than my father holding me in his arms.

Even now, with feet firmly planted on the banks of the South Platte in South Park, I am once again hoping and waiting for God to reach me again. I can wait. I have learned to wait. Even a glimpse of one rising fish is enough to sustain me and remind me of the ultimate connection that is forever possible. I am blessed to experience this sometimes, if only in part.

This memory, leaves me forever trying to emerge. I remain largely ignorant of the process and how, once again, to achieve this dramatic sensation.

College Life: The Genesis Story

I went to Rutgers on a full scholarship for wrestling, studied to become a teacher, and majored in environmental science. During my college years, the memory of the state match and the mystical connections it provided kept me going. So too did the pond, which was my Eden. It kept me connected, however fleetingly, to Something. The image of the pond, the sense of its otherness along with its quiet solitude, stayed with me. I held in my heart the hope that God might continue to meet me on an edge.

Learning to fly-fish and experiencing the otherness at the pond, along with the mysterious presence I encountered at the end of my high-school wrestling career, were parts of my personal story. In time, I would learn of a bigger and older story, as found in the Old Testament. "A river flowed out of Eden" (Genesis 2:10) is a verse that connected the seemingly random events of my life. It helped me understand how my inner experiences related to the world around me.

Although Rutgers was a secular institution, I wrote a paper from a biblical perspective on the environmental crisis for one of my classes. This and the books I read helped me better understand my own spiritual human condition. Even back then I was intuitive enough to know that any problem, and especially a problem as complex as the ecological crisis, had deep spiritual roots.

As I try to unravel the mystery of my life today, I rely heavily on my own inner experiences and the lens of intuition developed at the pond. This intuition did not then and often still does not seem to fit entirely in either mainstream Christian thought or secular thought. Secular psychology proved to be too restrictive to help me understand my inner experiences, especially those related to my sense of belonging. I find most Christian thinking to be shallow. However, I was attracted to the idea that God as the spirit within my soul could provide a useful lens for helping me understand my life.

While I was writing this paper, I thought about the pond, my wrestling career in high school and college, and my deepest feelings. I tried to unravel the mystery of my social life and family relationships. Underneath all of these events and the rocks I began to turn over in my heart, a common theme of not belonging ran deep like a river. The river tumbled over stones and ran into deep canyons that seemed to mirror the deep chasms within myself. To varying degrees, the river ran under my relationships with others, my relationship with God, and even with nature. I thought I might understand this river someday.

At Rutgers, I often looked back to the glimpses of glory that I once experienced at the pond and during that fateful wrestling match. While psychologists and psychotherapists might explain my feelings of disconnection, detachment, and discontent on family dysfunction or biochemical imbalances, I looked to spirituality. In college, I began to discover a spiritual pattern in the deeper caverns of my soul and perhaps in the heart of humanity. To this day, I often find myself asking people I meet along the river, what is your story? Tell me what you experience deep inside your soul. Do you often feel alone? What is the meaning of your life? Are you ever afraid?

The Four Divisions

In my paper I often referred to *Pollution and the Death of Man* by Francis Schaeffer, particularly where he discusses in detail four primary relationships that were impacted after the Fall of Adam. Schaeffer used the first chapters in the book of Genesis to outline the four primary relationships: The human being's relationship with God, *himself or herself*, *others*, and *nature*. According to the Genesis text, Eden was perfect. All relationships were in harmony—until there was a problem. Since then, each of those relationships became difficult. Human beings struggle, become confused, and at times feel lost. Haunted by the loss of paradise, human beings strive to get back in to the garden. I now see how my wrestling career, my draw to the pond, and my whole way of being in life as one great unconscious drive to bring back Eden.

According to Schaeffer, a Christian view of ecology holds to the hope that healing in all these relationships takes place through Christ. Over the years, I have asked myself if my life is a reflection of that healing. This is not an easy question to answer. I have considered this question both in solitude and in dialogue with others. Often this takes place while fly-fishing in the wild places of Colorado. What better place is there than the mountainous regions and rushing rivers of Colorado to consider the condition of my relationships with nature, myself, others, and God?

When I do this, I always overlay the Garden of Eden with my own life story. I pay particular attention to my own inner experiences. I consider the changes that have taken place over the decades, starting at the pond and continuing onto the South Platte River and other great trout streams: the San Juan, Green, Taylor, Frying Pan, Roaring Fork, and Arkansas.

The Genesis narrative helps me put the distances in perspective, but it does not explain away the alienation I feel and my persistent sense of not quite belonging. An angel still guards the entrance to Eden and "a flaming sword turning every way" still guards the tree of life (Genesis 3:24). No matter how I approach my relationships, this story suggests that they will be problematic. I cannot just walk back into Eden. However, I find it comforting that the motif of paradise lost is found not only in the Bible but in ancient stories found all over the world. Regardless of what I think about the Bible and Christianity, the fact that these ancient stories have appeared all over the world makes them worthy of my attention.

To Know Or Not to Know Nature: We Are Not in Harmony

As a fly fisher, I have become particularly interested in how I might experience God through my relationship with nature. While fly-fishing, I sometimes feel profoundly connected to God, myself, others, and nature. I feel powerfully connected when I hook a fish and experience the pulsation of life at the end of the line. In this moment of what I call grace, I perceive that life finds me and responds to me. While I sense a mysterious connection, I must admit I am also aware of a disconnection. I suppose I feel the latter more strongly when a fish is not on my line. However, even when the fish *is* on the line, I know the moment of connection cannot last. I am not in Eden, and I acknowledge that the disconnect I feel is part of the human spiritual condition.

As a fly fisher, I often speak of truly knowing a river or lake. At the pond, I learned the behaviors of the fish, how and where to catch them. I knew when and where the fish were on the prowl in search of food. I knew when they were in the shallows and when they were deep. I learned what and when they ate. I knew what flies to use and the proper techniques to catch fish. Sometimes, I feel really in tune with a river and its fish. This can happen whether I am alone or with a client.

I might instruct a client; "Cast your mayfly two inches off of that rock." If a fish takes the fly in that moment, I think I can walk on water. I feel I know the fish personally and know them by name. However, that moment slips away and drifts down river. The next fish can refuse our every offering or simply not be there. Then I can barely hold my own footing in the raging currents.

I have learned not to be so quick to conclude I know the rivers I fish. Conditions change quickly. I miscalculate. I become focused on the fish I just caught and lose any sense of what is happening. An opportunity may be there, but I fail to recognize it and the moment is gone, downriver.

Can I really say I know these places? The more I think about it the more inclined I am to answer, "Not really," or, at best, "Maybe, at times." On certain days, I am inclined to say, "Not at all." When I look back, I remember the highlights, the moments of catching fish. If I am honest, I need to reflect upon the long periods of time waiting for a strike. Still, the ritual of fly-fishing is familiar and comforting. When I look back to those early years at the pond, I realize I experienced the pond more as a mysterious unknown rather than a place to call home. It had the strange sounds of bullfrogs, dragonflies, cicadas, and slithering snakes. It had large bass dispelling water in wild pursuit of prey. Even the bass were mysterious. They were strange-looking creatures.

The groundskeeper was mysterious and a threat of sorts. He looked shifty and unstable. I worried that he might decide to drive me out of the valley. He was unpredictable, like the fish. Within the mysteries, sometimes a fish found its way to me, pulled on the line, leaped out of its watery world, and entered my world. This too was mysterious.

My current experiences are still filled with a sense of otherness, mystery, and places beyond my control. The rivers and lakes I fish are places where I feel transported away from mainstream life. My visits leave me feeling unsure of where I belong. In spite of the mysteries, there is something wonderful, comforting, and calming about these places. At the same time, they are unsettling. I'm never sure if I belong there. Paradoxically, my sense of feeling drawn to nature and the places I fish stems from my sense of *not* quite belonging. That I am drawn to such places gives me hope that Eden still exists.

Sometimes I think I have found the key that unlocks a fishery. Such moments are golden, yet forty-five years of fly-fishing has taught me that such moments are fleeting. A fish takes the fly, gets hooked on the line, and then is gone. And there I am, unable to hook another fish. For as many times as I find the key, there are just as many times when I am out of tune, lost in the midst of rising fish who refuse everything I throw at them. I then feel out of Eden and out of harmony.

Whenever I see migratory geese overhead, I think of how little I truly know in my blood as instinct. I do not have much blood remembering, as Rilke suggested. Many days, I am simply not in harmony. I am unable to find the right fly, unable to cast to the right spot at the right time. All it takes is one selective fish rising to tiny mayflies, in its own rhythm, and my repeated clumsy attempts to place the fly at just the right time and in just the right place. My frustration intensifies and further separates me from the life around me. My longing to connect intensifies.

Of course, sometimes I get it right and I place the correct fly at the opportune time, perfectly over the fish. This gives me a wonderful satisfaction. Sometimes, friends and clients who have watched guides fish will say, "Wow, how do you do that?" However, I know that the moment is fleeting. The irony is that the moment I think I know a place, and how to fish it, I lose it. I might have a great day of fishing using a certain fly in a certain section of river with a certain technique. I conclude that I have cracked the code and have found the key. I *know* these fish. My clients and I proclaim that the "fish gods" are with us. We go back the next day to the same spot, at the same time, with the same fly, and use the same technique—and it doesn't work. The way has vanished. We lost the key. Now we need to start all over again and have to apologize to the friend we dragged into the woods and promised all these fish! In post-Eden waters, I have to relinquish control over nature. Fortunately, there can be beauty and serenity in not being in control.

I have a tendency to simplify my relationship to God and my relationship to the fish, only to discover repeatedly I do not really know as much as I thought. I tend to flatter myself, forgetting I am no longer in Eden. I take these complex relationships and try to understand them in quick three-step formulas. I almost have to laugh when I see advertisements for fly-fishing schools that promise mastery of the art in three short days or guides who speak of five years of knowledge delivered in one guide trip.

Three-step processes are part of a culture that wants immediate gratification. Even the Christian culture follows this simplistic approach. Neither life nor fly-fishing is that simple. The moment I say, "This is how I experience God," or "This is how I live a more purposeful life," or, "This is how I catch these fish," the *way* does not work. Upon closer examination, there is not a clear-cut path with signs.

Sometimes the path through the woods to the fish is quite elusive and more difficult than I imagined. Perhaps the only awareness that can help me find a new starting place is to admit that I am lost.

The Way through the Woods

Rudyard Kipling's poem, "The Way through the Woods," describes an elusive, mysterious path. Throughout the poem, he tells in vivid detail how you will see trout feeding in pools if you take this road through the woods. This sounds wonderful—until the poet seemingly contradicts himself and says there is no road in the woods.

What happened? Where is the road through the woods that leads to the trout-ringed pools and the mystical experience of the Divine? Where is the path to Eden? Where did the *way* go? The poem implies that the plant growth covers the road and that only a mysterious unknown keeper knows the way. As a fly fisher, I want to know who the keeper is and what has happened to the trout.

This poem, which often reflects the reality of fly-fishing, suggests that mysteries persist even for the advanced fly-fisher and expert guide. I do not see everything; Kipling implies that the only one who sees is the keeper. Who is the keeper? I do not know. I get glimpses of the way, nothing more. These glimpses, evanescent as the dew, also vanish. However, I do not need to become hopeless; rather I can allow the mystery to teach me of the true nature of God.

The minute I tell another person on how to find the Divine in fly-fishing, my words vaporize. I get lost in the mystery. Sometimes, I feel Something tug at my soul. I might mumble, "I feel a tug down deep, but it may only be a snag," Or, "I think I see a fish flashing under water." At other times, I feel nothing and catch nothing for long stretches. Yet there is this slight awareness of Something in the nothingness.

If someone asks me for advice on how to experience God while fly-fishing, I stumble. I might suggest that he needs to look at nature in a certain way. I might suggest she needs to be intentional about what she is doing. I might invite him to think more deeply about what is behind or under the river. I might ask her to put her ego aside and "consider the lily of the field." I might suggest he borrow a page from Norman Maclean, author of *A River Runs Through It*, and bring a bible or a book of poetry and spend some time sitting on the bank reading. Sometimes, the best I can do for my clients is to sit with them. We stare at flowers, rocks, and fish, knowing that God and the fish will still elude us.

I might tell them how fly-fishing has a cadence all of its own. I might invite them to contemplate how the river will remain long after we are gone. I might tell them that fly-fishing provides a much-needed pause so that they can reflect on their lives. I might suggest that fly-fishing could become a form of spiritual meditation for them; it could get them in touch with their deepest longings and with the ancient cycles of the earth. Sometimes, I invite them to turn over some rocks at the bottom of the river and learn to distinguish a stonefly from a mayfly. I can teach them to "match the hatch." The most important thing to learn is this: in spite of anything I can tell them or anything they can do, both fish and the presence of God will often continue to elude them.

Since I cannot guarantee that God or the fish will show up on the river, I often suggest the other extreme, "Shut up and fish," as one T-shirt puts it. I simply fish with them. We pay no attention to what we are hoping to experience. We give up the search and let go. We quit looking for metaphors and meanings. A fish is just a fish, a stonefly is a stonefly, a mayfly is a mayfly, a lily is a lily, and a rock is just a rock. We empty ourselves of expectation and then, when we least expect it and when we are not looking, Something might happen. Some might call this the Zen of fly-fishing. Before enlightenment, a fish is just a fish; after enlightenment, a fish returns to just being a fish. We let go, we give up, and then, maybe we catch a fish and a glimpse of God. There is a Zen concept that if we try really hard, it will take twice as long to master an art. C.S. Lewis said the same thing about trying too hard to find a spiritual experience out in the garden. He implies that we must just let it happen to us.

When I search for God, I always sense there is something wrong with my approach and my vision. I need to remember I only "see dimly as through a glass, darkly" (1 Corinthians 13:12). Ever since I left Eden, connections and experiences of true clarity are difficult. At times fly-fishing can connect me to Something. Nevertheless, I must remember that God is not under my control.

While I believe by faith that God is in everything, I do *not* find God under every rock or tree, I do not experience God with each fish I catch. The one deep hole on the river that I keep returning to in hope of catching the elusive one may become an empty void. Perhaps I start there, in the deep hole with no fish. I start in the void and wonder why the fish is not there. I ask why God is *not* speaking. I ask, "Where are you God?"

I often project my desire to find God within nature to the fact that, at least in terms of my experience, I have *not* found Him. While I do value the projections of what I hope for, and believe ultimately that God is found in all things, I try to be aware of my own wishful-thinking. Just because I wish something to be true does not make it true. I need to pay attention to what I am doing and consider who is rolling the camera. My own projected images distort my perception of reality and of God. It is my understanding of Rilke that he implies we create our own images of God. Yet, these images actually wall us away from God. And we often do this religiously.

During those times, I might feel close to God. On the other hand, I *might* be feeling close to the "god" that I have made in my own image. This is often the "nice" god who grants me my every request. This is the god of sunny summer and flowery meadows where the fish jump on my flies all day long. However, I might be on the other side of a thousand walls, quite far away from the reality of God who seemingly ignores me and might drench the flowery meadow with a dark thunderhead and lightning.

I find it difficult to let go of my projections or to have them challenged. My pious walls of religiosity are difficult to knock down. Guarded day and night by aspects of my own psyche, and even by religious institutions I sometimes dismiss, these walls endure. At times, I push on them. I try to be careful. I fear that when one of the stones wobbles off the wall, someone on the other side might cast it at my head.

While fishing with clients and friends, I have tried all sorts of ways to find the sacred in fly-fishing. The result usually is this: rather than God being marvelously present in nature and in the art of fly-fishing, God is somewhere else. God may be seemingly absent or hidden and beyond the perception of my experience. While I am focused on the river, God may be hidden in a field. I walk on by and miss the treasure. I wander and become lost. However, being lost, and admitting I am lost, is sometimes a good starting point.

When I admit I am lost, I may then learn that there is no road through the woods. I discover that the way, which I thought was the way, is not the way. The wood vines and the heather have spread and grown over the road I knew. I no longer know the way. I learn to know by knowing I do not know. And even this way of *not* knowing may not be the way. All I know is I am lost.

We Are Naïve about Nature Revealing God

As a fly-fishing guide of more than thirty years, I know that many people (myself included), Christian and non-Christian alike, religious and nonreligious, spiritual and non-spiritual, agnostic and atheist, have a naïve relationship with nature. Often in fly-fishing, there is this sense of immediate gratification and entitlement that is characteristic of our culture. I am naïve to think I can charge into the river and catch fish after fish, as though there are no complications, misunderstandings, or issues to workout. I see this tendency in my clients. I remember one client of mine who never fly-fished before. Before we left the parking lot, he spread his hands and said, "Well, Anthony, I would like to go to a place where I can catch some really nice ones, about this big because that is the perfect size to eat."

I politely explained that catching fish on a fly is not that easy. He was going to have to learn some skills first. He was a wonderful person, just naïve. He had no idea how uncooperative the fish can be. He did not know he had to learn *skill sets*—not a single skill—to even hope to catch a fish on a fly. However, once humbled by how challenging a fish could be, he was ready to learn. He learned slowly, but as he did he became mesmerized by the process. By the time he started catching fish, he had lost all interest in eating them for his dinner (which I was grateful for). He had become lost in the art of fly-fishing. Such a transformation, which occasionally takes place, is one of the most beautiful aspects of fly-fishing.

I am naïve to think I can so easily have it all: fish in the net, beauty, tranquility, peace, identity, and belonging. "Hard and narrow is the path that leads to life and few find it" (Matthew 7:14). I fail to remember my frequent disregard of the garden, nature, and the way. If I can turn my back on Eden so easily, why do I think it's such a simple thing to find a sense of belonging among the fish in the river?

I am not always conscious of this, but I am forever trying to return to Eden. I am forever hoping to find a sense of belonging I once knew, even if it is only in the recesses of my distant memory. I try to enter the woods, the garden, and the meadow stream. Yet I often feel far away, perhaps because I have been away for a long time. I have learned some bad habits that can make a respectful entry difficult. I possess a clumsy irreverence. I do not know how to mind my manners and embrace a proper etiquette.

While I am trying to find my own way, I sometimes notice other fly fishers stomp into the river, start slapping flies and line on the water, and scare all the fish away. They might then conclude that the fish are not biting or even that there are no fish in the river. Some fly fishers are like rude dates, who show up late, miss the hatch, and the most active feeding time of the fish.

Guides like myself sometimes think we truly know the river. I may feel I know the river like the back of my hand. I think the fish are mine and that I know them by name. I have suggested jokingly to my client that my name or his name is written on the fish. In such a self-inflated moment, I may identify with the client who called me a "fish whisperer." However, I am not a fish whisperer, and I would be better to remember that fact. The fish can be just as indifferent to me as to anyone else. I cannot call these fish by name, whisper to them to take the fly. I am not in Eden, and these fish are God's creation, of which I am only a small and dysfunctional part. Furthermore, I am too often the part that is out of sync and does not belong in the fluid and quiet world of the fish.

I find it astonishing that so many Christians, from fundamentalists to progressives, know of the Garden of Eden but rarely speak of this text and its implications. Many of my clients get hung up on the literal verses and miss all the meaning. I am just as guilty. Too often, the story no longer lives inside of me. I don't connect to the power, significance, and mythological radiance of the story. I refuse to look at the injury and alienation implied in the story. It is as though I am trying to stomp past the guarding angel and the whirling sword of fire that is warning me to proceed with discretion and reverence. As a human species, we do not have a good record of being respectful to the creation. The turning sword and the guarding angel is, when I pay attention, a reminder to fish with respect.

Many Christians profess to be in tune with nature, even if they rarely visit places of natural beauty on a regular basis. Some Christians resist an intimate relationship with nature because they feel it is pagan or new age to hold nature in high regard. Yet many scriptures speak of the spiritual value of nature.

In Romans 1:28, it says that God "clearly reveals" his eternal nature and divine attributes through nature. Jesus asks us to "consider the lily of the field" (Matthew 6:28). In parables he often taught by making reference to different aspects of nature: flowers, seeds, streams of living water, and rocks. I spoke earlier of how Job, when under interrogation by his friends and does not know how to defend himself, tells his friends to speak to nature. He believes nature will teach them.

> "But now ask the beasts and let them teach you.
> And the birds of the heavens, and let them tell you.
> Or, speak to the earth, and let it teach you. And let
> the fish of the sea declare to you."—Job 12:7-8

Sometimes, a creature of God's creation can teach me about my place and reveal the true longings of my heart. If fish of the waters I fish can teach me a great spiritual truth, then such a creature is worthy of my respect. Perhaps a large part of modern society can no longer listen to creatures that live on the outer edges of our hearts. Society as a whole seems caught up in the affairs of modern life and is too busy to connect to the wild. Ask a fly fisher, though. He or she fishes, hoping for a connection! Ask the fish of the earth. Ask the fish of the river that you might hook. Ask the fish why it does not want to take the fly you are presenting. Speak to the earth. It is God's creation, and it can teach. Fly-fishing offers me the unique opportunity to savor brief connections with a wild creature. Alas, it is a unique nature of this art—with its long hours of changing flies, and casting techniques, and presentations—to leave me disappointed that I have not achieved the connection I seek.

Perhaps the fish that consider my flies are asking me to consider the longings of my heart. The fish that consider taking my flies declare something to me. As I pursue fish, I am compelled to ask myself how much I might sacrifice in terms of my time, resources, and finances, to experience even a brief moment of connection to wildness and beauty. I have often stalked one fish all day, hoping for a single strike and that brief surge of life on the line. At some level, I am seeking a connection to creation. However, I am often reminded that all relationships are complex and have unique demands. All relationships have problems. They require time and work. They require an often delicate, tactful, and thoughtful approach. In the case of fly-fishing, often the fish swims off, in spite of my innocent and gentle intentions. I wind up standing there, bewildered that my fish does not want to play. Fly-fishing brings to the surface a child-like longing or connection with creation. When my daughter was seven years old, she noticed that the deer and rabbits of the meadow would move away from her when she approached. She came to me and asked, "Dad, how come the animals run away from us?" The profoundness of her child-like question stunned me. She, like many children, was speaking from the innocence of Eden. She was not afraid of the animals; however, from her own observation of the natural world, she concluded that the animals were afraid of her.

It has often occurred to me that the sport of fly-fishing exists because the fish are afraid and move away from me. Fear has entered my relationships. Perhaps it has not always been this way. My longing for Eden is, in part, a longing to end all fear.

Have We Been Invited to Wilderness?

I find all post-Eden relationships potentially difficult. To walk into nature once a year, and claim that I am "close" to nature, is foolish. It's like a father thinking that he can have an intimate relationship with his daughter if he takes her to Disneyland once a year. It is like a husband believing that his relationship with his wife will be fine if he brings home flowers once a year.

Underneath my relationship with nature are these questions: Have I been *invited* into these wild places to fish? Can I be trusted? Can I step into this river without muddying the waters? Has nature invited me to enter? Some Christians, maybe most, do not want to work out this relationship with "fear and trembling" (Philippians 2:12). They fall back on bible verses that seem to suggest that human beings need to place every wild creature (including all the fish) under our dominion. Of course, these verses are misquoted and taken out of context. Many of these folks lack not only reverence for nature but also the skills needed to catch a fish.

If the waters are public, does that mean I am automatically invited? From a spiritual perspective, this is not the case. It's certainly not what I mean by being invited. I am part of a public that does not have a good track-record with wild places. Over the decades, I have seen many fisheries collapse under the weight of too much fishing pressure, even those that are catch and release.

Paradise Lost: Milton

The last lines of John Milton's *Paradise Lost* imply that, even with providence as my guide, I will be confused in this new world of paradise lost. Yet the poem also offers hope. I can see the possibilities of the whole creation being before me. I am free to choose. I can also see the paradox in Milton's suggestion that our steps should be a slow wander. This to me implies a concern for how I am to proceed on my solitary way.

Often I do not consider my own steps, and my own movements are not slow, careful or thoughtful. In contrast, I rush to my favorite holes and stake my territory. I sit on my favorite runs, trying to catch as many fish as possible, particularly for my paying clients. At times, I can come across as though I own the river, speaking arrogantly and loudly. I can be quite territorial. The fly-fishing community often does not appreciate my aggressiveness and possessiveness.

I have spoken to many veteran fly-fishers who have grown tired of guides crowding the river and claiming it as their own. They can't be talking about me, can they?

These are complex issues. They become even more complex with the exchange of money. Money speaks loudly, complicates matters, and certainly affects our relationship to one another, the earth, and the flowing gardens we fish. These gardens are the rivers entrusted to us as fly fishers.

I like to think I have been called to enter these wild places and fish. If so, I must consider that the call also comes with an obligation to give an account of how well (or poorly) I have taken care of the places I fish. In "The Wind One Brilliant Day" by Antonio Machado, it is my opinion that the poet wants me to consider the question of asking myself directly what I have done with the rivers I fish. It is also a biblical teaching that someday I will give an account.

How will I answer the question of what I have done with the rivers, lakes, and fountains of living waters entrusted to me? What have I done with the garden entrusted to me? When I am called and asked to respond to the question, might I just weep?

Complex Interrelationships

I can see how all these relationships are interrelated in *Perelandra*, a fantasy by C.S. Lewis. Perelandra is a perfect world, one not fallen. It is the original Eden. Ransom, the main character, is a human sent to help this planet in some way. Once there, he begins to experience complex interrelationships. For just a moment, he has a less than honorable thought and he notices the consequence of his thought upon the natural world around him. His inappropriate thought took something away from the colors and scents of the landscape.

If I am rude to others on the river or I carelessly disregard small fish and fail to revive each captured fish, there is something wrong going on inside of me. These slight changes in my heart can reflect excessive pride, self-centeredness, and ingratitude. These changes in one moment impact all my relationships. I cannot separate out any one relationship from all of my others. Each relationship affects all the others. Every relationship is downstream of the other, and it all pours into the waters I fish.

When I was a child, I made a choice to break away from my peer group. As I look back at this choice, I am not sure I can justify it. On the other hand, I realize now that I possessed a deep sensitivity that prevented me from trying to please others. Was this sensitivity God's grace at work in my life? As an adult, I understand that Jesus became quite frustrated with the "people pleasers," those who sought "human praise more than praise from God" (John 12:43). While I have done my share of merely pleasing others, I have also felt a responsibility to resist belonging to churches or other clubs, where I might seek the approval of others. Just as I prefer the edges of the rivers and lakes I fish, I prefer lingering on the edge of religious institutions and social groups.

It is difficult for me to say that I could have handled my friendships in a better manner when I was a child. As an adult now, I am more capable of watching a different story unfold. As an adult I imagine myself making a different choice. I can see myself as a boy picking up the pace and running that extra mile to catch up to my childhood friends. I can see myself fishing together. I can see myself talking and sharing a lunch on the banks of the pond. I can see myself giving classmates some of my hand-tied flies. Then I show them how to cast and retrieve. Maybe we catch some fish together.

In my imagination, I can let go of my projections, fears, and blaming. In my mind, I can choose to go the extra mile for someone. If I can relive these moments, perhaps I can learn Something of love.

In so doing, perhaps I could get closer to Eden.

Forty-five years later, I am in a new land with new lakes and rivers—and new peers. I still long for connection, and I still long for Eden. However, I am free now to fish with my peers. In a sense, I can slip back in time to the banks of the pond. I can go back to the edges of the pond, as well as to the edges of the rivers I fish in Colorado. Rather than a place of division, the edges of ponds and rivers can be places of bonding.

It is easy for me to play out the same old story of my life and project everything I do not like about myself onto others. However, I have a choice, and I can treat where I am today as the next cross-roads in my life. I am walking on a path that suddenly diverges, and once again I must choose one path or the other.

I recognize that I have a tendency to walk alone, out of fear of being hurt. Yet there is another part of me that wants to invite the first person I meet to walk with me. There is something right and wrong in both of these impulses.

Why do I often live in fear, failing to love others and myself as I ought? Why do I live with such hesitancy? What do I fear? Am I echoing the same fear that Adam spoke of when he said, "I heard thee, and I was afraid because I was naked, so I hid myself" (Genesis 3:10). What is this fear and hiding really about? Is this the existential condition of a human being?

I am older and more mature. At least I now know that I cannot turn away the stranger upstream who needs my help without some consequences to my other relationships: people, fish, and God.

With this thought in mind, I cast. Just as I do so, I notice someone moving on the ridge along the river. Or at least I think I saw someone. Or was it a deer, bear, or a phantom?

Fearing My Nakedness

Eden, I still have a fear problem. In the Genesis story, Adam is in separation from himself and God. When God called to him, "Where are you?" Adam said, "I heard the sound of thee, in the garden and I was afraid, because I was naked so I hid myself." Adam now hides himself behind masks and is afraid to be naked. While being aware that I am naked and fearful can be a good starting place, fear is problematic. When I am afraid and alone, I have a tendency to blame others. This is exactly what Adam does (Genesis 3:10).

I have done my share of hiding in fear. I hide from myself, from others, and from God. When I am afraid and feeling alone, I tend to blame others. The text tells me that Adam blames Eve. When God asks him if he has eaten from the tree, which He commanded him not to eat from, Adam replies, "The woman who thou gavest to be with me, she gave me from the tree, and I ate" (Genesis 3:12).

I have a tendency to blame the problems I experience in my relationships on someone else. If I feel alone and fearful, or I cannot get the fish to bite, I look for someone to blame. I have started many sentences with these two blaming words, "But you ..."

Whenever something goes wrong, such as a fish getting away or a line getting tangled, my first impulse is to blame someone. If my wife is around, I will blame her. If she is not around, I might still blame her for not being around to help. I need to get a grip on this blame game, but it has been going on for a long time, and it is a difficult impulse to break. It takes courage to not blame.

With all these complications, I want to scream, "Where is God?" Now and then, I need to scream this question into the vast places I fish. If I do not yell out this question to God, I might just keep blaming those around me. My spouse and friends won't put up with this. Another option: I could blame the fish, which is really quite silly. So is blaming my new $800 fly rod.

Why Do I Feel Alone In My World?

Toward the end of *Perelandra*, Ransom finally ends up meeting with the king and queen, the first father and mother, and the first man and woman of this unfallen planet. They are in their true form. On earth, Ransom has never truly experienced a man or a woman in their true form. When Ransom first sees the king and queen, he falls to the ground and lies there. He says he has never seen a true man or woman and that he has only lived among shadows and broken images. He declares how lonely he has been.

Since I have been only on earth for my whole life, and have not spent any time on an unfallen world, I have an understandable tendency to assume that what I see and experience is the only reality. Every day I see various people—men, women, and children. I naturally assume that what I see before me is what it looks like to be human. It is difficult for me to consider the possibility that I am seeing broken images and shadows of men, women, and children who are not in their true form. At the deepest level, I am alone. I have no other reality, no other way of seeing what it means truly to be human. However, I do know the story of Eden. I know—or believe—that this points to a reality above and beyond what I see with my own eyes. Even these thoughts, beliefs, and memories are broken images.

If by some miracle I could ever see a whole, un-fallen person, I could move out of the land of shadows and broken images. Even if it was only for a moment, an intense longing to become what I just took into my vision would pierce my soul. Then I too

might fall to the ground in awe of what was before me and of who
I could become.

I Do Not See Fish in Their True Form

I am good at spotting fish in a river. Yet the fish I spot are not
fish in their true form. Even in this reality, I see only broken images.
I catch only glimpses. Because I spend so much time on the river, I
often can piece together the images and conclude it is a big fish.

Sometimes I will spot a big fish and whisper to a client, "It's
huge, can you see it?"

If the client is a beginner, he usually will have a difficult time
seeing the fish at all. He might catch a glimpse of the fish and mis-
judge its size. This is no surprise. I can come closer to the true size of
a fish because of my past experiences and my ability to piece together
the broken images.

In addition to that, I have learned from experience that the
biggest fish, particularly brown trout, have an uncanny ability to
hide their true size. They have the ability to lay low, blend in, and
remain concealed. Armed with this experience, I might say to the
client who is casting to this quarry, You are not seeing its true size;
trust me, this fish is 25-plus inches; get ready."

This "not seeing"—seeing only shadows and broken images—applies to fish, the wild flowers in the meadow, and the rocks
along the bottom of the river. I see only the shadows and broken images of the strangers I sometimes meet on the other side of the river.
They could be angels without my knowing (Hebrews 13:2). I see
everything and all the creation "only [as] a reflection as in a mirror"
(1 Corinthians 13:12).

Being on the other side of Eden, I have often wondered if my
nervous system has been changed in some way, perhaps tuned down

so as to protect me from fully experiencing the beauty and vastness of the world. In *The Great Divorce* by C.S. Lewis, the narrator describes a heavenly waterfall of such vastness, power, and beauty that he concluded something had happened to his senses. He realized that if he were on Earth, the waterfall, and its sound, would have been too big to comprehend. His senses would have been overloaded. The character is also convinced that the water spoke to him.

Can a waterfall speak? Can the meandering river speak to us "clapping its hands"? (Psalm 98:8).

I Ache With Creation

Nevertheless, even though I cannot see what is *really* there, Something in me remembers what was lost. Deep in my soul, I ache *with* the creation in an indescribable manner. I ache, moan, and groan for another life as I await my true adoption (Romans 8:23). I long for transformation with the creation into my complete and true form, as I once was in Eden. I do not even know how to pray for this transformation (Romans 8:26), but Something deep inside urges me forward. The same Spirit in creation that moans and groans tells me what to pray as I wait, aware of my incompleteness and brokenness (Romans 8:26).

While I wait, I often feel lost and forgotten. The world may forget me, and not know me, yet, my true family waits. I have the creation with me. I have the fish, the rivers, the stones, and the trees that all ache with me. Perhaps they too feel alone, waiting for God, and longing for Eden. Perhaps I have a few loved ones with me. Together we walk the river.

However, I do not think I can sing myself into a state of belonging by going to church on Sunday morning. In order to experience how connected I am to everything, I first need to admit how desperately out of place I feel. I have to know who I am down deep and where I do *not* belong, and then, perhaps, I can embrace and connect to the whole creation in new ways. At any moment, I am both connected and disconnected to the river, the fish, and to human beings.

The biblical narrative gives me insight into my dilemma. I am an "alien and stranger," sojourning in a strange land (1 Peter 2:11). During my time on Earth, it is difficult to be completely at ease with any of the simplistic ways of belonging. During this premature stage of my transformation, it feels as though I am orphaned and do not know my true parentage. I am an ugly duckling wandering from pond to pond forever seeking a place where I might belong. As I walk and wander the river, I also wander in my imagination. I seek my ancient home among flowing waters, ponds, trees, rocks, fish, and vast skies.

Let's follow the ugly duckling's wandering. One day he sees magnificent birds overhead. They cry down to him in the most beautiful sounds the ugly duckling has ever heard. To him, the sounds of those birds overhead possess a beautiful "otherness" that speaks to his soul. The sounds broke the ugly duckling's heart and at the same time gave him great hope, filling him with incredible longing. He cried back up to them in a sound he had never made before and did not recognize as his own. He was beside himself. He swam in circles and then tried to fly to them, but he was too late. He watched the beautiful creatures fly away. He was bewildered and unable to respond, but he would never forget his experience. I often feel as though life is flying past me and I am unable to respond and that I am haunted by powerful experiences of where I might truly belong.

Sometimes I get similar glimpses of Something. When I was at the pond as a child, I heard (but did not hear) a strange, yet beautiful sound *under* everything. It was, as Emily Dickenson implied, a melody without words. It could be heard over and over again—but not heard. I saw glimpses of beauty on and below the surface waters of the pond. These sensations reached my inner soul. I looked up and around but could never quite find where the sound came from. Even my pond, my Eden, was a shadowy world of broken images that I could only see and hear dimly.

A Story that Could Be True

A poem by William Stafford suggested to me that, if I can remember who I truly am, this truth might help ease my constant attempts to please others and to belong. If I can know who I am and where I truly belong, this truth could prevent me from compulsively trying to eliminate the confusion and alienation I feel. These truths could help me deal with the cold harsh winds.

The opening lines of the poem describe a man's condition of being born in a world that does not know him. He does not know where he belongs. He is without a mother, and no one told him the story of what happened. No one knows his name. He stands feeling the cold alienation of life, the harsh wind, and the rain falling. He watches the people walk by seemingly content in their world.

Sometimes I feel this way. I watch people walking the streets. I watch people fishing the rivers and lakes. They are in their world, and I am in mine. I wonder if they know what I am thinking; I often feel alone and uncertain of where I belong even as I catch fish or I guide my clients to fish. I might even look successful, but I still hear them ask me who I am and where I belong.

I remember fishing the pond alone and how, at least at times, I was able to claim that place as my own. I remember belonging there, at least in part. If I hear those questions now, even if only in my mind, how can I answer?

Even though life can be dark and cold, it is my interpretation that William Stafford has the character in his poem answer this
existential question (where do I belong?) by claiming Something of
an inner royalty. To me, the poem also suggests that often the world
will miss that deep inner conviction of the soul because it is not easy
to believe that deep down we are really kings and queens.

Knowing who I am involves knowing Something about the
Divine royalty I truly came from. I am part of a "royal priesthood, a
people for God's own possession ... who called me out of darkness
into the marvelous light" (1 Peter 2:9). Perhaps I can believe by faith
that I am back home, even as I fly off to a far off country where the
rivers run wild and free, and I belong. The far off country is both
here and far away, and I hope the choices I make can help bring me
home.

Choices in Reality

I now can see that I chose fly-fishing partly to protect myself.
Of course, I had other reasons, perhaps even sacred ones, for choosing particular paths, including the path to fly-fish. These choices
came from deep inside my soul and are a part of my personal story.
Perhaps my soul knew the way that would lead me to my personal
destiny. My choices are the exact places where my personal story
seems to overlap the bigger story, just as a small creek merges with a
large river or a creek meanders into a pond.

How I interpreted my choices and where they took me de-
pended on my vantage point. As a child, I walked the outer edges of
the pond. This was my vantage point. I was conscious of those edges;
maybe it made me open to thinking I was walking along the edges of
Eden, while Something bigger pulled me inward toward home—the
way a fish pulls me into deeper waters. For those of us who fish, per-

haps the best way to know the truth of a matter is to walk around a piece of water that reminds us of Eden.

There is Something powerful about the choices I made. Life does not simply happen to me. I can see how I made a choice to fish the pond as a child and, regardless of my motives (some honorable and some less than honorable), my choice was real. It wasn't arbitrary. It wasn't an accident. It resulted in a series of real steps taken on a dirt path that led to a real pond. The steps were not imaginary, symbolic, or allegorical. The pond had a name. The locals called it Fishers Pond. I could take a trip, even now, to north Jersey, walk the same path, and perhaps find dirt still displaced by my comings and goings forty-five and more years ago. I might be able to find a tree branch still slightly bent down by my hands when I tried to pull my fly free from a snag. Some of the fish that swim in those waters are descendants of fish I caught and released. I could walk around the pond and consider how my steps connected to the bigger story of Eden.

As a child, I did not always live in present time. Sometimes, I lived ahead of time, yearning to fish in the future in some imaginary place. Sometimes, I lived back in time, caught in some delightful memory. Did I think that by looking back I could slow the passage of time and the passing of a summer? Yet, the pond had a way of bringing me back to the truth of the moment. The pond was a real, concrete place in real moments of time. I was in reality, in the moment, casting and catching fish. As I watch myself back then, I cannot but help notice the importance of my fly rod. Next to me, that rod is too long to escape notice. That rod was real—an 8-foot Browning 6-weight rod with a green floating-level fly line. The rod was center stage in the small story of my life. As I cast, golden sparks flew off the rod and my fingertips. How could I not have noticed the beautiful arcs of line shooting above the water?

That fly rod helped me through the loneliness and disconnection of my youth. Now as an adult at midlife, I still consider the
ways that rod provided me with connection, solace, and fascination.
Fly-fishing provided me with the calm and courage to seek the heart
and mystery of God. Fly-fishing did not enable me to transcend the
existential condition of life, but it provided just enough foundation
for me to remain on my feet while I cast my hopes, aches, and longings to the wind.

As a fly fisher, there is hope for me. I can learn to cast to the
fish rising on the far bank so delicately that the fish will take the fly.
The first choice is to be on the river. Then there is rhythmic casting
of the rod and the laying out of the fly on the water so that the fish
rises and takes the imitation. The art of fly-fishing is with me. It eases
my heart and mind as I deal with the complex distances of the soul.

I have both my own story and the bigger story of God, which
is mysteriously a part of me. While the bigger biblical story reminds
me that there is distance, alienation, confusion, and exclusion from
Eden, there is also grace for the broken-hearted. Finding love and a
place where I belong is as elusive as trying to catch a 30-inch trout.
It is a place and a love I do not deserve, but I can receive it, at least
in part.

One of the most rewarding aspects of guiding happens when
my client and I experience grace. This can happen while teaching
beginners to fly-fish. Sometimes, my clients in their innocence and
ignorance stumble into a river they do not know and hook into a
giant fish. Caught off guard, we connect with nature in a surprising
manner. We have no idea how it happened. I refer to this as a minor
miracle, and I think this is fair. We experience Something of unfath-
omable beauty, thanks to the river's grace. I try to remember these
experiences when all feels hopeless. For me as a guide, doing all I can
to help an inexperienced client catch a fish, while not losing hope, is

an act of love. Sometimes, this hope, which I can choose for myself and in part for my client, manifests itself against all odds with a fish pulling on the line.

Sometimes, when I fish with a client and have one of those amazing experiences, I become aware that I might not be as alone as I thought. I almost hear something. Almost. Something calls to me, beckons me to be open to what the river offers. At times, I hear a faint call, an angel's whisper in the breeze asking me to take my fly rod and follow. That whisper can make all the difference in our world.

IV

The Call

෴

Coming out from under the Tarp

If God were going to speak to me, I am not certain how He would accomplish this act. When I look at my busy life, I notice that I am quite well protected from such intrusions. In truth, I do not welcome divine visitations.

I have not learned well how to listen to messages that come from the silence of nature. It is something of a paradox that I should have so much trouble discerning God's voice when it comes in the natural world. In truth, I pay more attention to the noise around me because noise gives me a sense of belonging. I am more in tune to the pinging of email entering my mailbox than visitations from some place of silence. As long as I feel some sense of belonging, however superficially, I settle in and I am not all that open.

The culture lies over my heart like a thick tarp. What might lie beyond is too far away and cannot get through. What lies deep within cannot rise. The constant bombardment from entertainment is deafening and hides what the wind might whisper to me. If the dominating culture is a thick tarp, then fishing out in mountain meadows and lonely quiet canyons can leave my soul exposed in a manner most needed.

Long before the tarp slipped over me, I learned to fly-fish a pond. As a child, perhaps this was when I was exposed to Something in nature. If God ever spoke to me, it was at this pond when I walked the edge of its banks and cast for fish. This was a time of solitude and of quiet vulnerability. This was a time of innocence when my eyes could see and my ears could hear. It was a place where I was vulnerable to a deeper connection.

I cannot describe exactly what I saw, heard, or felt at the pond, but Something brought me back there again and again. Sometimes I could see fish, and perhaps that was enough. I could cast to those fish and feel them tug on the end of my line. I could hear the fish splash out of the water chasing dragonflies. I could smell the sweet grass and clover. I could feel the morning dew on my ankles. These sensations filled my soul and brought me into another world.

Fishing the edges of the pond was a way out and away from my peer group and the prevailing culture. It was as though I moved out from under the thick tarp and found an opening to a green valley surrounded by trees. How refreshing! What solace! I walked in mystery in the valley of God. It was there, without a tarp, where God could reach down to me through the membrane of the natural world and speak to me. For a brief time, I walked and fished in Eden, and found a place I could belong. Did I have a hand in this? Did I venture out in such a way that God caught me?

If God is going to get through to me, I need to move out to that edge. I have to get out from under the tarp, at least for a little while. I have to make a choice to go there. Some level of intention and commitment, joined with faith, is necessary if I am to meet God. The wilderness is tarp-free, a thin place where God might speak tenderly to me.

Some churches still provide thin places where people might sense Something, of God, but many churches are tangled up in mainstream culture. They have become businesses. They are stuck under a suffocating tarp, trapped in a building with a huge mortgage. Rather than experiencing God in the vast skies, open meadows, flowing rivers—and each other—people find themselves fighting over budgets, words, doctrines, status, money, and power. In many churches, Christians idolize their celebrities much as people do in the secular world.

I know churchgoers who insist they are inspired by the preaching and the music. They claim the preacher has fed them. They are satisfied and filled. So be it. If people are satisfied with what they are getting, what can I say? It's just that I don't identify with the idea of satisfaction here. If I am satisfied, I am not hungry. I am not thirsty. I am not longing for more. It's not good to be too easily satisfied. I would rather remain in a state of hunger and thirst—and not ruin my appetite for more.

I would rather go to nature. I would rather climb through a forest to a mountain lake or follow a meadow stream and experience the quiet. I would rather hear nothing. I would rather ask God to fill the nothingness with Himself. I prefer to stand in a meadow stream, awaiting a fish to rise or a spring rain shower. "He will come to us like the rain, like the spring rain watering the earth" (Hosea 6:3). Bring me the spring rains rather than the church budget or dramatic altar calls.

I would rather be called out of the mainstream, at least at times, to a place where God can speak to me. Even if I do not hear Him, even if I am not fed, I will have my hunger as evidence of God's longing within me for what I truly need. I do not think I am called out of the world as a result of following strict moral codes or by passing judgment on others. Rather, it is a movement of my soul, together with the souls of others, toward the heart of God. It is a movement of two or three gathered in his name, into where we truly belong, knowing that we belong nowhere else. It is a place where we become and know ourselves as a peculiar people for God's own possession (I Peter 2:9).

The culture resists my going out to meet God. The culture is possessive of me, wants me, and needs me. The culture has a life of its own. It will fight to have me. In fact, the culture is quite effective at keeping me under its tarp. This gives me all the more reason to get out. If I do not get out, I will have a hard time hearing fish slurping after bugs, smelling the sweet grass, or seeing the morning dew. I will find no reason to cast.

The culture is particularly effective at throwing its tarp over children. I was lucky that way, or maybe Something was just looking after me. When I was a boy, I spent my summers fly-fishing at the pond. Few children today have comparable experiences. They have no quiet place where God might enter. Does God call to children through pop music, TV comedies, professional athletes, violent computer games, and smart phones? Will God be able to find a way through their demanding schedules? Will God find a way to speak truth to children through modern day ministries, preachers, Sunday-school teachers, youth pastors and priests, whose efforts must be relevant to the culture.

My hope lies in being called out. My hope lies in my choice to move out of the mainstream culture into nature. In that wilderness, under a blue sky, I might actually regain my divine hearing and sight. I might really see fish below the surface. In that fresh air, I might remember where I wanted to be and what I wanted to do with my life. I might hear a whisper from above—or feel a tug from below—helping me to catch a glimpse of where I truly belong.

I began to catch these glimpses when I first learned to cast to a fish. I could hear the fish slurp the surface of the water and see them hiding below. I would turn to the sound and cast, hoping for the fish to take my fly. I learned to wait for the rise. Like any good fly fisher, I would pause and take a deep breath before setting the hook. Even now, when I cast and wait, my lungs fill with air from a far-off country. Then I remember a place I once knew, a place I barely remember. I set the hook, the strong fish peels off the line and in that moment, the line connects me to this other place that feels both far away and strangely familiar. My heart softens, and aches. My head spins, and I remember a place where I belonged and felt wonderfully lost.

Becoming lost might be a good way to get out from under the tarp. Admitting I am lost might be a good starting place.

Called for No Good Reason

Did I hear a voice? Was I called? I can't know for certain I was called to fish the pond in Northern New Jersey. I do have an "uncertain certainty," as Emily Dickenson once wrote. How could I ever know with absolute certainty? It is a weighty thought. To consider the possibility that God called me requires pondering, an uncertain process for sure. It compares in my mind to meandering backwards and forwards along the river in search of that one large and elusive trout. When I do this, I am likely to walk too quickly and pass the fish hiding in the undercut. Or, I might wrongly assume the fish can only be in a deep hole and fail to see the fish in a shallow riffle.

The possibility of being called to do any single task in this life is beyond my wildest dreams. For example: just once, one cast, to one rising fish. That would be enough. Ah, but surely there are worthier pursuits. I would love to know I am not alone. What could mean more to this lonely, lost soul walking this earth outside of Eden? How beautiful to consider the possibility that the tears of my homesickness and lovesickness were not the futile grieving over a delusion. To entertain the possibility that I am not alone brings joy and touches the deepest longings of my soul.

To consider the possibility that I am not alone moves me deeply with reverence and humility. I do know with certainty that I am not always in this spiritual place. When I am fishing, sometimes I see nothing. I feel nothing. Clearly, I am lost, but I may not feel even that. At best, I feel deeply alone. And then, suddenly, there is a movement from below, a huge swirl. A fish rises, takes the fly, and then plunges to the bottom of the pool, tugging both rod and soul. Once again, I live in the "uncertain certainty" of God perhaps trying to speak to me through glimpses, tugs, and swirls.

Can I be open to all possibilities? Do I believe a fish can rise in the next moment? Are there times when it is impossible for me to believe that God could call me, because of my lack of faith? It was said that, "[Jesus] did not do many mighty works there, because of their unbelief (Matthew 3:58). Is it my lack of faith that denies me the enchanting world of Eden, where anything can happen?

What could be more hopeful, exciting, and terrifying than feeling Something that calls me? It is terrifying because it requires a response. If I feel a tug on my line, I might respond by lifting the rod. In that situation, I would probably respond. But I might not. I notice that many beginners will sense a tug on the line and not respond. In this case, I usually ask outright, "Why did you not strike?"

Often their response is, "I didn't think it was a fish." In life I might do the same, nothing. I might refuse to believe that God is speaking to me.

It is a miracle that a call is even in the realm of possibility. Moreover, in return, my response requires a miraculous leap of faith. Here is another miracle. "How blessed are those who have not seen and believe" (John 20:29). Even though I cannot sense that God is calling me, I could respond. This seems strange, but I have experienced this while fishing. In fact, I often sense that a fish is there, lift the rod, and then feel life tugging on the line. As in fishing so in life, I can learn to respond even while I doubt.

Doubting makes me look for reassurance, but I do not know how to look or what I am looking for. After God instructs Elijah to go stand on the mountain as He is passing by, Elijah sees only a glimpse of God's backside. Like Elijah, I might see the mountain crumbling before my eyes, the strong wind, the earthquake, and the fire. But I don't see God. If I hear God's voice at all, it is in the "still small voice, and in the gentle whisper" (1 Kings 19:11-13). This is not easy, because the culture insists on constant noise that distort and drowns out the gentle voice. Many churches have come to be noisy places, where I can no longer hear the still small voice. In addition, I have my own inner blow horn; the endless chatter of my rational mind prevents me from hearing a gentle whisper.

Stories around the world suggest that the common reaction to a call is to refuse, at least at first. Certainly, I am reluctant. I do not want to do the task. Maybe I am lazy or afraid. Maybe I feel completely unworthy and incompetent. "Who me? Oh no, not me. I am not worthy." In my defense, I might point out that some of the biblical prophets heard the call and refused at first. In popular literature, I think of *The Hobbit* by J.R.R. Tolkien, in which Bilbo Baggins passed out from fright in his own kitchen when Gandolf and the dwarves called him to adventure. Everyone in the room, except for Gandalf, thought they had the wrong man for the journey.

It seems to me, when God truly calls, it is not so easy to say yes. Out of fear of having no purpose or connection in life, I keep a full schedule. There are few time slots for God. Mainstream culture, on the other hand, seems to know how to get me to respond to its opportunities. I am susceptible to flattery. If someone says, "I have a job for you," I feel honored. I like being connected, however superficially, to clubs, causes, and projects. I pile more and more onto my plate. I am learning—slowly—to question the automatic "yes" response that can leave me exhausted and confused as to what or who I am serving and where I truly belong.

When I have the courage to refuse a request, it tends to have more to do with pragmatic reasons, such as finances, rather than what my soul needs. This bothers me. If I only say yes to the world, I may be selling my soul. I am becoming like the rich man, who took advantage of every opportunity that made him richer. He could only think in terms of tearing down his barns and building bigger ones. In the end, he could not find his soul (Luke 12:18).

Responding to economic opportunities is not the same thing as responding to the call of God. Soren Kierkegaard warned me that following the Christian faith does not have practical value. When Jesus called the fishermen to follow him, they dropped all their gear and left. The call of God had nothing do with increased economic opportunities for them or their place in the world.

If I ever sense a call from God, how could I not feel some fear? My favorite poet, Rainer Rilke, wrote that all angels are terrifying. If I am stepping into God's plan for my life, I will sense the weight, power, and magnitude of Who calls me. Under this weight,

I will fear failure while at the same time as I hope that my life may be connecting to some bigger story. It will be like catching so many fish my boat seems to be sinking. When I realize that God is doing Something in my life, I might be in such awe that I too might yell out, as Peter did, "Go away from me Lord" (Luke 5:7-9). Rather than feeling comfort, I might feel lost and not in control.

Losing my way and walking in the dark may be what my soul actually needs to hear the call. As much as I love to fish, I can find four or five good reasons not to listen when I feel the call. I should challenge those "good" reasons. If I hear myself saying, "First, let me," or, "But, I have to … " I need to be suspect of *those* voices, as Jesus was when he called individuals to follow him (Matthew 8:21; Luke 9:61-62).

It might also be a good idea to practice leaving behind my suit and tie or my paperwork. Leave them at home in the closet or at the office. Grab the fly rod instead. For no rational reason I should grab that fly rod and get out the door, barely clearing the tip of my fly rod from the closing door. I may not get another chance.

In terms of calculating what is safe and responsible, the math is meaningless. It is *always* safer, more economical, reasonable, and practical to stay home. For me, it is necessary to respond to the call and fish while I still have opportunity.

Over the decades, I have had several fly-fishing friends pass away. When we were younger, we planned fishing trips. I am grateful for those trips that became reality and yet many drifted away and such opportunities cannot return. It is truly difficult to grasp.

The lesson is that life is a gift, and I need to make the most of my time. I do not know how much time will be granted. While guiding, I often meet individuals who are trying to live life in some deeper, fuller manner. We talk about how we feel the years slipping away. Often we talk about working less and walking the river more often. We often speak of all the obstacles, fears, and responsibilities that stop us from getting out the door to fish. Most often, I am encouraged by these conversations, knowing that many of us still hear a call to pursue life in nature. I hope that we can still respond before another three, ten, twenty, or thirty years slip away. The river of time races on and we are powerless to stop its flow.

I know of many individuals who at midlife have said, "All I need is one more year before I retire," or "All I need is one more year before I have enough money saved," or, "All I need is three more hours to finish this house project, and then I will go fishing." Sometimes, no such gift is received.

And I wish I had a dollar for every time someone told me they could not fish because they had to clean the garage or fertilize the lawn.

Straying from the Path of the Routine Where Anything Can Happen

Hooking a monster fish at dawn has a strange effect on the individual. It feels like a calling of sorts. I ask myself, "Was I called to land this huge fish?" I ponder the meaning of what lurks in the dark depths, powerfully pulling on my line.

In *The Old Man and the Sea*, Santiago has not caught a fish in eighty-seven days. He decides to go farther than he has ever ventured before. In those unknown waters he hooks a giant marlin. This story touches me. When I venture further out, beyond my comfort zone, I feel as though I am fishing in the deeper aspects of my soul.

As Santiago battles the fish, his heroic qualities appear. He develops a reverence for the fish, no longer caring about his own life or responsibilities. He is determined to fight to the end, even if it costs him his own life.

When I hook a big fish, I start to wonder. Are the fish gods with me today? Is today my lucky day? Why me? Am I meant to land this fish? Of course, there can be more superstition than religion in these thoughts, but perhaps I need to acknowledge the fine line between the two. Alongside the hope that I will land this wonderful fish is the fear that I will lose it, the one that got away.

Complexities with the Call: What about Everyone Else?

There is a biblical notion that God controls the hearts of rulers for his purposes. For example, he changed the heart of Pharaoh. There is also an old proverb.

> "The king's heart is in the hand of the Lord, like the rivers of water, He turns it wherever he wishes."—Proverbs 21:1

I think back to the pond, just downstream of the upper meanders of Pearl Creek, where I received the benefits of the groundskeeper's changed heart. Did God change his heart for my benefit? And how did my own choices, however slightly, change the river and course of my life?

Sometimes when I am fishing, I wonder who is more important, I or the stranger standing on the other side of the river. I try to be open to the possibility that the stranger across the river has a purpose I am not aware of. Perhaps it is the stranger's day to catch a monster fish. I might have to stand there envious of this person who, I feel, may have encroached upon my sacred waters. Perhaps I have to learn that if someone asks me for my shirt, I have to surrender my fish as well.

I am hardheaded, slow to learn the deeper meanings of the call to love others. One day on the Dream Stream section of the

South Platte, I wanted to get in one of my favorite runs by the old barns. However, someone was fishing there already. Somewhat disappointed, I walked on to find other water. As I was walking away, the man in *my* hole started to yell at me. He was waving his arm, and wanted my help. He wanted to know if I had a net. Being the snob that I can sometimes be, I hesitated. I figured he was an inexperienced fly fisher who had hooked into a ten-inch wimpy rainbow. I had my reasons. He was wearing a goofy straw hat, outdated vest, and old-fashioned waders. His fly rod was an old, thick yellow fiberglass model, which was bending sharply from the weight of what had to be a firm snag. I was sure that his wimpy fish (if there was a fish at all) had hung him up on a rock or willow shoot.

In my arrogance, the epiphany was slow to come to me. I wondered if he might really be fighting a big fish. I still said to myself, "No way. What are the odds?" However, I have had too many experiences with the ironies of life not to consider *what* might be pulling on the other end of his line. I sense that I was about to learn a lesson in humility and picked up the pace.

"I have been fighting him for about twenty minutes," the man said when I reached his side."Sure glad you have a net." My eyes followed his short, stout, 5-foot heavy leader (if we could call it a leader as it looked like straight 20-pound test mono). It went down into the water where it connected to an angry brown shaking its massive head back and forth, trying to dislodge the size-4 hopper. I netted the 25-inch brown trout. I stood in envy and wondered if even God could call such a monster fish out of the depths.

Was this man called to catch a giant brown and I called to merely net it for him? And was my half-hearted compliment part of a sacred contract, about which I was ignorant?

Could God Call a Fish?

Since I was a child, I begged God to cause a fish to bite. In that begging I didn't realize that I was engaged in a form of prayer. I have made thousands of casts, and I can admit that somewhere along the way I have wondered if God could change the mind of a fish and make it strike my fly.

Even as a guide, I have desperately begged God for a fish to bite. Begging and praying can take many forms. Many of my clients talk to the fish, sometimes in childish language, "Here fishy, fishy; come on, come on, take the fly."

I have known guides of the most skeptical nature to thank God when they finally put a fish in the net for a client. Maybe I'm one of them. If I thank God for a fish, does that suggest I believe God would call a fish to strike?

When I think about this, I try to avoid making hasty conclusions about what God may or may not be doing. On one hand, it is not dignified for me to scream that God has blessed me and hooked this fish for me. On the other hand, after fishing for hours and catching nothing, I might declare that God is dead or that He does not pay attention to such petty concerns. This is equally foolish, which becomes obvious when a fish bites shortly after my tantrum.

Even when I am not in spiritual mode and just fishing with my skills and experience, I make wrong conclusions. Sometimes I will cast and cast until I conclude that there are no fish in the river or they are not hungry. Both conclusions may be false. Sometimes, I reach these ridiculous conclusions even when I can see the fish in the river and that they are feeding. And sometimes a large fish takes the fly, pulls out the line, and defies the false conclusion I made just a moment ago.

The story of God calling a whale to swallow a man reminds me of how small I am.

Small "god" in My Back Pocket

When I believe I am called, I flatter myself. There can be other explanations. To be *called* is big stuff. It tickles the ego and offers a grand defense against the existential meaninglessness of my life. If I am called, I feel good about myself. I have a sense of belonging. I might even use my calling to manipulate others and justify many things.

I am not ruling out the possibility that I am called to perform certain tasks on earth. It is wonderful notion to have a sense of calling to my work, relationships, and fishing. It gives my life meaning. However, when I speak so nonchalantly about a possible calling, it may sound like I am trying to convince myself. In addition, talking casually about such matters seems a little irreverent. It is a form of taking the Lord's name in vain. I may say, "God's will is this," and "God's will is that," and "the Lord told me to do such and such." Speaking so casually, yet absolutely and definitively about God calling, makes it seem as normal as receiving a call on my smart phone. Smart phones are technological wonders, but getting calls on them from God is a whole other matter. If I think God is calling me on my phone, I should take it back to the store and get a refund. Then I need to go fish the Dream Stream in the middle of South Park all alone, where I might only hear the wind howl and catch nothing all day.

If I'm getting calls from God, I may be guilty of thinking everything revolves around me. It is worse than putting God in a box. It is putting God on my smart phone. I've got Him in my back pocket. Any time I need to hear from Him, I just pull out my phone and push a button.

If I am going to talk about God calling me, I need a special language. I prefer the following phrases: "This is my best hope," "I got a glimpse," "I see dimly," "I heard faintly," and my favorite, "Perhaps." I like to add some doubt to the hope I proclaim. Ironically, doubt keeps my hope alive.

Here is another thing that bothers me. Having an almost intimate verbal communication with God defies the huge distances that were set up after Eden. Intimate conversation seems to defy the vastness and mystery of God. How can I possibly comprehend these distances, especially with such ease? If I stood on the rim of some great chasm and screamed across at the top of my lungs, I question whether God would hear me. I might hear only my own echo.

Anglers speaking across the river cannot easily hear one another over the roaring cataract. Perhaps it is good to scream to God anyway. Then I can wait and perhaps hear God's voice in the silence that almost overwhelms me. If on the other hand, I think I am able constantly to hear God talking to me, how could I ever feel any loneliness or long to span the distances? If God is constantly speaking to me, there is no chasm or void. I would never ache to span such short distances. It would be like jumping across a narrow, shallow creek. I could easily span such a short distance with a step or two and keep "god" in my pocket.

In my inner life, I am in search of home, which at times feels deep within and at other times a million meanders away. Is my search for a place of belonging also a search for God? Perhaps I was called to that search while I was casting to fish that belong more to the river than I ever could.

Something about That Fly Rod

The search for God can be quite complex, abstract, and elusive. Searching for fish with a fly rod is far more concrete. As a child,

I learned to grasp the fly rod in my hands and sense its every move and vibration. Through practice, I learned to exercise more and more control over the rod. With my fly rod, I could walk with purpose through the forest to the pond and better handle the existential conditions of life. I could endure the ambiguity of the search or even ignore the search all together.

When Moses came down from the mountain after seeing only God's backside, his face was shining so bright that the people could not look at him. How could I claim that I stood before God and heard Him speak? How could I claim that an angel spoke to me if my face never became radiant? Even so, I think there were times when I came back from the pond, the Eden of my youth, and my face was slightly radiant.

"No man can see God and yet live"(Exodus 33:20). This sure coincides with my inner experience in that the very thought of seeing God is terrifying. How dare I approach God? Where can I find Him? A fly rod in my hand would help. At least, it provides a comfort and eases the brilliance in the truth of God.

However skeptical I am, I do not rule out the possibility that I may have been called to certain tasks on Earth. It is my understanding that Emily Dickinson suggests that there are truths that are too intense and we must take them in gradually. It is a great mystery. Maybe at the pond, I was called and maybe I was not. While I am open to my own errors in the interpretation of such events, I am also open to the possibility that God or an angel drew me to that pond. If God did, it was not because I was brave, worthy, possessing great faith, or anything special at all. It was just the way the story of my life would ripple, meander, and merge into a bigger river.

Jesus often responded to those with the least amount of faith. He did not seem to care about anyone's spiritual accomplishments. For him, faith the size of a mustard seed was enough to move mountains. He was willing to help those with humble unbelief. My faith is tiny and alive with uncertainty, but it holds out the possibility that a 30-inch brown lying in the undercut bank *might* take my fly. How could real faith ever have certainty in a world of such mysteries?

Sometimes while fly-fishing alone, I wrestle with how God is involved in my life. Then I feel a comfort that I cannot explain with my rational mind. The more I question and the more I wrestle, the more alive and real my faith becomes. Perhaps grace meets me in my own weakness and doubt. I suspect that doubt provides the openings where God might enter—but only if I do not fill those openings with concrete certainty. The best starting place is where I am *unable* to believe. Then I might hear a call to Eden.

Looking for Proof of the Call

Did God or an angel call me to a little pond in the wood of northern New Jersey? While I cannot be certain I was called, I can at least be certain that I responded to an opportunity. I walked the trail through the opening in the woods that led to the pond. And I fished. Was I called and then walked to the pond? Or did I walk to the pond and then sensed that I was called to do so? I do not know. Perhaps it doesn't matter. God transcends all time and sequences.

Since those summer days at the pond, I have had a growing sense that Something did Something. Maybe it was a call, maybe it wasn't. All I retain is possibilities. I offer no proof. For the most important things in life, perhaps I never have proof. I can consider my own life story. I can look at the concrete reality of how I later became a fly-fishing guide and came to take hundreds of adults and kids fishing. While fishing with me, perhaps a client heard, saw, or sensed Something of the treasure I was trying to share with them. Perhaps he or she took it with them, however small the treasure.

As I continue to ponder these questions, I choose to follow the serpentine curves of the South Platte River through its mountain meadows and the trout-blessed pools of deep canyons.

Beyond Catching Fish

The goal of catching fish is complex, powerful, and primal. I would like to claim I focus primarily on more important things, but I am a fly-fishing guide. Catching fish tends to be my immediate goal when I approach a river. After forty-five years of fly-fishing, this is how I am wired. At the same time, I am also aware that I am seeking Something else. Henry David Thoreau did not actually say it, but he is often credited for saying that men fish all their lives without knowing that it is not the fish they are after.

I am past the age of looking for an adrenalin rush. I do not need to catch the biggest or the most fish. Sometimes my ego comes into play but less often than it used to. It does seem that pursuing a trophy fish or the biggest number of fish increases my frustration. If I think my catch for the day defines success, contentment eludes me. If I think the catch will define who I am, Eden feels far away.

The best approach for me is simply to be grateful for the opportunity to fish. As a child fishing the pond, I found a strange peace and contentment. I had a sense of thankfulness, knowing that I wanted to be at the pond, casting and peering into the water. It didn't matter so much if I concluded the day without being able to grasp the fish in my hands.

My sense that Something will happen increases if I have an attitude of gratitude when I visit the wild trout streams and lakes. I do know that Something will *not* happen while I am sitting on the couch watching TV. Therefore, I consider it my responsibility to show up at a canyon or meadow stream with a grateful heart

I also think that choosing to fish or wander the hills creates an opening where something out of the ordinary can happen. Fly-fishing can bring me to a place where I listen in new ways. I begin by showing up. I go to the river. I listen to the water tumbling over stones and to fish rising in quiet pools. I consider what might be under the rocks. I listen to the silence between the sounds of rising fish and rippling currents.

Perhaps, in that pause, I am called.

V

The Pause

◇◈◇

The Pause in the Cast

Something about casting a fly is beautiful: the effortless back and forth rhythm, the magical movements, the tight loops, and the arc of the line dancing in the morning light. As I cast I try to get in tune with the rhythms of the river and the fish.

Even as an experienced guide, I often feel somewhat out of tune with God's rhythms. I do not experience connectedness. Outside of Eden, I have a hard time finding my true rhythm and place. Even so, at times, fly-fishing provides me with unique moments of grace and connection to Something bigger than myself. In fact, it is because I feel out of tune that I am able to experience a hunger for a deeper grace. When I realize my true spiritual condition, then my desire for grace reaches deep within my heart. Where my heart is, there lies my treasure. If I know my true spiritual condition, I am less likely to fall into spiritual complacency.

As a guide, I know that it is difficult to teach the art of casting. Most beginners will be out of tune and take a fly rod too far back. If you take the rod too far back and or do not pause before starting the forward cast, you lose all the power. The rod simply does not load. In a sense, by not trusting in the pause, you lose power.

As an experienced fly fisher, it is tough to watch someone take the fly rod back too far or not allow the needed pause. Beginners tend to leave out the pause, then over-compensate by casting with more power forward. The harder they try the worse it gets. As a wrestler, I learned there was a time for more power and time to remain and wait. I would do well in life if I could learn the wisdom of knowing when and where to put power on. Even when I cast, I sometimes forget to pause.

When mastered, the cast is beautiful and graceful. It also offers a spiritual lesson. Perhaps it even provides a glimpse into the beauty and rhythm of God. However, I have to do my part by committing to making the back cast, just as in life I have to commit to certain tasks. Then there comes the crucial moment for the needed pause. Without the pause, I am driven by anxiety. When I wait in the tension of the pause, the line suspended in the air, I am engaging in an act of faith. I do nothing during the pause. In my anxiousness and compulsiveness, doing nothing is not easy for me. It is hard to do nothing well, but sometimes doing nothing is really Something.

The pause in fly-casting helps me consider the madness of my ways. Here I think of the story of Martha and Mary (Luke 10: 38-42). Martha is compulsively fretting, while Mary takes a pause at the feet of Jesus. Mary receives praise for her pause. Often in life, I compulsively do too much. I tend to be an overachiever, and my compulsions can set me off on self-defeating paths. The pause stops me from forcing my way through life. To pause and allow grace to meet me is a thing of overwhelming and immense beauty. I might then learn something of the peace, beauty, and power available to me.

The pause in the cast has parallels in my life and faith. "Be still, and know that I am God" (Psalms 46:10). The call to fly-fish can create the pause, and that pause can lead to rest. Each cast I make reminds me of a needed spiritual pause. If only I could learn to pause in the midst of my struggles. If only I could learn to be still before God, that moment could become a sacred moment and Something of grace. My hope is that my casting creates a pause where God might enter.

Pausing in the Midst of a Compulsive Culture

I have a sense that the culture in which I live does not wish for me to pause. It has its own agenda that does not include rest. The culture is quite effective at keeping me caught up in the madness of my life. When I allow the culture to overcome me, I live compulsively rather than in freedom, power, and grace.

Every time I pause and consider going fishing I sense some resistance, which comes from a mysterious place. Perhaps you feel this resistance yourself. Wherever this resistance is coming from, it can make it difficult to get out the door.

"Come unto me all who are weary and heavy laden and I will give you rest" (Matthew 11:28). This call to enter rest requires a response. Ironically, when I am being "responsible"—doing my job and chores at home, never getting out into wilderness—I rarely enter deep rest. On the other hand, fly-fishing, allows me the pause I need to let go of my compulsions. I can let go of the chatter in my head.

It's built in to the world of fly-fishing. I pause while the line lingers in the air, suspended during each cast. While spending a few hours fly-fishing a river, I might pause hundreds of time.

Am I More Than What You See?

Deep down it is my hope that I am not this anxious man that most people see. I hope there is more to me, inside me, and to my life than running myself ragged.

I am aware that Something deep inside me moves at a different pace, Sometimes it doesn't move at all. At times, I can rest in the pause. "Let us therefore be diligent to enter that rest" (Hebrew 4:11). Too often, I fall from this grace and rush away from this still point. Most often, I am not in a deep still place. I reject the rest offered.

As a guide, I can be anxious and frantic. I rush around trying to get a good piece of water for my clients. I am anxious to get fish in the net. While it is true that this is what they are paying me for, I am not relaxed and neither are the clients. They can sense my tension. Ironically, this state of mind is the antithesis of fly-fishing.

Deep down, perhaps when I feel most at peace with myself, I am at rest in between the self-imposed pressures of life. This resting point is a better indication of what my soul desires than the anxious rushing around trying to prove myself and find a place where I belong. I can be quite content in these in-between places and times. When I am walking a river alone, looking for fish and waiting for them to rise, I am at rest. In the pause during casting, I am at rest.

Sometimes while fishing for deeper dialogue, I may ask a client, "So, how is life?" Such inquiries tend to create a pause, and I have to learn to sit in the silence and allow the person to reflect. For those of us who fly-fish together, such pauses may provide the only interruptions from the hectic compulsiveness of our lives.

Being on the river is a great place to enjoy a pause. Sometimes, I'll ask someone, "Do you have a spirituality or religious faith that you practice?"

One morning on the river, a gentleman, after a substantial pause, responded this way: "You are only the second person who has ever asked me that question in the past fifty years. The other time was just last month."

Together, while casting, we had meaningful conversation. I find that many people long for dialogue that moves below the surface, but they do not know how to begin.

In a related manner, they do not know how to begin to drift a fly.

Letting Go: Drifting in the Quiet In-Between Places

In between the casts, there are countless drifts of the fly. I cast and then let the fly rest on the water and drift. I cast again. I try to make perfect casts with perfect drifts. Cast and rest. Cast and rest. Cast, let go, and drift. As I cast and let go, my mind sometimes enters a quiet place and a rhythm all its own. Between the cast and before the next is when the fish takes the fly. In this quiet interval, Something miraculous can happen. The fish takes the fly and enters my place of stillness. The fish enters my world as I enter theirs. I connect with creation in that in-between place. It is the briefest of encounters, but other fly fishers recognize the experience.

The first time a fish took my fly from the surface on a dead drift, I thought it was bizarre that I did not have to do anything but let go. I did not have to twitch or jiggle the fly in any manner. I did have to learn specific techniques that set up a drag-free drift, such as "mending" and "high sticking," but once I learned those tricks, all

I had to do was let the fly drift down the river. I had to let it go, no strings attached as it were.

My problem in fishing and in life is that I want strings attached to everything I do. I came to realize that my need to control things just messes everything up, including a good drag-free drift and a chance to connect to a good fish.

During some drifts, I sense deep within that Something is about to happen. The pace and exact place of the drift feels a tiny bit different. Time feels suspended. Words are inadequate to describe this awareness. How can I describe Something that lies beyond rational thought? How does a poet know to use a certain word and not another? How does an oil painter know when to streak an arc of blue across the canvas? How does the batter know when to swing for the fences? How does the quarterback know when to release the ball? How does a speaker know exactly when to use the right word? How does a fly fisher describe Something that borders on the mystical? How do I find the words to explain the mysteries of life?

Most often when I try to pray (for lack of a better word), I am not in a place of quiet flow where I sense something can happen. I am out of flow and not at rest. When I am rushed, chatty, or too cerebral, I do not feel comfortable being quiet for any length of time. Yet no matter how often I am unable to be at peace, deep down I am aware of a still place available to me, where I know Something can happen. Sometimes I avoid that place because I do not like the idea of Something happening that is beyond my control. Instead, I might choose to be anxious and miserable in the moment because I think I am somewhat in control, even though I am not.

Perhaps outside of Eden, I forever struggle to let go of my control on life. I clutch to hope and love in all the wrong places. I forever use a little bit too much force and fail to enter the flow of grace.

Learning to Wait Without False Hopes

Outside of Eden, I am not very good at waiting. I hate waiting in line for gas or for something in a store. I am not very good at waiting for love, a fish, or anything else I can think of. As for fly-fishing, instead of allowing the fly to drift, I often overreact in my desire for a fish—and scare the fish away. Experienced fly-fishers do not allow anything to cause them to react prematurely. Mature anglers know how to distinguish false cues from the real ones. They do not overreact. They know how to wait and strike only when they *know* a fish has taken the fly. This kind of knowledge and discernment comes with experience.

There is a parallel between the tendencies of beginner fly-fishers and immature people of faith. They both tend to be impatient and have a tendency to misinterpret events. They both tend to want immediate gratification. Being an enthusiastic, impatient, wishful thinker in fly-fishing is one thing, but wishful thinking in one's spiritual life seems more serious. It can keep the individual (and church communities) in a state of spiritual immaturity. Instead of ending up with spooked fish and a tangled leader, the immature Christian ends up reinforcing the skepticism of the secular world. I am quite familiar with these results, having practiced immaturity for a long time.

> "By this time you ought to be teachers ... Spiritual meat is for the mature, who through practice have their senses trained to discern good from evil."—
> Hebrews 5:12, 14.

The mature man or woman of faith and the mature fly-fisher have discernment. I love to watch a mature fly-fisher wait out a drift and strike at just the right time to hook a fish. It is equally rewarding to encounter a mature Christian who behaves in a similar way.

Grabbing at the Wrong Thing

If only I could learn to pause. Not many people in life or on the river are good at waiting. The human ego impatiently grabs at unrealistic hopes and the wrong thing. The fly-fisher desires to feel a fish tug and the believer longs to experience God. In both cases, it takes a mature individual who is willing to wait in hopelessness and who has learned to value the waiting in and of itself.

The mature individual knows there are no guarantees in either the physical or the spiritual world. The mature fly-fisher has learned to focus on the natural drift of the fly. He waits and waits for the right moment and only the right moment. The mature individual of faith likewise remains calm and focused on the flow of life. She allows all thoughts, expectations, and anxieties to flow down the river as she empties herself, waiting for the divine moment, a place where God *might* enter. She does not allow delusions or wishful thinking to distract her.

When I allow my illusions to dissipate like the morning mist off the river, I enter into an ancient tradition of negation called the *via negativa*. This tradition holds that God can be known only by first learning to discern what He is *not*. The individual engaged in this process in a sense says repeatedly, "No, this is not it; no, this is not God." He waits and he waits. He has discretion. Ironically, he is anything but negative because his hopeful heart is attempting to close in on the true God.

In the silence of waiting, my demands can fade. In spite of what is *not* experienced (and the absence of fish), true faith persists. Then, in the middle of my pause, a fish might rise to the fly, and I gently lift the rod. The discernment and patience required in fly-fishing helps me to be less hasty in my spiritual life. The pause, along with the waiting inherent in fly-fishing, helps me learn this discipline. The art and the grace of fly-fishing are all in the waiting.

My hope is that God might rise to meet me when I am waiting in the in-between places. When I stand between heaven and earth, between sky and water, between the church and the world, I am lost yet found.

Perhaps God delights in finding individuals in these in-between places because He is aware of those who whole-heartedly have said "no" to much of what the culture offers. He can find us in these in-between places, hungering and thirsting for what only God can give. For me, it is like standing on the bank, refusing to cast to the small fish, instead holding out for the one trophy brown trout lying in the deep undercut just beyond my hopes and dreams.

A Trout at Budd Lake

As a child, I spent a weekend with my uncle and aunt at Budd Lake, New Jersey. I asked my parents to help make such arrangements because I often wanted to get away from my own neighborhood. Perhaps, like the ugly duckling I was hoping to find a deeper sense of belonging in a faraway place even if that place existed mainly in my imagination. Like many anglers, I was hopeful that the larger waters of Budd Lake might hold monster fish. In addition, I enjoyed being with my uncle and talking about fishing. It was easy to be in his presence. He often smoked a cigar; its odor became familiar to me and therefore comforting.

My pond back home certainly provided me with solace and big fish, but sometimes I just needed to explore new waters. I loved the feeling of being completely alone in another town, a safe dis-

tance away from the anxieties I often associated with being around
my peer group back home. I loved the solitude. It did not bother me
when the fish were not biting, which should have been the case at
Budd Lake. It was the dog days of summer, and I expected that the
fishing would be difficult.

It always felt good to sit up front of the truck with my uncle
as we headed for the lake. I do not remember if we talked about
anything in particular. On this occasion, my uncle told me he was
going to drop me off to fish while he ran some errands. I don't recall
any disappointment at this. I must have assumed he had planned
on fishing with me. Yet, I was fine with the change in plans. Early
in my childhood, I must have gotten used to fishing alone. Maybe I
preferred it.

My uncle dropped me off on a rocky shore of Budd Lake and
drove off. I don't remember watching his truck fade away down the
road. He had not offered me any fishing advice or warnings to be
careful. Perhaps the world was safer then, or maybe that was only in
my imagination. Regardless, I fished alone, hour after hour without
lunch or drink, casting across a barren expanse of water that showed
little signs of life.

I wonder how I could have fished alone for so many hours
with so little hope of catching anything. I do recall being content
to stand before this barren expanse of water beneath a blue sky. I
found a rock jetty protruding out into the lake, thinking that trout
might prefer the structure of the drop off. I cast repeatedly in every
direction, waiting and waiting in the emptiness of the expanse of the
water meeting the expanse of the sky. Those expanses touched the
inner places of my heart.

My heart was not empty. My inner solitude comforted me
more than any fickle friendships I possessed back home. I also knew
there was a possibility, however remote, that a fish might find my fly.

I cast rhythmically back and forth, With each new expanding loop moving outward over the waters, I felt my heart reaching for something even more elusive. What was I seeking? Was there Something unreachable and unsayable lurking in the expanses? What could I do to capture the elusive? I waited in the nothingness, casting into the emptiness, hoping for just one tug from down deep.

As I revisit this memory, I consider the possibility that my hope and longing were a prayer of sorts. I was reaching out with the concrete image of a fish that *might* strike. Perhaps all of my longings are prayers. How blessed I was as a child to be alone in my enchanting inner world. My hopes could remain undisturbed as I cast out and over the waters of life. Perhaps this was a place of undisturbed solitude where God might enter in a pure form. Pure, because as a child, I did not even know what I wanted. I had no motive other than to be immersed in nature, hidden where no one else wanted anything for me or from me. Too often I had felt the so-called concern of others, which dragged me out of my peaceful solitude. Too often as an adult, I have watched parents not allow their child time to explore their inner world—and just allow them to fish.

I was in another place, mesmerized by the slight ripple on the surface of the waters and the deep hunger within my heart. I made one more looping cast, like so many others, but this time a fish moved up over the rocks, struck my fly, and tugged on the line. The line slipped past my fingertips. Here was life, pulling out the fly line and stirring something in my heart. I do not know exactly when or how, but I had learned to equate these sensations with God.

It was not a huge fish by any means, but to me it was miraculous. It was a skinny 14-inch brown trout chasing a fly up over the rocks. Still, my experience at the pond associated the frantic movements of my prey with Something mysterious and personal. It was only one fish for all those hours and hours of casting, but it became intensely memorable.

When I was young, I was less prone to evaluate myself based on productivity or other cultural standards. This modest fish was somehow magnificent to me. Looking back on it, I treasure the freedom I felt to bask in the experience and not be evaluated by others' standards. I was lost in innocence and hidden in a world all my own, a place between dream and reality. For one brief moment, that fish was *everything*. This little tug from below had come from a place both within and well beyond.

That one fish in the midst of all that nothingness mattered immensely to me. I have wondered if it was the nothingness that mattered most and the fish was merely a disruption of my solitude, a distraction from what was really important. As I look back on this experience, I believe this particular fish, perhaps because it was only one fish, was neither an intrusion nor a sign of success. It was Something else, a blessing that I could vaguely sense. I could experience this one fish as a blessing because it contrasted so starkly to the vast empty waters, the sky above, and the longings of my heart. If a guide, my uncle, or my parents, had been there providing me with a constant stream of instruction, validation, and attention, that one fish probably could not have been a blessing. The one fish would have drowned in a stream of noisy validations.

I have been an educator for thirty-one years, I am quite familiar with the way modern society, including my profession, bombards youth with rewards, recognition, and validations, all in the name of building self-esteem. I am not a fan. I believe it is causing an erosion of the souls of our young people. Thanks to this streaming—of rewards, programs, and entertainment—children rarely experience a big sky, an empty plain, the rippling surface of a lake, and repeated castings of apparent failure.

I am thankful there was not a guide present when I felt that tug on my line. The constant instructions, helpful hints, and fly changes would have filled the beautiful space of my solitude. One fish, just one fish that I could call my own, or God's own, was enough. In my solitude, I was in my own way present at creation. Within the void and empty space, I had a sense of the Spirit moving over the surface of the waters. Perhaps I could hear God speak. In my child-like way, I knew that God creates and that it is good (Genesis 1).

While I was in college, I came across a scripture passage that still haunts me. It is a reference to the Israelites' journey across the wilderness to the Promised Land and their struggle with the emptiness and challenges along the way. They complained repeatedly about the conditions and felt abandoned. They mumbled and grumbled to God. This grumbling *became* their prayer of sorts. "Then the Lord God gave them their hearts desire but gave them leanness of soul" (Psalm 106:15). This is quite profound, in that they got what they wanted, their heart's desire, but at a price to their souls.

Is our culture doing the same thing to individual souls, and particularly to the souls of the young? In a sense, the culture keeps giving the youth their hearts desire. The young receive feel-good encouragements through verbal validation, parties, rewards, trophies, toys, and electronic gadgets. If fishing were a subject in school, educators would find a way to make certain that students would catch plenty of fish. A particularly skillful teacher would probably invent a computerized fish programmed to strike and swim right into the net, ensuring that no one fails. As educators, we dare not allow anyone to feel emptiness or failure. No empty nets! For that matter, why bother to take children to the river to fish when we could allow them to fish on their computers. Of course, this is already taking place for the millions of children who remain indoors playing on computers.

In our culture, few would argue that guaranteed success is a block to the development of the soul. Still, how can a child learn that a fish is a blessing from God when he or she knows it was somehow arranged by his or her all-powerful parents, teachers, or coaches?

The larger culture fails to realize that young people (and adults for that matter) need failure, vulnerability, and emptiness for proper soul development. The culture does not want children to wait. They all have Attention Deficit Hyperactivity Disorder, after all. If they have to wait, they will begin to fear failure. We can't have that. If children are not catching fish, receiving A's, or scoring points, they might not feel good about themselves and their sense of accomplishment. God forbid! Would it be so traumatic if a child failed at something and concluded, "Maybe I need to work a little harder"?

There are many traps. If a school did take its students fishing, what happens if one child catches more fish than another child? Could a teacher allow a child to be vulnerable enough to consider why he or she may or may not have caught a fish? Often some vulnerability is what a child needs to contemplate the mystery of his own life and perhaps the life of God. This is hard to imagine. Who can tolerate the sight of a child sitting alone under a tree, along a creek or on the banks of a pond, wondering why she does not feel completely connected to her peer group. Can you imagine a child sitting by a stream, perhaps with a peculiar sadness, wondering why she does not feel at home on this earth like a fish feels at home in the currents.

After a few more hours fishing on Budd Lake, I hadn't got another strike or even seen another fish. Finally, my uncle came down the road to pick me up.

"I see you got yourself a nice brown trout," he said.

His praise apparently touched something inside me. He seemed surprised. I had had a vague feeling from the beginning of this outing that he knew the odds of catching a fish from the shore during the middle of summer were astronomical. Today, I still wonder why this man who loved to fish chose not to fish with me that day. Was he just too busy with adult weekend tasks? Was I an intrusion upon his routine? Could he have felt a bit guilty for just dropping me off to fish alone while he took care of his adult responsibilities?

Was he impressed that I caught something? Did he know how that one fish was an accomplishment of sorts, at least within my own inner world? Could he ever consider and know its meaning and significance to me? Did he remember? I will never know. I never asked. He died at age ninety-four several years ago.

And did I ever tell him how much it meant for me to go fishing with him? I don't remember.

VI

Thousands upon Thousands of Casts

❧☙

Thousands of Leaps

Martha Graham was referring to Vaslav Nijinsky when she mentioned the "thousands of leaps before the memorable one." For her as well there were thousands of leaps—and one that brought her into stardom.

In my life, I have become aware of the 10,000 repetitions needed to master a skill. In my wrestling days, I needed to do thousands of repetitions just to learn one hold, from which, when mastered, an angel could not escape. In the final seconds of the state final wrestling match, I executed the move I had practiced so faithfully. That single maneuver was my leap into the unknown. It secured a memorable victory.

Before I found my way to the wrestling mat, I executed thousands and thousands of casts at the pond. I did so much casting that the top guide on my Browning 8-foot 5-weight fly rod wore a groove in the metal that nearly broke through from the line moving back and forth. That childhood rod is on my wall in my home to remind me of the thousands of casts needed to learn any task well. Of course, I do not need any reminders because etched in my heart are the memories of those casts, the loyal companions of my soul.

My memories also take me back to the neighborhood ball fields and backyards. I can smell the freshly mowed grass. I see my father practicing baseball with me, giving me the opportunity to catch thousands and thousands of ground balls and fly balls. Over the years, we wore out several gloves. More grooves are etched in my heart. During batting practices, I swung the bat thousands of times in order to keep my eye focused on the ball, just as I learned to keep my eye on the fly and the fish about to engulf my fly. Whether it was baseball, wrestling, or fly-casting, I developed this ability to practice, thanks to my father.

As I grew, I applied this concept of practice to various outdoor activities that would help me develop connections to the natural world and ground me to the earth. This grounding helped me contemplate God. In the lonely alpine mountain meadows and shaded canyons of Colorado, I learned through countless repetitions the skills needed for telemark skiing. Each time I skied, I internalized the particular curves and slopes of a mountain trail, just as I memorized the meanders of the river. I experienced a slight sense of belonging when my skis touched the earth and flowed down a familiar slope, in much the same way that I experienced the meanders of the river when I went fly-fishing.

In all my chosen activities, I learned to associate the repetition of a task with a peculiar security that connected me to my father, memories of practice, and perhaps a bigger story. The ritualistic repetitions performed in the same places, particularly while fly-fishing, imparted a sense of familiarity and belonging, as though I stood on the edge of Eden. This wasn't perfect. I often missed the deeper meanings. I did not often feel fully at home, even though I would continue to seek my place among the creation through the disciplined art of fly-fishing.

In every river, there are places that hold some of the biggest fish and the ones that consistently rise to the fly. These places are familiar to me and where I often go to practice my art. In time, these places became somewhat like home to me. There are holes, runs, and riffles in the river that have changed only slightly over the decades. The constancy of the boulders and other structures is comforting to me. Sometimes, these familiar runs changed. The Tree Hole, a run where a client caught a 25-inch rainbow trout below a fallen tree, is now gone, swept away by heavy spring flows. Other holes have filled in with sediment and silt and no longer hold fish. Ironically, habitat improvement structures have changed the character of the river but not always for the better. Such changes remind me of the constant flow of time and changes that I cannot control.

As I cast again and again, the waters become familiar to me again. Each cast helps ground me in a place, allowing me to once again stand on the edge of the mainstream culture, waiting in a world that is somewhat my own, with the hope of meeting God. Repetitions, like loyal companions, comfort me. They invite me to participate in a place where I might get a better sense of belonging.

My sense of home develops slowly with thousands upon thousands of casts. If Eden comes to us, it does so slowly as Emily Dickinson implied.

Remaining in the Waiting

Often on a fishing trip, especially to some new water, it may take thousands of casts, slight adjustments in the angles of presentation, and many fly changes before I hook a fish. While making those casts, I sometimes remain patient by thinking about playing catch with Dad or fishing my pond alone as a child. Occasionally I slip into a dream of that one wrestling match where I held my ground, waiting for the perfect moment, and seemingly leapt into heaven with that thousandth leap. I have the capacity, at least some of the time, to remain and wait, knowing anything can happen. Sometimes, it *is* amazing.

Often, while walking the river and stalking fish, I feel poised like a strung bow, ready to shoot my arrow into the first giant fish I spot. I feel a certain satisfaction and sense of pride when I can cast to a specific fish that I target because it connects me to my past meanderings. I no longer fish with the consistent intensity of my younger years, which forces me to admit that today I often hook fish unintentionally. I may not even see the fish; it seems the fish catches me. Today I am more off guard than ready. At times, I am just not paying attention when I catch a fish. In some ways, this does not bother me. It adds to the mystery of life and fly-fishing. It is okay. When I least expect it, I can be surprised by grace in the form of a tugging, slashing fish. Life is not all about me and my concentrated efforts.

Turning My Back on a Fish

More than twenty-five years ago, I signed up for a weekend teacher workshop in Alamosa, Colorado. I left Colorado Springs at 3:30 A.M. After a few hours or so of driving in the dark, I dropped over La Veta Pass and saw the sign for Smith Reservoir. I had heard about Smith and its big trout. Glancing at my watch and the dawning sky, I considered the registration time of my class. I quickly did the math and found myself pulling over and taking the little dirt road to the reservoir. I calculated I had twenty minutes. I parked near the first sight of water, slipped on my waders, and started casting a small black and olive wooly bugger and an olive scud rigged in tandem. I made cast after cast, with varying retrieves and depths, all producing nothing; not a bump; not a pull. I scanned the surface water searching for a rise, but I found only stillness. After I made a long cast and waited for my flies to sink, I looked at my watch and realized it was time to leave. I turned around mildly disappointed and walked into shore, still dragging my flies in the water. Then a big rainbow trout struck. The large rainbow hooked itself and was powerfully pulling out line. I heard and felt it before I saw it in the dimly lit dawn. The fish caught me off guard, yet I was able to pivot and gently lift the rod in time to maintain contact. The fish made several powerful runs and leaps before I was able to battle the six-pound fish to my hand. Once again, something I might call grace surprised me after I had made a thousand casts. Sometimes mysterious events happen even when I have turned my back on a fish—or life. If I have practiced something well, the unexpected seems to happen more often; maybe it's because practice enables me to go on automatic pilot, and my movements blend in with the flow of life and creation.

I know that I have to do a lot of waiting for the unexpected.

Making Wrong Conclusions While Waiting

I teach the same patience and practice to the beginners I guide on the river. I encourage clients to expect to make thousands of casts before the memorable one—when they hook a fish. I also remind them to be alert for a sudden take at the end of the drift, when they have turned their backs to look up river in anticipation of where the next cast will land. Fish that strike at the end of the drift often get away because the angler is not ready and, in a panic, strikes the rod too hard.

Sometimes beginners will cast for five minutes and then conclude the fish are not biting. I have to laugh because I can see the fish feeding. Beginners make many premature conclusions about fishing and about life. I encourage them to look deeper, maintain faith, and hold out the hope that a fish will strike out of nowhere. So be ready! One time a client, convinced there were no fish in the river, kept trying to roll-cast up stream. His line just stayed in the water.

"It won't cast," he said.

"Well maybe," I said, trying to keep from laughing. "You should unhook that 14-inch rainbow you are trying to cast through the air. It might cast better."

After a short debate, he was able to feel the fish, reel in some line, and we were able to net it.

Here lies a parallel to my spiritual life—and perhaps yours. I can utter thousands of intentions, prayers, hopes, and dreams—waiting for something to happen. Then it does. After all the waiting, a glimpse of God comes to me. If I have to wait a long time, I might make hundreds of wrong conclusions. When I am waiting for God to speak—or a fish to strike—and all I hear is the silence or the ripple of the river, I may conclude that God does not care and there are no fish. I might also conclude that God is not paying attention. I feel so alone.

Moses went up the mountain. Aaron was in charge. Moses, who was doing some wrestling with God on the mountain, was late. The Israelites concluded that God and Moses were gone for good. The Israelites erected a golden calf. I might do the same thing in many ways because I am not good at waiting. I am not good at re-maining in the tension of waiting in the unknown. If I feel aban-doned, I might erect my golden calf, based on premature conclusions and immature thinking.

Sometimes I take things too far the other way. I assume that because I caught a fish, it means that God blessed me. God gets the credit and the blame for everything that happens, which I suppose can be both true and not true at the same time. However, I remind myself to be careful in my hasty conclusions.

Even worse, sometimes my fly-fishing methods and ways of dealing with life become bad habits.

Bad Habits

On this side of Eden, I am inclined to develop bad habits. I know this is true of my clients. Those rare moments of immediate fulfillment can be trouble. Sometimes beginners get lucky and catch a big fish on their first cast—it happens—and now we've got a prob-lem. Their first cast could not have been good. They could not have already learned the art of the proper drift. Beginners who get lucky early are well on their way to a bad habit. Bad habits in fishing and in life are hard to break. In these instances, I have to spend the rest of the day undoing the potential bad habit. It will be frustrating for them because we are unlikely to catch any more fish. It's hard for them to ignore the fact that the technique (however bad) worked and brought about (at least once) a desired result. This is the nega-tive side of persistence. The lucky beginners persist in making thou-sands of casts, but each one is fundamentally wrong!

The same dynamic can happen in my spiritual life. I possess such a strong need to belong that I will remain within the conven-tions and expectations of the group, until I wake up, rebel, or fall from their grace. As a fly fisher, I might fall in the river several times before I realize how out of place I feel. What was that rock doing there? Then a powerful current sweeps me away. It's a hard lesson. The rock belongs to the river, was there the whole time, and it is I who do not belong.

I might persist in my conformity to a group tradition because it is "God's way"; after all, it has been done this way since the dawn of time. I can insist that the way my family church has done things is the only way. On the other hand, I may know my group's way is not the only way, but I reason that any group is better than being alone. I might never move beyond their habits, customs, traditions, and conventions, even if I know, deep down, that I need transformation. In my soul, I belong somewhere else.

VII

Moving Out of Convention

❦

Entering a Deeper Rhythm

In the movie, *A River Runs Through It*, there is a beautiful scene where Norman, Paul, and their father are fly-fishing on the Big Black Foot River. Paul wanders off and, figuratively speaking, crosses over an edge; he starts casting in a  different direction with a different technique. Paul moves beyond his father's instruction. He catches fish after fish with his own technique. He goes beyond convention and enters liminal space.

When fly-fishing, I can get stuck on one way of doing things. I can lock onto the first and only instruction I received on a particularly technique. It worked. I caught some fish, so I stuck to it. When I try to apply this approach in all situations, I find it doesn't always work. This puts me at a new threshold. If I pass through this threshold, I can go to a whole other level and perhaps become an artist. This is what happened to Paul, who goes beyond his father's instruction and creates a new technique and approach to his casting. It is in this liminal space where Paul is free to explore possibilities beyond the conventions of the mainstream.

I move into a liminal space when I am willing to go beyond my previous way of doing things. It is a gate through which I can pass and discover something new. Perhaps true spiritual experience results when I allow myself to pass through liminal space. I cease using the same old wine skins, as Jesus suggested. If I move beyond the convention of church, who knows where I might end up? If I step into the unknown. I might end up on the edge of a river casting, which may be where perhaps I belong anyway. Then again, I might slip off an edge, and the river will sweep me away.

A "New" Fly-fishing Technique

While I cannot claim to have created any new way of casting, I can understand the need to go beyond conventional ways of casting. Like many experienced fly fishers, I have learned from other anglers and added their techniques to my bag of tricks. Sometimes a somewhat new approach emerges that is a blending of several different techniques.

Like many fly fishers, I received the initial instruction to cast a fly by quartering upstream and then mending or high-sticking the line. This technique works quite well, but I got to the point of where I found that more challenging fish and waters needed a different approach. When it comes to fooling the biggest and most wary fish on a river, I rely on an across-and-down technique to provide the most natural fly first presentation. This is particularly true when dry fly-fishing. The trick is to present "fly first" to the fish so that when the fish is looking upstream and overhead all it sees is the fly and not the tippet.

If you are wondering how to achieve this type of a presentation, I invite you to enter a place of liminality. If you try the technique, your casting will look unconventional to others. Casting across and down does things backwards—inverted and upside down at the same time. It is casting downstream when everyone else is facing and casting upstream. It is doing an about-face and looking in a different direction. It is deliberately stopping casts in midair, which can feel counter-intuitive. Yet this is what I need to do—lay the leader and tippet upstream of the fly.

It may also involve casting to a spot where (to others) fish are least likely. It is casting to that tiny slot, an edge, carved out by a narrow riffle when everyone else is fishing a big obvious hole. I often fish the in-between places that the crowds ignore. When fishing in liminal space, anything can happen. Sometimes the biggest fish is lying in that narrow slot; it takes the fly and then comes exploding out of the water.

Who can predict such a thing. Still, in the silence of my heart, sometimes I have sensed the fish was there all along. Then again, there have been Sunday mornings at church when I stand up, walk out the door, and go to the river. And I knew all along that God was there waiting for me.

First Cast Big Fish: Breaking the Rules

The odds against catching a fish on the first cast are astronomical, but it does happen. Fifteen years ago, I took a client to the Dream Stream. He had never held a rod. Fly-fishing was on his bucket list. We approached a meander that held two large 22-inch rainbows that were sipping tricos on the surface. Just because I could see them didn't mean we were going to catch them. I was up for the challenge. Sometimes as a guide, I get bored with teaching the same old way. I grow tired of hearing myself talk. This was one of those times. Without any instruction, lecture, or casting lesson, I handed the rigged dry fly rod to my client and said, "So, have you ever cast a fly rod before?"

"No."

I tried again, "What about a spinning rod?"

"No."

I tried again, "I know you have never cast before, but maybe you have seen someone casting."

"Not really."

Of course, I had to ask, "Ever see *A River Runs Through It?*"

"No, Anthony."

At this point, I questioned my unconventional tactic of just handing him the rod. However, I decided to play the scene out. "Well, we are now standing in a situation that captures the essence of fly-fishing. Do you see those two big fish over there?" Of course, he could not see the feeding fish. Do you see all the bugs in the air?" Of course, he could not see the bugs. "Well, those fish are feeding on these bugs." I showed him a trico, on my fingertip, which he could barely see. "This is what they call matching the hatch. I want you to just use any ideas or instincts you might have about casting and fly-fishing." I said this realizing that he had just told me he had none! "Just try to cast it over there by those rising fish."

His cast was a mess, a minor disaster that resulted in a big pile of leader and fly line all over the water. Somehow, the fly landed perfectly, in front of the fish. It drifted a few feet, and the fish took the fly. I yelled at my client to lift the rod. My yelling did not help; he did nothing. He hadn't even seen the fish rise to the fly. It did not matter; the fish somehow hooked itself and leaped out of the water several times. Since we had so much slack line sitting on the water, the fish did not break the leader with each run and leap.

During each leap, I assured him, "Yes that is your fish! You have it on *your* line." Of course, with all the slack he could not feel the fish. I kept yelling for this rookie to reel in line. When he finally got the line back in the reel and could feel the fish, I had to yell at him to let go of the line because the fish made another run. After much screaming, and running up and down the river, the fish was still on the line. We wound up in a stalemate with the big fish lying alongside a boulder. Finally, the man was tight to the fish with his rod held high, and he was ready to let go if the fish bolted.

I quickly explained the game plan. I would come up from below the fish with my net, while he slowly lifted the rod and put pressure on the fish. If he could raise the fish, I could make a quick stab with the net. I worked my way into position, still fifteen feet away from the fish. I placed the net down in the water. Just as I was getting ready to tell my client to start putting pressure with the rod, the fish bolted downstream and swam right into the net! I lifted the net up out of the water and stared at this slab of rainbow straining and bending in the net. I had never seen anything like this before.

My client was smart enough to be perplexed. "Do the fish always swim in the net like that? Are they attracted to the net?"

All I could say was, "Sir, please go buy a lottery ticket today." I explained to him that experienced fly fishers rarely catch a 22-inch rainbow on a size-24 dry fly, certainly not on their first cast of the day, and nets usually scare fish away.

Then I gave up. I just stood there, dazed and surprised by grace.

Cheap Grace: Easy Art

Such moments are quite wonderful, rare, and difficult to understand. While I am often critical of petty spiritual claims and wary of what Dietrich Bonhoeffer called "cheap grace," I have to acknowledge that grace does seem to come our way on occasion. I've seen it in fly-fishing. It's more difficult to define it in my spiritual life. How could I define the life of Jesus as a "success"? Everything is a bit upside down in the true spiritual life. For example, my financial assets don't define me as a success in my spiritual life.

I live in a culture of easy religion. I have such easy access to churches, books, prayer groups, bible study groups, Christian music, and other forms of religious entertainment. Television and the internet can bring in spiritual messages and information into my home minute-by-minute if I want. I can become saturated with spiritual information and tools. And here lies the problem. In the midst of all these resources, I may never pause to ask, "Am I hungry? Am I thirsty?" If I am full of all this information, how could I ever feel my hunger and thirst for God? If I want to keep my hunger and thirst, I might have to say a firm "no" to conventional spiritual nourishment.

Perhaps Christians have been grazing so long on spiritual junk foods that their true hunger is falsely satisfied and rarely felt. These spiritual materials are not necessarily bad for me. They are not necessarily unsound. It is more that their goodness—their tastiness, if you will—tempts me to consume more than I can absorb. After devouring all this cotton candy, I may no longer feel the true appetite for food of greater sustenance. I am likely to miss the quiet revelations that could feed my soul. I am addicted to the sugar. I am as dumb as the newly stocked fish that will bite on anything,

In this culture, it is difficult for me to discern what is truly soul food. I am not like the disciples who, when asked by Jesus how many loaves of bread were available to feed the 5,000, replied, "Five—and two fish" (Mark 6:38). The disciples felt the hunger of the crowds. They felt their own hunger. They knew how few the resources they possessed were. In my culture, it is difficult to feel there is a shortage of soul food. As long as I keep feeding on the sweet resources of my culture, I may never feel the need for real nourishment. I doubt I will understand what Jesus meant by the "bread of life" (John 6:35).

It is also difficult for me to feel my thirst. I wish I were like the deer that thirsts for water and finds it at the river. I have been party to discussions in churches about what dulls our hunger and thirst, but those discussions rarely go beyond the usual suspects: money, television, and lust.

To be honest, I live in a quasi-Christian culture. I can walk into a church and join without paying a price. Churches cannot afford to hold me accountable. They make few demands. I can put on a smiley face, be a member, and pretend I belong. There is no cost—emotional, psychological or social—to join.

Once I am in the club, I look and sound the same as the others. It's easy to learn the language. A few simple clichés apply to any issue.

"I will pray for you."

"God will provide."

"God's timing is not our timing."

"Our preacher really teaches the Word."

These clichés provide no need for me to change. I don't need to be in the process of transforming my life. The smiley face and the clichés will do as long as no one reveals their true hunger and thirst. It is easy to learn the language, to go along, to keep it positive, and to not ask questions. In some sense, the evangelical church often is the perfect place to hide, to pretend, to be shallow. I don't have to grow up to belong.

While such places make it easy to experience a superficial sense of belonging (as long as I do not speak my truth) and a false sense that I have my act together (but I dare not be honest about my life), deep down I know I do not quite belong. I would rather go to the river. On the river in the quiet hours of a trico mayfly hatch, I do not have to listen to the clichés. I can more deeply contemplate my true condition, be it belonging or not belonging.

Trico Hatch: An Unconventional Church Service on the River?

In the next bend of the river lies one of the most complicated meanders I will fish. My thoughts, plans and hopes, can run deep in this very technical water. This morning the fish have moved up from a depth and are rising to tiny insects with glistening wings. These are trico mayflies. As the hatch progresses, I notice thousands and thousands of tricos on the water, and as is often the case, I will need to make thousands and thousands of casts. Perhaps the rising fish can teach me and reveal Something to me.

Mystery lies at the heart of fly-fishing and my faith. I will not completely understand my faith, the waters I fish, or the answer to life's deepest questions. I may not know why the fish ignore me on a particular day, take my fly on another, or why God seems strangely absent during those times when I desperately need him most. Like Emily Dickinson's poetry reflects, I also feel a continual flip-flop between belief and doubt.

I present fly-fishing as a practice that can bring anglers to wonderful places, both spiritually and geographically, places I might feel I belong and yet do not belong. Fly-fishing helps me contemplate the deep existential questions of life. I dare to ask to what extent I belong in the beautiful places I fish. I both belong and don't belong, a hundred times an hour.

There is much mystery standing in a beautiful river, rhythmically casting, as I wait for a fish to take the fly. At times, a fish might interrupt the rhythm of my casting, and then I find myself connecting to a fish; at other times, I am simply casting in a gentle summer breeze, dangling my offering without a response. As a fly fisher, both connection and disconnection are quite familiar to me.

How many times have even the most experienced of fly fishers suddenly felt a fish pulling on the line; they do not understand precisely how or why it struck nor how it hooked itself. On the other hand, how many times have I persistently and tactfully performed the exact right technique with the precise correct fly, from thirty or forty years of experience, and caught nothing? The fish ignore me.

It is often while fishing when I myself become "caught" in a state of wonderful ignorance that leaves me in a deepened sense of humility as I try to contemplate the meaning of the strange events that sometimes transpire.

There are moments while fly-fishing when I live in the beauty of my ignorance and insignificance as I contemplate the deepest questions about life. Where do I belong? Am I loved? Is there anyone out there?

I often feel caught up in this ignorance and insignificance when I am casting in the middle of a trico mayfly hatch on the South Platte River. The fish are feeding all around me as I repeatedly attempt with the greatest efforts to entice a fish to take the fly. No doubt, while engaged in this ritual, I not only miss catching a fish but I miss the full meaning of the event. The fish appear at home. The insects know the exact time to emerge. The fish follow the mayflies, keep their appointment with the river, and feed in a complex relationship. I stand in ignorance, and I stand in isolation.

I watch the fish feeding rhythmically and efficiently, moving methodically and only slightly to each side of a seam line on the surface. The fish do not waste any energy as they feed. Nothing is forced. The fish do not go too far off to either side to chase an insect. There is no haste and waste. The fish and the insects go with the flow; it is I who am out of tune.

I am mesmerized by the fish. In comparison, I often veer off in life, away from my true-life source. I waste time and energy, willing to compromise my soul to fit in any place I can. I move to the right to belong, or to the left, back and forth, forever trying to please. I lose my focus and pay attention to the wrong thing.

However tragic this may be, it is often while fly-fishing where I can honestly consider that the life I am living may not be the life I long for deep in my soul. While casting to fish, I sometimes feel a sense of belonging and at other times a sense of not belonging. I find myself grieving for the life I desire but am not living. I remember the times I sold out rather than held out. While fly-fishing I become aware of my desperate attempts to hook a fish when I am really trying to find out where I belong.

As I cast to the trout with trico mayflies all around, I try to unravel the mystery of how I fit in to this place: the feeding cycle, the flow of the river, and my sense of a bigger world around me. I consider the best fly and the best casting technique to use, hoping I might place the fly precisely in the current so it will drift perfectly in front of the fish. At the same time, I struggle to know where and if I belong in the midst of this phenomenon of nature. Yet I am beginning to discover there is beauty in my ignorance as I learn to respect nature's autonomy, intricacy, purposes.

As the hatch continues, I consider again the advice of Job.

"But ask the animals, and let them teach you,
    or the birds of the sky, and let they will tell you;
    or speak to the earth, and it will teach you,
    and let the fish of the sea inform you."—Job 12:7-8

As I consider what this complex set of experiences and feelings is trying to teach me, I realize there can be beauty in not quite knowing where I belong even while I sense that every trico mayfly and every fish has just tried to speak me. To consider the possibility that God could teach me through the creation and that sometimes I am the focus of God's love is too wonderful for me to comprehend. To consider such possibilities is perhaps what it means to have faith and can be an opening to a whole other world.

For the past thirty summers, I have stood in the South Platte River in the midst of these trico mayfly hatches. I tie on the best trico imitation I can find in my fly box and cast it through the thousands upon thousands of swarming naturals. My fly lands among the thousands of spent wing spinners, drifting in the currents as dozens of trout are sipping in the bugs. If I am lucky I might spot my tiny fly drifting among the thousands of naturals on the water. Luckier still, I might see one trout among the dozens that are rising almost imperceptibly sip in *my* fly from the surface. Almost instinctively, in a flow with the river, I raise the rod and the fish upon feeling the hook leaps out of the water and bolts downstream. As I remain in contact with this fish, I marvel that this leaves me feeling a part of this flowing world. What a precarious situation I find myself in. It all seems bigger than any world I have experienced in years, maybe decades, and in some sense too wonderful explain to anyone when I get back home.

The only drawback is that I must return to a much smaller world. As I reflect more deeply, I realize that the trick is not to fool the trout but to learn the art of living with wisdom, integrity, vitality, and wonder in both worlds. Even as I stand among dozens of fish feeding, I realize that their hunger cannot exceed the hunger in my own heart to belong to this beautiful place. If I could only feed like those gulping, sipping mouths, I would lie beside them, with them, take this whole world in to my soul, and perhaps then feel at home.

Perhaps, as Emily Dickinson suggested, trying to take in this paradise is my true occupation. If I read the waters correctly, I understand that I do not belong completely to either world. Or perhaps the deeper reality is that I do completely belong to both worlds, and I am simply not aware. I remain ignorant. However this humble realization allows me to let go and simply become a part of the serpentine flow of the river and this beautiful cycle of life. Fly-fishing, accompanied with frustration and a demand for the fish to take my fly, does not place me in the flow of life within God's paradise. I have to let go of my control.

In order to best contemplate such questions I need to step back to the edge of the river.

Stepping Back to the Edge: Achieving Better Resolution

Sometimes, right in the middle of a hatch, I have said to my client, "Stop, let's step back and just watch." Then I asked him or her to step out of the river with me and climb the bank or sit on top of a boulder and look at the run we were trying to fish. The distance gave us some perspective and better resolution. As we observed the water from the river's fringe, we then saw exactly where the fish were located, what their feeding patterns were, and what were the best drift lines. We then came up with a game plan for making the best presentations for these circumstances.

In other parts of my life, I have also stepped back and observed from a distance. At times, I have needed to step back from the influence of people in my life, regardless of their often loving intentions. Often I have needed to go off, fish by myself away from people, and ponder things. Even though this is taboo for many, I often feel a need to distance myself from organized church institutions and its conventions. If I am an active part of the clan, I might be too close to see accurately.

Stepping back to the edges is a familiar tactic to me; it reminds me of the edges I stepped back to at the pond, a place where I could cast freely without the influence of others. In another area of my life, I tended to sit on the edge of my peer group, which enabled me to see what was going on with some clarity. Stepping back enabled me to see below the surface of the waters and the surface of my social group.

When I am too close to mainstream culture—be it church, work, or school—I can't see what is going on. I need space and perspective, away from the influence of others. In essence, I would rather step back, look at things through my own eyes, and make decisions based on what I perceive. Of course, sometimes it is quite wonderful to associate with another person, who has eyes you can trust and can give you another opinion.

Can I step back, get some distance, and at the same time not fall backwards out of my responsibilities? I hope so. I need to. That is my calling. I must. It is tricky, I must admit. Whenever I step away from mainstream culture, I risk losing my balance and falling off the edge. How far can I move back before my eyes lose their power of resolution? You can answer this question on your own, but my hunch is that if you attend church regularly, you have rarely tried to step back. It's too risky.

It *is* risky. If you dare to step back, you may become a threat to the mainstream, and that includes your church. You may earn the label of one who rocks the boat. You may be perceived as negative, rebellious, or contrary. People generally do not like their boats rocked while fishing. And those who are religious can be particularly sensitive. Yet this is what Jesus did over and over again, and that is why he made certain people, particularly religious leaders, very nervous.

Does it make sense that a "good Christian" is one who slavishly follows the conventions of a church? Does it make sense that good Christians must be forever positive and go along with everything and everyone? Is there not a time for good Christians to turn things upside down and tip over some tables?

Many times I have gone to church only to bite my tongue because I know that what the minister is saying is the polar opposite of what I know to be true. It is like standing behind another fly fisher and watching him cast in the wrong place with the wrong technique and the wrong fly—and not say anything. I appreciate Wendell Berry's contrariness to speak out in a poem titled, "The Contrariness of the Mad Farmer." I relate and apply Berry's insights to my own life. When well meaning folks tell me that I have to go to church to see God, I counter with, "But why, I see him on the river."

I arrive at a place of substantial power when, for the sake of truth, I can say honestly that I no longer care if I lose money, status, emotional security, or a sense of belonging. Can I stand back and not be disturbed while I watch the temple tables get turned upside down—even if it means I will suffer personal loss. If I get to that place, then I am able to live life on the edge. I no longer care what others think of me. This is truly a place of power.

When I no longer care about my place of belonging, I live with a new freedom and power. I am not afraid to see things as I see them or hear things as I hear them or say things as I mean them, even if it means I am not part of the mainstream. This is a place on the edge where I have nothing to lose. This is the path that might lead to Eden.

I would rather try to please the One who truly lived on the fringe, who had no place to rest his head, and who did not belong to this world system. If I do not belong to the mainstream culture, perhaps a place remains for me in the natural world of God's creation where I cast my flies. However, to enter that place, I might have to make some adjustments.

Repentance

After making thousands of casts, I get to the point where my casting loses its rhythm. Perhaps I lose my focus. For whatever reason, something in my timing takes the power and vitality out of the cast. Something is out of balance. I can feel it. I am out of Eden.

This happens too often both in fly-fishing and in life. Over the years the errors pile up and weigh me down. There are too many to count and too many to correct in one cast or even one lifetime. I try to mend the errors with thousands of adjustments, but it doesn't matter. Those thousands of errors pile up like a tangled cast. No pause can make it fly. It will collapse even as I collapse. I then have to start all over again. I have no other choice. I might have to change the direction in which I cast. The good news, for me, is that it is wonderful to be able to start all over again and make another thousand or ten thousand casts. The Christian tradition calls this repentance, and it is at the heart of the faith.

This reminds me of a poem by D.H. Lawrence called "Healing," in which he describes an individual making a mistake and trying to free oneself from repeating that mistake again and again. He describes the individual as being ill to the level of the deep soul because of wounds. A form of repentance is needed.

Fly-fishing helps me realize my life mistakes and the need to start again from the beginning. I may cast thousands of times conventionally and unconventionally, but D.H. Lawrence teaches me that I am not a mechanism simply with uncoordinated arm movements. My problems are deeper. I feel wounded in my soul and out of Eden.

When I consider this, I begin to know I am not alone. I appreciate the need for patience and long-term repentance. Conceivably, I can deal more effectively with the deep wounds to my soul when I fly-fish with others. Standing and casting in the healing waters of rivers deepens my soul. I know that. I always have. However, when I choose to fish with others, I may be forming a church community on the river.

Someday, I may have to give an account for all the times I failed to meet God, not in church but with a friend on the river.

VIII

Shallow Fishing: Going Deeper

❧❧

Deep Water Nymphing in Silent Pools

I ventured into Cheesman Canyon for the first time in the early 1980s. I learned quickly that deepwater nymphing tactics were the best way to entice the big rainbows at the bottom of boulder-formed pools. When I was not getting strikes, I kept  adding more weight to get the fly down deeper. Often this adjustment was the ticket to get the fish to take the fly. Going deeper also worked on other stretches of river. I added weight to leeches and wooly buggers while streamer fishing on the Platte above and below Spinney during the spring spawning run and then again in the fall for browns in the Tomahawk section. Eleven Mile Canyon's unique deep plunge pools also required going down with weight and often not using a strike indicator. The Arkansas River below Pueblo Dam had extensive habitat improvement structures that created deep pools and runs, which also required more weight. This was also the case on the Taylor River, which had massive mysis-fed fish. Time and time again, getting down and going deep seemed to be the way. Big fish prefer to lay low and deep, having learned to survive by staying slightly under the radar of anglers and the vision of predators. Rarely do big fish come up from the bottom to take a fly. They seem to sense their own vulnerability. I have watched the biggest fish in a run lay low, taking tiny morsels off the bottom while all the smaller fish in the run are feeding aggressively at mid-depth and or on the surface.

There are other ways of going deeper. If I take my floating strike indicators off and rely on other cues for detecting strikes, more than likely I will get down deeper and achieve a better presentation. Strike indicators can cause problems. This is particularly true of the larger floating varieties. Strike indicators, in all forms but some more than others, send warning signals to fish, especially to the wary ones that have been in the river a long time. Many fly fishers are experimenting with a variety of different techniques such as straight-line nymphing and czech-nymphing. These techniques provide a more natural drift and get the fly deeper and more consistently in front of the fishes face. Some fly fishers do not use tapered leaders in favor of a straight tippet, which is finer and sinks faster to lower depths. Others use monofilament instead of a fly line.

It takes some courage at first, particularly for the novice, to go deeper while nymph fishing. It can be intimidating. The immediate problem is the awkwardness of casting more weight in a way that does not make a mess of things. There is more potential to snag on rocks at the bottom of the river. I have to choose my drift lines carefully. In deeper water there can be swirling undercurrents that make the presentation of the fly unpredictable. Finally, it's just tough to see anything in deeper water. Is that a giant rainbow or a log or a rock? I think I saw it move. Did it just take my fly?

Going Deeper Spiritually: The Shallow Net

Going deeper while fly-fishing reminds me of the need to go deeper in my spiritual life. I tend to stay on the surface. I often do not feel comfortable looking down at the deeper waters of my soul. I may approach the edge of a deep pool, take a quick look, and back away.

In Luke 5:4, Jesus said to Peter, who had not caught a fish all night, "Put out into deep water, and let down the nets for a catch." This Greek word here for deep, *bathos*, is the same word used in Genesis 1:2 where it is written, "... darkness was over the surface of the *deep*," which literally means "chaos." If I go deeper for big fish, I may have to deal with a little chaos. If I enter the deeper waters of life, I must take responsibility for what I find in those deep places.

Throwing the net down into the deep of my own heart could end up in a tangled mess. I may have to deal with the messier aspects of my life—and the lives of people I am involved with. There could be some nasty snarls. This can happen when I and my clients have to fish around others. We can cross our lines and end up in a tangled mess. This is not a rare occurrence. In fact, I spend more time than I would like on tangles. It takes time to figure out what line belongs to whom. In relationships, I have to take responsibility for my own stuff. Instead of blaming others, I have to ask myself why similar entanglements keep occurring. Maybe it's something about me. In fishing, I might keep getting frustrated with other fishers crowding me, when it is I who needs to learn better boundaries. Or maybe I need to learn to care about someone besides myself.

It is far easier for me to live on the surface, keeping my net in the shallows. It is less complicated if I keep casting on the surface, not asking the deep questions. This is typical of my culture. It is far too common for churches. They have grown fond of only shallow fishing. This is no surprise. Things are just less messy this way. Even when the church does try to go deeper, the cast is often aimed at some legalistic, pious, moral issue that misses the heart of Christ's message. Perhaps, it is like the fly fisher who keeps casting the fly into the rocks or the willows instead of to the fish.

For me, the net that churches cast in the name of saving souls is too often an example of fishing too shallow. It catches the easy ones and misses the broken-hearted, the poor, the weary, the sick, the prisoners, the orphans, the outcasts, and those who are asking questions of depth. It misses the prophets, poets, the true teachers, and individuals who possess a deep discernment. Some are hiding, just like fish, because they are bored with and burned out by the superficial forms of Christianity. I have seen *that* net move over my head several times, and I am glad I was able to avoid its shallow sweep. I want to go deeper, even if it terrifies me. I want to cast and drift to the depths of a God I do not understand.

Throwing my net down into those chaotic waters might sift through the distorted images of God that I have netted before. I know I have been dragging them along for a long time now. I will have to decide which to throw away. Some of these distorted images I have picked up from my religious upbringing, my family, the culture, or the gurus I prop up. Sorting through these idols can be a tedious task. It isn't pretty, all that untangling, all those bones, pieces of drift wood, and rusted hooks. As a believer, I will have to learn to avoid the shallow nets. Many church gurus boast about how many fish they have caught in their shallow nets. The shallow nets are easy to recognize. They are often nice and fancy, especially for fishing nets. The nets may be fancy buildings, comfortable seats, entertaining music, or feel-good sermons. The net Jesus wanted Peter to throw into the depths was about catching the deeper aspects of the soul. There should be something deep inside my heart that yearns for *that* net far more than all the shallow things offered by the culture. I yearn to be caught in the deep net that Jesus threw, to be pulled out of the unconscious, chaotic waters of my life and of this culture, in hope of being transformed.

I will have to ignore the flashy trinkets and the surface lures of culture. I will have to ignore the catch phrases found on the surface of spirituality:

"I must always feel good and happy."

"It's all about me."

"I must be popular and successful."

"I want to catch more big fish now."

The church promises a superficial sense of belonging. If you just join the club, you will be connected to everyone. If you just join, you will never have to ask:

"Where do I most deeply belong?"

"Who am I really?

"Where is God?"

It is difficult to avoid getting all tangled up in those shallow nets. It is getting more so. Unfortunately, I live in a shallow culture that does not encourage depth of soul. As a member of this culture, I am sorely tempted to throw myself into the first shallow net that comes drifting by. If it gives me a sense of belonging, I'm in. I can drift along with the others and conform to their thinking. I can maintain a superficial sense of belonging by cheering on some football team or toting the lines of a political party. Such parroting gives me a shallow language that keeps me on the same page, which is at a sub-mediocre level. Such language does not help my soul grow deep like a river. Nor does it get me closer to the heart of God.

There are also liberal and progressive forms of Christianity, where it is trendy to question and be open-minded. However, if I am only following the latest trend, then I am merely conforming to a different crowd. If I am part of a trend, I can pretend to belong. However, Jesus still stands on a narrow path and invites me to follow him and, at least at times, to stand alone.

Avoiding the Shallow Net

I would like to avoid the shallow nets thrown by my culture, including those of the church. I certainly can hold out for a while, but there is a cost. If I am going to say no to the cultural chaos, I will have to spend some time on the bottom of some deep holes. I am less certain of my ability to remain alone on the bottom for very long. I might have to learn to breathe like a fish. I know when I go down there, I get anxious. I quickly come back up to the surface gasping for air. My best chance to survive in the depths for any length of time is to first undergo some transformation. I will have to become like a fish.

My constant hope is that fly-fishing will help me avoid the shallow nets. It is on the river where I have the best hope of getting below the surface, connecting to something that is bigger than me. While fly-fishing, I am participating in life. I am playing. I am problem solving. I am an artist. I am creating, thinking deeply, hoping for that tug from deep below the surface. When I am fly-fishing, I am actively searching for something deeper. Literally. It is better than following a step-be-step guide to fly-fishing or a self-help book about how to live.

Few things are as foolish as trying to follow a manual, be it for fly-fishing or for life. Throw them away. Unfortunately, many preachers use step-by-step manuals. Throw those away also. Let them drift away to be brought up in one of those shallow nets.

Deeper Thinking: Not Merely Following Principles

In *A River Runs Through It,* the Reverend Maclean is always pondering deep spiritual issues. He asked the deep questions and shared his thoughts with his sons Norman and Paul. At the river, he picked up stones and sometimes talked about how they were formed. He talked about God's words being under the rocks and how his boys needed to listen to the river. In addition, he would contemplate which came first, the water or the word. He sat alongside of the river with his bible opened to the first page of the Gospel of John contemplating the Logos, the word that become flesh. The reverend was aware that to the ancient philosophers, the Logos was the underlying unifying force of reality. It was beneath everything and within everything. It was the "glue" of the universe. I am quite certain the reverend was aware of other passages, such as Colossians 1:17: "He is before all things, and in him all things hold together." Or Hebrews 1:3, "The Son ... [sustains] all things by his powerful word." The Logos fascinated the reverend; he pictured it being under the rocks of the river he fished. It was the fabric of all life and the bedrock of all of creation.

In the novel, the eldest son, Norman, recalls a conversation he had with his father. He remembers his father discussing the question of which came first, the water or the Word. The Reverend Maclean encouraged Norman to listen carefully, and he would hear that the words are underneath the water.

It seems that Norman did not necessarily accept his father's conclusion. He thinks his father's belief might be based on his role as a preacher. Norman argues that if you look at the issue from the perspective of a fisherman, such as Paul, then one can see that the words came from the water.

His father counters saying that Norman is not listening; that he needs to listen more carefully.

The father's response is significant because it indicates that he is not a man who merely follows Christian doctrines and principles. His connection to God is much deeper. It is a living, breathing, fluid, and dynamic relationship. He does not believe what he believes, as Norman suggests, because he is a "preacher first" of certain church theological doctrines. He does not believe what he believes to maintain his religious social status within his community. He has *heard* for himself and has used his own rational mind to form a belief. We could say he uses his own inner authority, relying largely on his own inner experience as he personally interacts with the creation—the tumbling river, the rocks, and the Word.

Even while under interrogation, Jesus challenged those around him. It seems that Jesus is quite interested in not only what I believe but my motives. He wants to know if I discovered my beliefs on my own initiative or if I am following the crowd. As was mentioned earlier, when Pilate questioned Jesus asking if he were a king, Jesus responds with another question, "Is that your own idea ... or did others talk to you about me?" (John 18:34). Perhaps I should ask myself this question regarding many of my beliefs. Do I believe what I believe merely because someone has told me, or do I believe it for myself and of my own initiative?

In essence, the Reverend Maclean does not believe what he believes because someone told him what to believe or because he *should*. He believes in what he believes because he has listened carefully. He has *heard*; he has heard from the river he fishes ritualistically.

He repeats his accusation that his sons are not listening carefully. In so doing, perhaps he challenged all of us. Are you listening? Are you listening carefully? What have you heard? What do you hear, if anything at all while you fly-fish?

While fly-fishing, I sometimes become locked into a familiar pattern or set of principles that prevents me from hearing anything else. It is common to see fish rising to caddis. On occasion, I have assumed this calls for a dry fly when, in reality, the fish are chasing the swimming pupa below the surface. The fish propel themselves upward toward the surface in pursuit of the swimming caddis but then, after inhaling the pupa, turn downward with a splash. My old assumption that they were eating the adults on the surface was wrong. In such situations, an emerging swimming caddis pupa in the surface film or just below the surface can be very effective.

I know many fly fishers who insist on following the textbook principle that you present a fly by quartering the cast upstream— even though a down-and-across presentation can be far more effective. Fly fishers who are taught to "match the hatch" may discover there are times when it is better *not* to match the hatch. There is a time to show the fish a different fly.

There are countless other examples of how I get hung-up following rigid principles that do not work in every situation. The river and the fish are a living dynamic. Fly-fishing is a fluid process, an art that requires countless adjustments to an endless set of changing dynamics. Likewise, living the day-to-day spiritual life is a living dynamic; following principles is often ineffective and contrary to the true spiritual life.

The writer to the Hebrews says we need to leave behind the "elementary teachings about Christ and be taken forward to maturity" (Hebrews 6:1).

I know that if I merely follow self-made forms of religion and the principles of others, I will spiritually stagnate.

If I fish more deeply or use a technique that violates all the principles of fly-fishing, who knows what will come up from the depths? Huge browns like to lie deep down at the bottom of the river. For reasons that elude me, sometimes these fish rise upward from the depths toward my fly. If I try something unconventional, sometimes fish manifest themselves, almost as though from another realm. When they rise to my fly, it stirs something in the depths of my heart. In my spiritual life, I might need to try something completely "nonreligious" and against convention. In so doing, I might discover that this is the way Jesus lived. Perhaps I can meet him on an edge.

Over the years, I have had clients pull out of their own fly box a strange-looking fly that they have successfully used elsewhere.

"Mind if I try this?" they said. "This works everywhere I fish."

"Sure, give it a chance," I have reluctantly learned to say. Some, ugly, monstrous flies have produced amazing results. One time, I was fishing with a client in Cheesman Canyon. He was catching fish on a large-size 10 renegade fly that looked like a bird's nest compared to the size 22-26 nymphs I was accustomed to using. Another time on the Dream Stream, a client was using a fat chocolate W-D40 nymph that produced wonders. Perhaps the lesson is to trust in what you know and have experienced for yourself rather than obeying the guide—or the preacher.

There is a price to be paid. When I violate principles in fly-fishing or in life, I can't expect support from anyone. At least at first, I will have to stand alone. I may have to get down on my knees. While fishing, this may take the form of kneeling on the bank while I try to figure out how to make an unconventional cast with an unconventional fly. I try not to bow down to anyone except that huge fish I am trying to entice. I might look foolish to everyone on my knees, trying some new unconventional technique, but I try to stick with it. There is a time to be a maverick and an outlaw. It's a test. I have to commit myself to what I believe, even if I do not receive support from those around me. I give myself to what I have personally heard deep in my heart.

On the Sabbath, who is to say I might not be better to go to the river and help someone catch a fish? On the river, I might have to reach out my hand to someone who has fallen. Perhaps the rushing river and the leaping fish may awaken something in both of us. I think it is better to fish with those awake on the river than with those sleeping in church. This is how Jesus lived; he pushed the outer edges of convention. I might try to do the same.

If I reject the shallow net of the culture and of the church, what remains for me? Am I alone? Is God with me?

IX

Perhaps There Persists

❧❦

Fly-Fishing as a Ritual: Images

God remains large-
ly hidden from me. If God
were to reveal himself directly to me, how could I
endure God's radiance?
Wouldn't the angel I seek,
if it ever were to come to
me, overwhelm me? It is
my opinion, as Rilke sug-
gests, that we could not
endure an angel moving
toward us. Therefore, I
see, if at all, only in part.
I catch glimpses of God in
images. While fly-fishing,

sometimes a large fish surfaces out of the water before my eyes, and
it is almost too much for me to endure.

This makes me wonder if I saw even a single fish in all its

glory, it might be too much for me to endure. Perhaps my nervous system tones down the incoming images I receive so that I am better able to behold what is before me. The toning down of my nervous system could be a blessing. By limiting what I see, the beauty does not overwhelm me.

If I could fully see the beauty of a single fish coming to the surface, only to watch it break free, how could I endure it? My longing to become one with these beautiful creatures is so great that truly connecting with a single one of them—and then losing the connection—would be too hard to endure. I write this and then realize that I have in many ways lost this connection, not only with the many big fish I have lost, but also when I lost the Eden of my youth.

When I hold a fish in my hands, however briefly, I have a vague sense that I have touched Something. Perhaps this is why it is sometimes so difficult to set a fish free. Surely, it is not so hard because of the loss of a meal or the chance to mount the fish on the wall. Not for me anyway. It is Something more. Yet I cannot drop the image of eating a fish too quickly. The desire to eat Something represents a longing to be one with Something. Think of how adoring parents speak to their babies, "You are so cute I could just eat you."

God, and the true beauty of his creation, remains largely hidden. A veil lies over my eyes. However, on occasion, I get a glimpse. I see a fish flashing to the surface, then darting below, just beyond my full gaze. Romans 1:19-20 explains the paradox of creation *clearly* revealing God's *invisible* attributes. How can I clearly see what is invisible? Perhaps rituals can help manifest what is invisible, even the invisible attributes of God. For me, fly-fishing is a ritual in which I am able to see, at least a little, what ordinarily lies hidden from me. In this ritual, I can sometimes glimpse the heart of God.

God in nature lingers just below the surface, like a large brown trout in a seam line barely disturbing the surface as it sips in blue-winged olive mayflies. As the brown participates in its daily ritual, methodically and repetitively rising, I engage with my own ritual: casting. In my own repetitive ritual, I experience Something. I tend to keep my appointment with this ritual at specific places on the river. In so doing, my hope is that I will meet God. I must admit, though, I am seldom fully conscious of what I am doing. However, fly-fishing, for me, has a quality of prayer about it. Jesus "went out to a mountainside to pray, and spent the night praying to God" (Luke 6:12). Going to a particular side of the mountain was his ritual. Fly fishers often have their own rituals, returning to the same particular places repeatedly, casting out our prayers and hopes with a fly on the water.

For my fly-fishing ritual, I return to the same river, hearing again its familiar sounds. I visualize my cast and its rhythm, remembering the images, words, and stories of loved ones, all closing in on the hope that a fish might take the fly. With each cast, I have the hope that Something might rise up inside me, reminding me that I am not alone. The ritual anchors me, steadying my heart as I cast into the powerful currents of both river and soul. I cast into mystery and hope for what eludes me. Sometimes, the cast, which lasts only a moment, becomes eternal. The spiritual becomes physical, as real as the person who fishes by my side, the stranger across the river, and the fish that tugs on the line. Fly-fishing, unlike many religious customs, is as physical as a giant rainbow trout taking an emerging mayfly off the surface of a pool, as physical as the tension I feel in the bend of the rod as the fish plunges downriver. This sensation, the connection between the spiritual and the physical, is not automatic. It comes with ritual, with time and frequency on the river.

When a client tells me he had the "best day of fishing ever," I tell him that the true spiritual beauty of fly-fishing is still beyond us. As exciting as a single day on a river can be, it is only a day on the river. In order for fly-fishing to transform my life, which it has, I needed to visit the same river repeatedly. I needed to experience it in the different seasons, weather, and hatches. I needed empty days full of waiting for a fish to rise. I needed other days when I could not keep fish off my line. All these experiences connect to memories of the people I fished with, of friends lost and found, and of fish caught and lost.

The ritual of fly-fishing causes images to stir in my soul. These images rise like mist off the river at dawn and are gone. Some of the images linger, perhaps by my choosing, and are caught on the surface of my heart like an emerging mayfly stuck on the surface film of the river. The images come and go like trout in a riffle feeding. A few images stick with me. I recognize faces. I see a familiar tree. I see the wake of a big fish moving in the water toward my fly. I recognize a path I once walked as a child to the pond. My soul knows the way. I remember the faithfulness of God.

The images flow from the labyrinthine passageways of my heart. They form sequences as I continue to fish. At times, the sequences form words. The images, the sequences, and the words tug at me, asking me to pay attention to what these messages on my heart might mean. My soul awaits in eager anticipation. While I ponder these things, a fish might rise to my fly, and I might raise the rod to hook the fish. This moment is all moments. Images from the past, the present, and the future, all merge. It is a moment of eternity, Eden here and now, brought to me by the ritual of fly-fishing.

Sometimes, in such a sacred and wild moment, I hear faintly what I might perceive as a word from God.

I think back to the pond, wondering if as a child I followed the whisper of God.

Is There Anyone Out There?

Searching the waters by casting a fly is a way for me to ask: Is there anyone out there? Is anyone at home? Am I at home? Am I just searching for what is at the surface of the waters of the river? Or am I searching below the surface of my life. Rainer Maria Rilke, in *Duino Elegies*, opens the series of poems with a question. He ponders what would happen if he yelled out. Would anyone hear him? This question sets the whole tone for the elegies, which became his most significant work, rich in existential thought. In these poems, I believe Rilke asks all my questions: Am I alone? Why is life so fleeting? Where do I belong? What is the meaning of my life?

Rilke challenges me to consider to whom I can turn in my need. In the first of the elegies, he suggests that neither people nor angels can truly help me. At the deepest level, without God I am truly alone. Even with God, my *experience* is often of being alone. The fish I seek in fly-fishing, ultimately are small comfort. I connect with a fish, but then it swims away from me in fear. How can I derive comfort from a beautiful creature whose first instinct is to get away from me?

In spite of my faith, or maybe because of it, I need to ask these questions repeatedly. Such questions are an honest response to the human condition. These questions are for the religious and non-religious, the spiritual and non-spiritual, or those who believe and those who do not. I ask these questions because deep down I live with frustration, ignorance, and a sense of incompleteness. I live in the frustration of not knowing or experiencing God completely. I only see in part. I only hear in part. Even as a believer, I must ask, "Where are you God?"

Over and over, I howl these questions into the wilderness areas. What do I get? Silence. No one responds. There is no one there; I am alone. Ironically, it is this experience that draws me to God and leads me to reject idols, be they religious or secular. If I do not know by experience that I am alone and all is hopeless, how could I ever solely put my faith in God?

I look to Jacob, who wrestled with the angel of the Lord and would not let him go. Perhaps I should wrestle with an angel, demanding to know where I belong, where is my place in the world. I could hold the angel until he blessed me and tells me if he was the one who led me to the pond.

I want to know if anyone heard me when I cried out, if anyone claimed me as his or her own. Jesus is the alpha and the omega, the beginning and the end. As a believer, I am no longer seeking a doctrinal answer. Perhaps I just want to wrestle with the possibility of knowing God and the day-to-day incompleteness of my experience. Although I consider myself a believer, I am still at the beginning of the journey.

How ironic that as a *true* believer, I do not quite completely believe. I feel most alive when I am asking the real questions, often behind a curtain of doubt. I have learned to live in the tension of not completely knowing. I don't need my questions to be immediately resolved. I may try to hold the angel, only to remain locked in the tension of a stalemate.

A Familiar Tree

Among other things, Rilke's poetry invites me to find spiritual comfort in performing a simple task over and over in a familiar place. Doing so grounds a person. That's what fly-fishing does for me.

In the first elegy, Rilke describes certain aspects of nature that can remain with me and comfort me. He asks me to remember a familiar tree on a hillside. Just visualizing the tree accomplishes part of the task. When I fly-fish, I like to go to favorite meanders of the river. There may be a familiar tree in one spot, or a rock, or another landmark. When I combine favorite places with the familiar task of casting over and over again, I create some stability in a world where time slips away and all is transitory.

Of course, this does not answer my existential questions, but it does make me comfortable enough to explore the deeper questions. My ordinary fears, my inability to control my life, and my wrestling with meaning and belonging can be overwhelming. Fly-fishing eases my soul just enough to stand in the middle of the river and ask the deeper questions. Do I belong to this creation? What do these fish declare to me? Does God care if I catch a fish? Who is the stranger across the river? With whom do I fish? Does anyone care about me? Would it matter to anyone if I slipped and the river swept me away? Do I matter? Where is home?

These questions can be terrifying. Fly-fishing reduces my fears, and I am not so inclined to resort to defensive mechanisms that shield me against the answers. If I allow fly-fishing to help me remain with the river, then perhaps the river will remain with me. It will be easier to ask the questions and build my relationship to God.

Fly-fishing can provide the stability that allows the fearful truth of my condition to penetrate deep into my heart. I can maintain the stability I need to keep from falling into the abyss, the deep hole lying just beyond the gravel bar of the river. While this stability helps me, it does not sustain me. The swirling currents, the deep holes, and the elusive fish remind me of my vulnerability. At any moment, I could take a fall and the river might swallow me up, leaving me and without a prayer—or perhaps with *only* a prayer.

I have uttered many prayers for a fish to bite. When I do so, does anyone hear me? Am I religious, spiritual, or superstitious? I always wonder about this. Does God intervene in this world? Does God cause a fish to strike? Does God enter into any of these events?

One spring morning on the Arkansas River tailwater in Pueblo, my daughter and I were fishing in a run strangely called the Carp Hole. We could see the dark forms of large rainbows along the bottom. She was fishing the run patiently when a large fish took her fly.

After landing the bulky rainbow, she asked a difficult question. "Dad, I wonder what made *this* particular fish bite and not another one? I wonder what it was thinking and seeing."

I did not know how to answer her, but I realized she was thinking in terms of *one specific* fish rather than the group of fish, which is a unique and personal way to look at things. In essence, she was trying to think like a fish. Of course, this made me think of my own questions about whether God caused a fish to bite. If God does intervene in such life events, it seems reasonable that God could influence the one fish needed to accomplish his intention rather than a whole school of fish. This seems consistent with how Jesus spoke of God noticing *one* sparrow that falls to the ground or how God called a whale to swallow Jonah.

As an individual who often prays in one form or another and to varying degrees for catching a fish, winning a wrestling match, and finding the job of my dreams, I have to admit my prayers become mixed with paganism, superstitions, and egocentric motives.

At some level, I pray often, even when I do not know it. Can the rational fly fisher pray to God without knowing it, perhaps without even believing in God? Can the pious Christian admit that sometimes she asks the animals, the birds of the heavens, and the earth itself to teach her (Job 12:7-8). Perhaps the important issue for me is to be aware of what I am really doing, to be honest with myself, and to pay attention to my reaction to the events that may unfold.

The Foundation Provided by Fly-Fishing

The familiar places where I stand while fly-fishing are a foundation that provides me enough comfort to accept my true spiritual predicament. Ironically, the more aware I am of my aloneness the more I seek the true comfort that is in God. Fly-fishing eases my heart and gives me the courage to meet God in my loneliness, stripped bare of emotional and religious pretense. Stripped of defense mechanisms, I stand naked and alone before God. I empty myself and stand ignorant with only my fly rod in hand. This vulnerability creates the opening to Spirit—as long as I do not seal off the opening with religious constructs. Carl Jung suggested that people will often use religion as defense from God.

As a fly fisher, I am able—sometimes—to stand in this vulnerable place because the rocks under my feet have become somewhat familiar to me. Because I have gone to this river so often, I can recognize individual trees, boulders, and currents. In this river, I am comfortable. I can let my feet settle securely on the bottom while the currents rush past my legs. This place becomes my meeting place for God and other human beings. It is the place where I can lean against a familiar boulder, or sit under a favorite tree, and do no more than watch the river flow past me. It is as close as I get to being home. Familiar landscapes give me a sense of place in the world.

When I stand and settle into my familiar places, I can more freely cast out my questions, fears, and hopes into the heart of God. My favorite word, *perhaps*, is relevant to this discussion. I am not suggesting that the fly-fishing will produce comfort that makes a spiritual experience a given. Fly-fishing is different every time. One day I may have a wonderful experience. Another day, I may I catch nothing. Worse, I may feel nothing. A lightning storm over the mountains may threaten to blow over me. I might feel no tugs from below or within. The best I can do is realize that I am not in control, and this realization might be my greatest spiritual experience.

On the other hand, I may think I'm the greatest fly fisher in the area, one who has mastered fly-fishing techniques and is forever looking for the next great adventure. I may be at a place where it is like being caught in a back eddy, and I need to find more exotic places with new and unique fish species. Before I know it, fishing has become an addiction that only numbs and no longer comforts.

The tension remains. I am uncertain of being able to catch either the fish or the God who remains out of my reach. Even so, I can lean against the boulder. I can sit under the shade of a tree. I have my rod. I have a place. I have a task. It is Something.

I have not arrived. I am only trying to live in the tension of uncertainty.

Living in Existential Tension

Living with my unresolved issues with God, nature, and other human beings can lead to a peculiar madness. Accepting this requires courage and endurance. I am not very good at waiting in tension. The culture seems to prefer that I live in constant happiness, comfort, stimulation, and resolution. If I am not happy and do not know where I belong, it is tempting to conclude that something is wrong with me. The culture is always offering options that will make me happy and feel like I belong.

However, there is a price. Literally. Many of the options require money. For example: drugs, legal and otherwise; exotic fishing trips; fancy vacations; electronic gadgets; toys; or the latest therapy. There is an emotional price as well. I may delude myself that this or that idol will make me happy. I can chase idol after idol in much the same way that I chase fish after fish in different lands.

"How long will you people turn my glory into shame?"—Psalms 4:2

What it means to live in the tension will vary for each person. I offer a few thoughts. For me, living in the tension means I cannot expect to know God with complete understanding. God will largely remain a mystery unresolved. Likewise, my relationships with others, nature, and myself, will also remain incomplete and metaphorically unconsummated.

However, I can remain in the apprehension of the dark forest and not know it completely. It is okay that my questions will remain largely unanswered. My existential questions about God, who I am, and where I belong will remain for the most part unresolved. I can choose to acknowledge this reality and choose to remain in the tension of not knowing with certainty.

Ronald Rolheiser, in *The Holy Longing*, suggests that we need to learn to live in the tension of issues being left unresolved. Yet when I consider myself and observe people around me, it seems that to live in the tension is not easy.

It is tempting for me to break the tension by resolving these issues—or pretending to resolve them. As a fly fisher, I know the tension of battling a big fish. If I doubt that I can land the fish, I might decide to horse in the fish, which often does not work. Deep down, I know that. However, I just want to relieve myself of the tension. So I will rush things, break the fish off, and feel the line go limp. The tension is broken.

Sometimes I am too tired to maintain the tension required to reel in my catch. Sometimes, I do not have the patience to keep reminding, encouraging, and instructing my client. I forget that the life of faith and catching big fish requires this type of endurance. Perhaps, I need instruction on how to run my race, finish my course, and keep my faith (2 Timothy 4:7).

My clients (both children and adults) are often not prepared to endure the physical and emotional fatigue required to maintain the tension. I can be part of this. We might fail to move with the fish, chasing it downstream and getting the proper cross-current angle. Instead, we hold our ground thinking we are in control and can drag the fish up river. This often results in a break off.

Tension is critical. The fly fisher has to keep the rod up, which maintains the proper tension. The proper tension keeps the slack out of the line, which prevents the hook from dislodging. The proper tension also transfers the pressure and strain of the fish into the rod, which enables the angler to enter a give and take relationship with the fish. The rod acts like a shock absorber. This skill set is also a needed in human relationships—and even with God.

One of the quickest ways I end the tension in any situation is by not taking any responsibility. I might end the tension in a spiritual situation by submitting to the instruction of a spiritual guru. I let someone else resolve my issues. Unlike the mother of Jesus, I fail to treasure these things and ponder them in my heart (Luke 2:19). I may stop pondering the complexities of life. I might consider all these issues a done deal because a guru, whoever that may be, told me so. I might ignore the inner authority of the word inside of me. Doing so is the opposite of what it means to live in spiritual tension. In fly-fishing, the comparison would be to use only one fly, one technique, and one fishing hole because this is what the guide instructed me to do ten years ago.

Returning to the Question at the Pond

The question remains: Did God or an angel help me find the pond of my youth? If God just once had walked a single step with me, helped me make just one cast, or nudged a solitary fish to strike at my own hand-tied fly, this would have constituted a miracle. It wouldn't have taken much: the slight redirecting of my gaze so I would notice a fish, a little push to adjust the angle of my rod, or a gentle touch upon my shoulder. Something tiny could have confirmed that I was not alone. I'm afraid I am doomed to wrestle with this issue as both a believer and a skeptic. I am willing to concede to the argument that it is *possible* that no intervention occurred. Perhaps I always walked the banks of the pond alone. Perhaps the fish were simply fish, and I was just a child who acquired some skills with a fly rod. Yet, I am also open to the amazing possibility that God was and is forever with me and in everything—fish, pond, sky, Earth.

My own life story suggests Something happened at the pond—and at other key moments in my life—that I cannot explain. This is the basis of my claim to faith. The seemingly random meanders of my life, the deep pools of my feelings, and my haunted longings to connect merge and then emerge into a river that reveals there is more to my life than my perceptions that I do not belong. As I follow the river's meanders, a widening meander turns me around to face an endless sky—and I glimpse a place of belonging that may be Eden.

X

A Sense of Place, a Habitus

❧☙

Living in Nature: Is this My Home?

I often imagine the un-fallen world as described in C.S's Lewis's fantasy, *Perelandra*. Within my imagination, I have lived in this book and this other unfallen place for decades. On Perelandra, there is no sin, and there are no divisions between nature and me.

I have often imagined meeting the Green Lady. She too is un-fallen and intimately connected to her world. She has no experience of alienation in any form. In my personal fantasy, I ask her where her home is.

She looks confused and does not understand my question. Then, she understands my question. She points to the towering trees teeming with life; the flowing waters with leaping fish and swarming insects. I slowly understand her answer. To her, the entire natural world *is* her home.

The Green Lady has a sense of place that I, in my own fallen world, cannot even imagine. To her, home is all of the natural world and the wilderness surrounding her. The animals follow her around and are not afraid. She in turn does not scare the animals. When she steps in the water, the fish come to her. If she were a fly fisher, she would not need to cast. She lives in Eden.

Since the loss of Eden, I am separated from the natural world. Modern life largely widens the gulf between nature and myself. This is true in spite of my profession as a fly-fishing guide. For the most part, I no longer hunt, fish, farm, or gather my own food. These acts are distant memories. I go straight to the grocery store and bypass the natural way. This is a world I have grown accustomed; it offers conveniences but at a horrible price to my soul. Being severed from the natural processes of the creation leaves me alienated. I am disconnected from my roots.

D.H Lawrence spoke of our culture's disconnection from the natural world. I think for him this disconnection was like a severing and left humanity bleeding at the roots. It was a horrible loss. It was like a marring of a former love relationship. It is my opinion that D.H. Lawrence thought that this marring and loss is what is wrong with us; me, humanity.

Indeed, the wounding to my soul is terrible. How did I trade my relationship with nature, my first love, for a few modern comforts and conveniences? How did I allow this to happen without protest? How did I so easily go along? However, at times, I still feel the loss, even as I try to forget. At times, I awaken and am forced to remember the Eden of my youth.

Here is a catastrophe. Many Christian churches, instead of

healing this division between human beings and nature, remain suspicious of anything pertaining to the earth. If I speak of healing my relationship to the trees, fish, or beasts of the earth, the Christian culture accuses me of being "new age," even though these values are as old as the earth itself. They go back to my roots in Eden.

The modern world will deepen my alienation from nature if I allow it. However, I can choose to challenge this. Fly-fishing, as a tool and ritual, allows me to enter the natural world. Fly-fishing can help restore the intimate connections of Eden. As I fly-fish, I glimpse a paradise barely remembered. However, the memory still flows in my veins. The blood flowing in my veins can help heal my spiritual wounds—like waters flowing over a scorched land.

In the opening lines of *A River Runs Through It*, the author makes two important observations. First, there is no clear line between fly-fishing and religion for the Maclean family. Second, family members grew up at the junction of great trout rivers in western Montana. The family was rooted in a specific place. This sense of place was the foundation that enabled the Macleans to experience fly-fishing as something spiritual. The river itself erased the dividing lines between fly-fishing and religion.

Am I Without a Home?

I try to allow the waters I fish to erase the dividing lines between religion and the natural world. I try to seek a spiritual connection to the natural world, even as I live in the conveniences of modern society. However, I always run into obstacles. I realize how the severing of my life from natural processes has left me ignorant. On a practical level, my life has virtually nothing to do with the natural world.

Even when I would attend church regularly, I might hear

talk about connecting with creation, but there is little practical in-
teraction with nature. The church's spiritual practice consists mainly of worship services, bible study groups, prayer groups, discussion
groups, and community outreach programs. These activities, most
often, have virtually nothing to do with place, the natural landscape,
and nature itself. The practice of religion is largely indoors severed
from the natural world. I stay *inside* and watch "church" on stage
or, worse, on the big screen. If a preacher comments on the beauty
of creation, he or she must point *outside* or to a projected image of
a natural landscape that few in the congregation have ever visited.
In church, my relationship with nature is reduced to a few romanti-
cized comments expressed indoors. I look out of the windows of the
church, aching to be outside. Yet to be honest, I am usually no more
intimate with nature than the preacher. I feel largely severed from
my ecological roots—and, not coincidentally, from the biblical narrative that honors creation. As a practical matter, it is assumed that
the best way to experience God is within a man-made church building. In order to experience Eden, I would do better to gather with
two of three others on the river, breaking bread and giving thanks.

Churches do retreats into nature, but these occur rarely,
perhaps once a year; certainly not enough to become a ritualized
habit or a habitus. There are sunrise services on Easter. It's hard to
call this a ritual. I need rituals that bring me into nature regularly.
I need habitual opportunities to connect me to particular places in
nature. Since this rarely happens or develops in church life, I prefer
to leave the stage, the spotlight, and the music and instead listen to
the sounds of the river.

Beldon Lane in the opening lines of his wonderful work, *The
Solace of Fierce Landscapes*, suggests that discussions about God cannot be removed from the context of place. He goes on to describe
how landscape plays an important role in the way we envision the

holy and how we relate to others, the larger world, and even God. The biblical narrative is full of texts indicating the significance of place: Sinai, the Promised Land, the desert wilderness, and the tree on the banks of the river. These places shape people and change their perspective of God.

Fly-fishing is one way I move out into nature on a regular basis. I can create with others my own habit of fly-fishing in nature. If I do this, I might then hope to hold on to the fish stories of my youth.

More Than Fish Stories

Conservationist Terry Tempest Williams emphasized the importance of putting one's personal story in the context of a "homeland." Unfortunately, in modern life people tend to leave their homeland in search of work, which winds up serving a global market instead of our roots. The fish stories shared with me on my fly-fishing trips give me hope that some of us are rooted in a place. I encourage this. When I ask people to search their lives for stories about fishing, their stories push upward and crack through the hardened shells of modern living. Fishing can be a link, perhaps *the* link, that binds a person's faith to the land and its waters.

For the Maclean family, fly-fishing was a ritual that connected where they lived to God's words. I like to imagine that for the rest of Norman Maclean's life, he tried to listen to God's words every time he fished—as his father hoped. For Norman Maclean, God's words were under the rocks in his home river. Fly-fishing in a specific place became repetitive contemplation, which took the form of a ritual. Their Maclean family story is rooted in the river, as perhaps it is with those of us who fly fish, along with the bigger story that we hear, however faintly.

My hope is that all these fish stories merge into a deep river, where they expose roots that reach into the rocks in the undercut banks. When you and I follow those roots down far enough, they might connect us to a bigger story. For my part, if I ever had to leave the places I fish, I would lose a part of my life story and perhaps the bigger story of God.

What Would I Miss If I Had to Leave the Places I Fish?

After living in Colorado for thirty-five years and fishing the South Platte in canyons and the vast expanses of South Park, I sometimes ask myself what I would miss if I had to move away. What would I remember? As I ponder this question, I quickly feel the weight and intensity of my attachments to river, landscape, and sky.

If I had to leave, I could never forget morning's first light on the granite walls of Eleven Mile and Cheesman Canyons, their deep emerald pools and trout gently rising to blue winged olive mayflies. Most of all, I would miss the mysterious South Platte River meandering through South Park, where I have taught many to catch their first fish. As I consider the thought of someday having to leave these places, I begin to grieve. I grieve for particular places. I recall a specific curve in the river where every summer I—or my clients or my daughters—hooked a large rainbow who was sipping tricos along the willows. I recall a particular meander where a big brown engulfed a streamer and took me deep into the undercut bank. This is the place where my daughters made their first casts while wading in shorts and jelly flip-flops. This place has twisted its way into my soul.

Even now, when I think back to a small valley in New Jersey, I sigh, remembering my childhood pond, with its tranquil surface, and the surrounding forest hills that once protected me. I remember the odors of a particular dampness found in a warm humid air, and the smell of sweet grass and clover. I can still remember the sense of excitement I had when I walked along its banks and saw big bass moving through the coves. I miss seeing and hearing the movement of water displaced by a large fish chasing food in the shallows. As a solitary hunter, I learned to cast ahead of the moving fish with a streamer fly and was rewarded sometimes with the tug of a heavy fish on the other end. Even now, I miss the feeling of having this beautiful valley, the Eden of my youth, all to myself.

The pond is a place I still go back to in my mind, remembering the connections that enabled me to stand strong alone in my solitude. I remember my footing and, at least at times, a sense of stability. Whatever it was I was reaching for back then, I still reach for. Back then, I experienced Something of Eden. Yet there were parts of me that I could not find. The longing stays with me. If I ever have to leave the places I fish now (and someday I will), I will miss both the remains of what I could and could not find. As a child, there was much I could not find. However, my hope is that nothing is lost as the river tumbles through the valley of my heart, only to merge with the heart of God, which I can only hope is inside me.

When I leave South Park and the South Platte River, I will forever look back to the times I spent in this enormous valley. I will miss whatever glimpses of divine beauty I was able to retrieve back into myself with each cast. I will miss the beautiful fish that I was able to hold so briefly in my hands. Those fish bore the fingerprints of God. When I leave the vast meadows of South Park, I will miss the elusive fish and the longing I expressed with each cast, casts that came from the deepest places of my soul. Perhaps some of those casts are still reaching beyond the skies to another realm.

I will miss these places. In some sense, even without leaving, I already do. Every time I fish these wonderful, waters and greet these beautiful places, I am already saying good-bye. I am both griev-

ing and praising, arriving and leaving. I am forever aware of the transitory nature of my life and my time on the earth. What can remain?
Who can remain? Where can I belong? Have not all the wonderful
fisheries that I have greeted in their days of glory already faded like
the Indian paintbrush flowers of South Park in autumn? And have
not I, in some sense, also faded with them?

I hope some of the beauty will remain long after I am gone.
Wherever I may go, I hope that Something will remain within my
heart, forever in bloom along the river's edge.

Could the Places I Fish Miss Me?

While it is easy for me to know how I would miss different
aspects of nature, I sometimes contemplate a more difficult question.
If I had to leave this area and the places I love to fish, would the
natural world miss me? Another way to ponder this question is to ask
if God, who resides in creation, would lament my absence *through*
the creation? Could the Spirit of God remember my former place
in his natural world? Could the branches of the trees that I gently
pushed aside, while making my way to the pond, feel my absence and
remember me? Would God *feel* my absence? Would God remember
how I once walked in the cool of the morning in this Garden of
Eden, the garden of my youth?

Sometimes in the early morning, I push through the brushy
willows along the banks of the river, I remember how beautiful the
river looked just a few days ago. Caught off guard, I sigh because I
am reuniting with creation in an intense way. I wonder if in a similar
manner, the river breathes a sigh of relief because I have returned.

As a child, I routinely stood on the banks of the pond and
received comfort from the trees and the beauty around me. As I aged
from a boy to a young man, the time came for me to move on and

leave the pond. Did God notice that I was no longer standing on the banks of the pond and casting under the shade of a tree? Did God miss the solitude we once shared? Could the fish themselves miss me standing over them, not as predator and conqueror but as a guardian who meant no harm?

If the rocks themselves are capable of praising their creator, if the rivers can clap their hands (Psalms 98:8), if the heavens can declare the glory of God (Psalm 19:1), if the mountains and hills can burst into song (Isaiah 55:12), is it possible that nature itself is capable of feeling and emitting emotion. I am a part of the creation, which leads me to wonder if God's creation sometimes misses *itself*. I realize I am attributing human emotions to nature, but did not God incarnate himself in Jesus, a man of human emotions and deep longings? Did not God in Christ long to restore our relationship to him and creation? I think of Jesus weeping over Jerusalem, "Oh how I longed to gather you up ... how often I have longed to gather your children together, as a hen gathers her chicks under her wings, but you were unwilling!" (Matthew 23:37). It is quite easy to over-spiritualize Jesus and forget that he was a part of the creation, a man of flesh and blood quite similar to me, longing for his place of belonging.

It seems reasonable to me, and at the same time utterly astonishing, to believe that God could speak through the creation. Throughout my life, I have thought that God spoke to me through another person. Is it so different to believe that God speaks to me through the animals, the trees, and other aspects of the creation? Scripture states that the natural world reveals God to me (Romans 1:23). And scripture invites us to, speak to the animals, the birds of the heavens, the fish of the sea, and the earth itself, and allow them to teach us (Job 12-8-9). Why can't I interact with the fish, trees, lilies of the field, the rivers, and the stones under the river and then remember the oneness and sense of belonging we once shared?

Why couldn't the small piece of earth that held my pond remember a boy? Why couldn't the birds cry out to me from their lonely gray sky, perhaps in an attempt to comfort me? Why couldn't a fish I once released remember me? Why couldn't the meandering river I now fish as an adult, but will one day leave, remember me?

I like to meander along the South Platte looking for fish. Sometimes, I am surprised to realize I have followed the meander backwards. It's a strange sensation. It feels like the river is trying to wrap itself around me. Is the river trying to teach me? Equally strange, I do not notice the large fish rising by a boulder the first time I pass, but the fish is now in plain sight as I prepare to cast. Was the river trying to bring me to a new viewing point, where I would realize how it was trying to enclose me—or maybe it was just trying to give me a second chance to see the fish I missed. Was the river trying to speak to me? This makes me think about all the other things I have missed in life because I refused to take a different viewing place and change the angle of my heart.

I also wonder if by following the meander backwards, I was walking back in time, being given a second chance and experiencing the longing of my youth? As a child, I often wanted to move back in time to relive a memory. These feelings, while quite fanciful, reflect the deeper longings I once experienced. Maybe this was what it was like in Eden. Perhaps this is what it was like to walk in the garden, connected with creation and able to walk along the time continuum. If I look from a different perspective, I can see how, regardless of where on the time continuum, all of life as good. Is all goodness forever before me? If I truly believe in the goodness of life, my life in particular, then I wonder if given a second chance, would I choose this same life over again?

How can I dismiss the call I felt to go to the pond—or to fish a meadow stream. Isn't that the voice of God in creation, brokenhearted, missing me, wooing me, and longing for my return? If everything is connected and if God upholds all things by the power of his *logos* (Hebrews 1:3), then perhaps I may have heard his words whispered to me.

If for some reason I am unable to return to the river I once knew, or if I choose to stop fishing, could the river remember and mourn my absence? Perhaps I might forget. I might no longer have the faith to believe such so-called nonsense, but God is not forgetful. Perhaps God forever remembers me, even how I dare to love and follow the rivers I fished.

> "I remember the devotion of your youth,
> how as a bride you loved me
> and followed me through the wilderness,
> through a land not sown."—Jeremiah 2:2

Perhaps it means something to God when I follow paths back into wildness.

God remembers when he called me and I followed, although I did not know where I was going or if I heard. While I may not remember, God remembers when I walked upon the soul of the earth even as I walked the banks of the pond. Perhaps I can learn to remember my creator in the wild places I fish and how He once spoke tenderly to me before it became too difficult to hear.

If God takes notice of a single sparrow that falls to the ground and expresses heartfelt care for the flowers of the field, then what grief God must endure as we, his beloved, stand outside of the Eden we can hardly remember.

Awash in Exile

As a young child, I felt the weight of the existential human condition. Below the surface of my heart, I felt my aloneness, the passage of time, the fleeting nature of everything that seemed to be flying past me. I wondered at the meaning of life, where I came from, where I was going, and where I could truly belong. My inner soul was forever remembering Eden. I felt the exile in my bones or like the dampness in my leaky waders on a cold morning fishing.

If I am forever remembering Eden, then, to some extent, I must feel in exile. I did not sense this exile because I experienced unjust treatment from the world. If anything, I was born with a silver spoon in my mouth. Throughout my life, I have heard stories of true survivors and of incredible hardships endured. In some sense, these stories put my personal story to shame—but perhaps not completely. If I really did know Eden and somehow lost it, then what greater loss could I experience? In spite of the wonderful life I was given, I still feel some form of undefined exile and loss.

As a child, I was always remembering Eden and experiencing its loss. Was I always sensing Eden, glimpsing it from a distance, much as I could look below the surface of the pond and sense the presence of a fish? I still do not know why I felt so deeply at a young age. It is only now that I am older that I can look back and better handle the weight of what I felt and consider it a strange blessing.

When I look back at my life at the pond, I do feel blessed to have possessed an awareness of the human condition. Even now, I feel blessed to be someone who lives on this edge of faint awareness, remembering what life could be. My best guess is that some of us have "thin skin," a peculiar sensitivity that is part of our story. This sensitivity allows us to feel our true exile and the Eden of our memories.

Through my thin skin, I feel the wonder, the beauty, the mystery, and the vast distances I am barely able to endure. I experience the beauty and power around me at an intensity that makes me homesick for Something I cannot define. I feel the warmth of a summer breeze, the flowing waters, as well as the great storms of life. I am aware of the whirlwind that in one moment threatens to annihilate me and in the next moment speaks gently to me. I confront the cold, slanting rain as well as gentle snowflakes on my face. I see and feel the droplets of dew in the grass as I walk to a meadow stream. I possess the sensitivity to perceive a fish before it strikes. I feel life itself moving toward my fly and then tugging on the line. With this peculiar sensitivity, I feel connected and disconnected both at once. I feel at home and not at home; I belong and do not belong. If nothing else, this sensitivity has helped me become a better fly fisher.

It has taken honesty, courage, and intense self-awareness to admit I do not want to feel my true predicament and vulnerability. However, at least at times, I can unravel my protective layers and expose myself to my true state of aloneness. I can feel the exile and, at the same time, experience the beauties and passions of life. Entwined in the passions and beauty of life are the vast and frightful energies of life. The dark abyss I fear is the very place I need to venture. The deep dark hole full of potential snags may hold a trophy trout. I do not quite belong here, but I feel compelled to cast.

Sensitive individuals often live in what the Celtics call a thin place. In a thin place, I feel vulnerable to the depths of life. I feel the cold and the stiff breezes of the night while I am wondrously aware of the yearnings of my soul. My soul gives me hope that the next cast may connect me to the large brown trout that lies deep in the undercut of a deep dark hole. I do not know how deep and how far back that fish lies. Even if I knew, I do not know if I can hook it or, if I do, how deep it will go. If I hook it, I do not know if I can move the fish back out into my world.

Heavy Existential Thoughts and Insights

As a child, what could I do with all the heavy thoughts running inside my head? What could any child do with such intense thoughts? What a blessing it was to have the pond within walking distance of my home. It became a sacred place for casting all of my lonely feelings, longings, and hopes. I cast and cast, not knowing that all my longings for a more tender communion with the world would fill the whole valley and overflow it.

As a child, I experienced the transitory nature of life. The fleeting nature of life stirred something deep inside me; I understood that I could not go back along the time continuum and relive memories. But, like a child who stubbornly insists on wanting things to be a certain way, I desired to be able to go back. I was slow to learn that I could not stop time. When I did learn, it saddened me. I knew that a great day of fishing was in some sense already a distant memory. In a sense, I lived in anxious anticipation of the inevitable farewell to Eden. I was not good at yielding to the loss of a season or a love. In this, I was not alone. Robert Frost, in "Reluctance," called it treason to accept such things so easily.

How childlike of me to think I could forever remain in Eden in the springtime of my life. How could I as a mere child stop the pond from freezing? Although my melancholy was great, it could not slow the passage of time. How naïve to think I could enter the garden of bliss and live there forever. How caught off guard was I to discover that the world I was living in was not a place of permanence and glory. How youthful of me to think the angel standing guard of the garden was there merely to comfort, lead, and whisper to me.

Maybe now I can understand why the angel could not allow me to remain. I had to become aware, if only faintly, of the bigger story in my heart.

Preserving Time: Buried Notes

What could I, as a child, do with time racing faster than a river? How desperate were my attempts to deal with the passage of time. I wrote little notes on scraps of paper, describing where I fished and the fish caught. I dated the scraps of paper, folded them up, placed them in small plastic boxes, and buried them like time cap-sules—as if the dates on the notes would preserve time itself. They were my secret treasure. I was thinking I could relive those events by opening the boxes and reading about them. I tried to do so. How feeble and desperate were my attempts to deal with the existential condition of life.

Even so, my attempt to preserve those memories foreshad-owed a resurrection and a real connection to the past. All that I buried, along with my hopes and longings, came back, resurrected in a way, and transformed into higher understanding of time. Fly-fishing helped me think this way. Sometimes late in the evening I or one of my clients would hook a large fish, a happening that extended the day under the darkened sky. Furthermore, as the fish went racing downstream, I realized there was a brief window of time in which I could slowly turn the fish by changing the direction and angle of the rod. I could defy the rushing river by skillfully bringing the fish back up the river along the edge of the bank. The possibility seemed to suspend the passage of time and defy the space. For just a moment, I could reverse time and space. Sometimes I could net the fish. Did God the eternal enter that space and that time. This experience provided me with a short-lived sense of power over the overwhelming existential forces of life. This was a time continuum that I would become a part of and that would sweep me away.

Glimpses of Divinity

As a child and an adult, I had glimpses of divinity. In some moments of difficulty, I felt overcome with a peculiar calm. Other times, I was on the point of giving up when I had an awareness that I had somehow stumbled onto my destiny. Such experiences were so wonderful, even in the form of a glimpse, that it made it difficult for me to stay in that moment. These glimpses hinted of destiny, divinity, and meaning. They haunted me because they reminded me of how life could be. Even the memory of one of these glimpses could tug at my heart and pull me out of the mundane world. I wanted to feel the sense of mission and weight in my steps *all the time*. I wanted all of life to feel like the path to the pond, where I so often had the sense that I was walking into my destiny and into a land I belonged in. In addition, I wanted to feel the divine moments when a fish appeared out of the depths to take my fly. Such glimpses often were a revelation, revealing to me some greater purpose.

These glimpses of God, even though infrequent, were powerful enough to become both my distraction and my hope. The memories still rise up inside me. Such memories became my hope, allowing my heart to open to the possibility that a fish might rise to my last cast in the fading light of the evening. In a sense, I was distracted with hope. Do I blame my distracted heart upon God who led me to believe that all things are possible? I cannot blame or demand. I don't dare blame my distracted heart upon God or demand more of God because He made belief and genuine hope possible. Still, experiencing the vague sense of destiny, even just once, is not easy to endure.

How do I as a mere mortal, largely out of tune with divinity, endure my menial life when I have experienced, as Paul claimed, something of "the third heaven?" (2 Corinthians 12:2) How can I avoid comparing my day-to-day menial life to this one moment when I felt the dazzling presence of God and something of eternity? For a fly fisher like myself, this can happen the moment I glimpse a huge fish roll on my fly. Perhaps the fish are rising all around me, and I know I am in the right place at the right time; I make the perfect cast and it feels as though I just walked into my destiny.

Sometimes I feel this sense of destiny while guiding or fishing with a friend or a loved one. For a brief moment, and only a moment, the window opens and we enter. The fish also enters this space with us. The fish may have been waiting for us, but we did not notice until now. I have had more than one such experience while fishing with others. Perhaps they remember, as I remember, when together we walked in the brilliance of Eden. We may have rationalized the experience as luck in conjunction with our so-called skill. Yet, deep down, we knew better. I knew better anyway. I am forever leery of my own guiding ability and of the skill level of my clients. Somehow the fish rose to greet us. Some of us choose to acknowledge these destined moments while others attributed it to skill, luck, or something else.

I have had other glimpses of eternity on the river. I have had chance encounters with strangers across the river. Sometimes I feel a wonderful connection with them. These experiences while usually brief can be of a peculiar intensity and stay with me. I have a sense that we will never meet again, but the connection expands my soul like a cast reaching up and shooting across to the heavens. As William Shakespeare suggested in "Sonnet 18," such heavenly connections shine too brightly for me to understand.

How wonderful and at the same time how cruel it is to experience such glimpses; cruel because, in comparison, I live most of life in the day-to-day mundane world. I never know when similar experience will occur again. However, fly-fishing encourages me to hope for the large fish, the mysterious phantom, the entrancing beauty, the arching rainbow, or the big brown that engulfs my fly.

Alone on the planet Perelandra, Ransom felt how cruel it was for him to catch only a glimpse of the Green Lady. Catching a glimpse of her gave him great hope, but his inability to close in and see her once again was a form of torture. His solitude, once bearable, became intolerable because of that glimpse of divine beauty. He felt imprisoned, utterly alone, trapped in a world of only occasional glimpses. The Green Lady became a form he could only glimpse from a distance. I identify with Ransom. There are times when I think I am better off having never seen Something. I may even choose not to see or feel because it is easier to give up and become numb.

While divine glimpses can be a profound blessing, such experiences can cause intense loneliness in my soul. I often find myself lonely after the experience, in part because I cannot accurately describe what I felt. As a lone fly fisher on the river, how do I bear witness to the beauty perceived in the glimpse of 30-inch rainbow that slowly comes out of the dark waters and rises to my fly? It is gone in an instant, and I am the sole witness. I have no proof that I even saw it, which leaves me dumbfounded and alone. Will the fish rise again?

Watching a fish rise to meet my fly can feel as though it came from some faraway place. I will ask myself, "Where did that come from?" This reaction unconsciously reflects my suspicion that Something just entered my world. This is a wonderful feeling, but it is painful living with the magnificent.

On Perelandra, Ransom did not feel sharp loneliness until he was given a glimpse of another human form. The glimpse gave him great hope and deeply touched his lonely soul but now he was aware of his deep loneliness. In a sense, the glimpse of the Green Lady ruined, or at the very least, disturbed his solitude. For a moment, a mere glimpse, he knew he was not alone.

When I read this fantasy story, I find myself relating to Ransom's experience. His experience feels similar to my own real life, in which my day-to-day experience is one of receiving intermittent images of the divine, and yet I am unable fully to close in on what I desire. When I experience a glimpse of God's glory, I remain haunted, hoping for the next encounter and longing for how life could be. I greet life hoping Something will once again reflect God's glory, but much of life seems to fade and disappear like a phantom. I remain alone holding to the glimpse of glory while hoping that the next meander of the river brings Something of God, a phantom of a fish that is large, beautiful, and powerful. I throw my hope into the next cast. And what is strange is that I want to know that such a fish rose, not due to my own skill, but by Something else. Such knowledge gives me a greater sensation.

Haunted by the mere shadows of fish, love, and belonging, I long for more glimpses of God. Divine glimpses are extremely powerful even though I most often only experience them in the slightest form. These glimpses are like trout that slowly rise to the surface, take the fly, and then disappear. I barely notice them. Divine glimpses are like those days when the fish find themselves on the line. Or like those days when I walk into the meadow, make a cast, and connect to a fish in the river that appears to teem with life. I am caught up in an intense vibration.

Divine glimpses can also be like the star that streaks across the vast distances of the night sky, lingering until I finally notice. They can be the memory of the silhouette of a large fish fading into deeper water. These images can stay with me if I allow room for them in my cluttered heart and remove the vanity from my eyes.

Feeling the Distances of Time

I knew that neither the glimpses of divinity in my past nor the hope for a rising fish in my future truly belonged to me. All the events flowed down the river and would not come back. Those approaching events were in some sense already gone. Having learned that beautiful moments do not last, I clutch at them, the very thing Jesus said not to do: "For whoever wants to save their life will lose it …" (Luke 9:24).

Every time I or my client quickly reels in a line to keep a fish, only to feel it break it off, I am reminded of how I cling to my own life, or to a moment, only to lose it. I am still learning that the only way to live freely and in joy is to let go. In his poem, "Eternity," William Blake spoke of this need to let go and not to cling to joy and happiness.

Furthermore, the only way to find my own life is to lose it. I must let go of all those things I compulsively hold onto—even at the fish I hook. I have been slow to learn that clutching onto things cannot preserve Eden, a sense of belonging, or time itself.

For me, having faith means believing that God will be present time after time, wherever I find myself on the time continuum or wherever I find myself geographically. Perhaps, with hope and faith, I can choose to believe that the God of all creation is in control of time, upholding all things by the word of his power; in God, nothing, not even time, is lost. As I walk the meanders of the river, I can choose to believe that God will provide in these new wilderness areas and in the future years of my life. I can choose to believe that He has set me on a pilgrimage (Psalm 84:5) and is with me in each moment.

While glimpses of divinity can distract me—because they remind me of Eden—fly-fishing helps me focus in the moment. The present moment is where eternity touches me. I cast and focus on the fly in each present moment as it drifts. When a fish rises in that spot of time, and I can in that moment live in eternity. I can raise the rod and let go. I can choose not to clutch onto the line or the reel. I can let the fish run and let the moment pass, however beautiful it is.

A Bigger Story of Hope

While I cling to the fragments of my personal story, a bigger story remains. I can only hope that my story mysteriously joins with God's creation and his story. I sometimes feel that eternity reaches down through the vast distances and touches me. It touches my life story, however insignificant and meaningless it might feel to me. I hope for the coming together of all things, the merging of all rivers and creeks and ponds. All the fish caught and lost, the loved ones here and the ones lost, all of my tears and joys, will come together. I wonder if there will be an end to my longing and a bridge that spans all the distances. Will it all be swallowed up in eternity, which many call God?

I am trying not to convince you of the validity of my story. It's just that I cannot package up my life into a certain way of believing, thinking, or being. I know of no special way of praying, meditating, or finding contentment and peace in life. In fact, most people I meet appear happier and more together than I do. Who am I to prescribe a way of living for others? In these pages, I have only told my story hoping that in some small ways my story might overlap with yours and perhaps, together, with the big story of Eden.

I can only hope that a meandering meadow stream can symbolically be a narrow strip of Eden and, perhaps literally, the exact place where the bigger story of God overlaps with my individual story. If you are a fly fisher, perhaps your story can join mine as we share a similar meander on a river and cast to similar fish. In doing so, we might share a connection, not only to a fish but to a place we still remember.

Nevertheless, it is difficult to live and sustain oneself on such narrow ground. I grow tired, lonely, and desperate to live on so little in places where I feel at home. It is what I do.

XI

Daring to Exist?

✺

Casting in Desperation

As I live life, I tend to settle for too little. I allow the slightest sensations to provide relief and pacify my ego. I give in to whatever has come along to stimulate me, unaware that deep down I am seeking Eden.

I live with a certain degree of desperation. When I feel desperation, fear comes to the surface of my heart. I panic and try to ease my vulnerability as

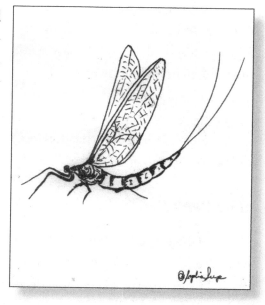

quickly as possible. Perhaps Thoreau was correct when, in *Walden and Civil Disobedience,* he wrote that the majority of society lived in quiet desperation. He went on to say that there was even a form of desperation in our games and amusements.

Am I a desperate person, concealing myself under the amusement of fly-fishing? Am I a desperate, fearful person simply trying to pacify my longings and emptiness? Yet I find little relief. It seems that nothing, not even catching the fish of a lifetime, can satisfy my deepest hunger. And yet I sense Something below the surface of my life and the waters I fish.

How do I appropriately bear witness to this longing and the Something that sustains me, at least some of the time? At times, I feel so lonely that I cannot bear witness to what I have received from fly-fishing in Eden. I'd rather throw it all away. However, when I try to abandon my solitude by breaking it and scattering it into the river, the broken pieces of my longings swirl, merge, and rejoin in my heart, forever to remain with me. I cannot get away from this longing. I have tried casting it all away. Sometimes, even when I made a powerful but deliberately sloppy cast and watch the swirls of line dragging every which way, the fly still mysteriously found its way in a current seam line, drifted properly, and a fish took the fly. In those moments of contact with the pulsing fish, I remember Something of my connection in Eden that forever seeks me and is the longing of my heart.

How Can I Endure?

Given the level of desperation I sometimes feel, I have often wondered how I make it through life. If I feel desperately disconnected from my true place, how do I endure relationships in which I feel painfully unfulfilled? How can I maintain my solitude with God, others, and even with myself, when I often demand too much of others, myself, and even the fish I seek. How do I endure?

I observe the large fish lurking just below the surface. The one fish I see rising on the far bank is too far away. Why do I cast repeatedly into *their* watery world, when the fish keep rejecting what I have to offer? The fish keep me outside of their world and increase my sense of not belonging? Where do I belong? How do I remain?

I have made the perfect cast and felt the fish take my fly. In those moments we connected. Our worlds join together and we *almost* merge in Eden. But even the perfect cast that lands a beautiful fish does not bring everything back that I long for. It is not enough. It is never enough.

But it is Something.

How did I survive the hours upon hours of fishing alone waiting for one bite from a fish below the mysterious, dark, waters I forever gaze upon with longing? How did I endure the approaching gray clouds that I knew would pour rain, bring lightning, and end my hope of hooking a fish? Did the innocence and radiance of childhood protect me from feeling overwhelmingly alone as it allowed the natural world of fish, earth, and water to comfort me?

Now I am adult. How do I survive the pretense that I belong and am part of a group, be it a fly-fishing club, a team, a political party, a church, or a family? Where can I ever remain and belong? And even the connections I make to the river are fleeting.

Enduring the Wandering

As I wander along the river, I have crossed paths with many. Some were strangers. Sometimes our solitudes touched for a moment. I would hide my innermost self, hoping nothing escaped and gave me away. In the spur of the moment, I might have shared a deep thought or feeling and just as quickly apologized for sharing too much of my soul. My apology was usually insincere, because I *was* hoping for a moment of deep connection with another soul. So, I tried to find another way.

I might have offered a fly that was working for me or the hole I was fishing but held back, not sure how the stranger would receive such an offering. I hoped such offerings would matter. At the deepest level, I still hide my loneliness, longings, and my hopes. I hide my desire to connect. I conceal my desperate attempts at seeking my true place of belonging. I often hide my unconscious despair under the small-talk of fly-fishing.

Over the years in my pursuit of fish, I have traveled over mountains, entered dense forests, fought through entanglements, crossed meadows of prickly nettles, all in an effort to *belong* to the places I fish. My sense of belonging is as elusive as the fish that always gets away, the one I cannot grasp in my hands. I struggle to belong to the moment even as I am distracted by the fish that got away and the even more magnificent fish that just rose upstream.

I have pursued fish on rivers that flow through lonely canyons like Cheesman and vast meadows like South Park. Of course, the fish sensed my intrusion upon their world and did their best to swim away and conceal themselves. Their hiding always reminded me of how I do not belong in their world. Sometimes, I would stomp around and howl into the wilderness, asking the question: Where do I belong?

When I look back over my life, I wonder how I could have survived with usually only slight sensations granted to me. It might have been nothing more than a pleasant breeze across a lake or river, when I ached for so much more. How did I survive the loneliness and the persistent sense that I did not quite belong? How did I survive those lonely days of fishing when I desperately hoped for just one tug from a fish (that never came) or a glance from the girl with the golden hair across the lake (who never looked my way) or a moment of connection to a fly-fishing stranger (who walked away)?

I always seemed to hope far more than reality could ever have given me or that I could have given to myself or others. I did sometimes have the sense that there is more Something in me than I or anyone will ever know. Perhaps this is true of all of us.

Enduring Childhood Loneliness at School

When I was a child, how did I endure those intense feelings of aloneness and longing while fishing the pond? How did I endure my loneliness in classrooms on rainy overcast mornings? How did I bear saying goodbye to my mother when I went off to my first kindergarten class? I remember standing there, confused and reluctant to leave her. For that matter, how did I endure a classroom poorly lit by dull yellowish lights? I can still see my mother waiting at the entrance to the school. I was standing in the hallway, between the cold gray of the outdoors and the dull lights of the classroom. I did not know if it was better to be inside or to go outside with her. I looked at the classroom, then back for her, but she was gone. I was standing there alone. Was I really alone? Surely other parents and children were there, but I don't see them in my memory. I felt a sense of betrayal, not because my mother wanted to betray me but because I felt I had lost Something. Did my inner solitude and true self remain, or were the broken parts lost in the yellowish dim light?

Loneliness and longing must have filled the room as I and the other children bumped into one another as we tried to hang up our coats in the classroom closet. I didn't know which hook was mine. I saw a girl, without a name, who gave me some hope. I just wanted to brush shoulders with her. What loneliness did that come from? Could I dare to live for such a moment of pure innocence? But was it innocence? Such an event can never be completely innocent or a mere accident. Looking back, I realized I hoped such a brief meeting would last forever, a child's version of the return to Eden.

Since then, I have lived for such brief moments. My hope that a fish will take my offering is an adult's everyday hope for eternity. As a child, I had the hope that a little girl could be an angel, my inner beloved that I had somehow lost. It seems silly now. Yet, sometimes I expect a single cast to pacify my deepest longing.

Enduring Church

Then there was church. How did a cup of coffee and pastry or comments about football, the weather, or the sermon satisfy my hunger for belonging? In church, I might have arranged to teach, preach, or serve on a committee. Then I might have been able to console myself with the thought that I was helping people—until I felt my own pretense and hypocrisy. That was when I would come to grips with my own sense of nakedness, and deep hunger, when I knew I did not belong.

I suppose I could have stood up and said, "The pastry does not satisfy my deepest hunger. The canned words of the preacher do not bind me. I do not belong here. I would rather be fishing on the river. At least it would be quiet, and I might catch a fish." Could I have gone against the conventions of the community knowing that, as Soren Kierkegaard suggested, the crowd distorts the truth. For a long time, I could not admit that becoming a "member"—belonging—was a compromise of my soul?

I'm not sure how I survived. I waited and waited for the church to give me a glimpse of Eden lost. It rarely did. It would have been far easier for me to just get rid of my solitude that remembered Eden, however vaguely. Was it too painful to remember the Eden I had lost? Perhaps I could have just left my solitude in a canyon, the vast meadow of South Park, or along the river, but I doubt it.

Enduring the Transitory Nature of Life

How did I survive the transitory nature of life that races on, sweeps me along against my will, and leaves me behind? In the name of God, how did I survive? How did I survive a trophy fish striking just as the sun was setting. I so wanted to stay connected to that fish for eternity. How did I survive not being able to relive significant moments—a fish caught, a competition won, a connection made with a loved one? How did I endure not finding the words to speak to the girl with golden hair before the last light of the evening faded from her face? How did I endure the disappointment when I waited for her on the banks of the pond and she never arrived? How did I accept the loss of a fishery to abuse, neglect, over-fishing, or drought? How did I ever let go of the glimpses I once received of Eden?

Accepting the passage of time and the contrasting longings of my heart requires a different kind of courage and endurance. It is not the same as enduring suffering from mistreatment or suffering from some kind of a hardship. Yes, the world is full of unjust brutalities. Surviving the loss of Eden is different. It requires a different kind of endurance to face the loss of Something incredibly beautiful, something I had in my hand, as it were, until it got away. I had it, saw it, felt it with an intensity that hurts. It was the connection I was longing for all my life. And it is gone. It takes courage to live without being able to pacify this deep longing.

Daring To Exist

In view of the transitory nature of life, Rilke asked how any human being dares to exist for so little. His challenge to me is to consider the ways I desperately try to establish some sense of permanence in this world. His message seems to be that my attempts are largely in vain; that nothing I try works or alleviates the loss. He challenges those who are beautiful to understand that beauty fades. He challenges those who have found love to understand that love does not reverse the arc of time. I cannot remain in the Eden of my youth, even while in love.

Still, I think there is hope in being honestly aware of my state. As a fly fisher, I can be honest with myself when I do dare to exist on very little. I have settled for catching a certain number of fish or fish of a certain size as if this will justify my existence. I have demanded photographs as proof. Proof of what, I should ask myself. I have taken these pictures and hung them on my walls or posted them on the internet. To what end? Do they prevent the passage of time? Do they justify my existence? If I can post them on the internet, am I immortal?

Perhaps I have shown even more desperation when I dared exist for those days when I hooked dozens of fish. With each catch, I proclaimed, "I got another one." I'm sure those around me could hear the fading excitement in each one of my proclamations. After the first few dozen fish, I barely felt the experience. It had become meaningless. The only feeling I had was in my aching shoulder and my numb heart. I found myself begging the fish to stop biting. If I was healthy, I chose to stop this compulsion and put the rod to rest. It took real courage to dare not to exist, not for this. As a fly fisher, I've had to face the truth that the next fish (or many things in life for that matter) may not bring the sensation I had hoped for. If that is so, how do I once again live in the pure, sustained quiet of Eden?

The Elusive Fish

It has occurred to me that there might be completely different fish out there, one who lives on the edge of Eden and who might sustain a deeper sensation in my soul. Of course, this fish has eluded me. At times, it moved up from the deep into the pool of water in front of me, but it would not be caught. For a long time, I did not realize that this fish, the fish I could *not* grasp in my hands, was the one that filled my soul and was the one I always remembered. It was the elusive one who *always* got away. This mysterious Something always eluded my grasp but never faded from my imagination. I could reverently spread my hands in front of me, and say, "It was this big." This was the Something that occupied a space in-between my hands. It was invisible, incomprehensible, just beyond my grasp. It was always in my heart, even when I did not know it was the one I sought.

Contrast this with my experiences catching dozens of fish or the record-breaking trout. I settled for so little when I ached for so much more, the one who would not be caught. When I settled for catching hundreds of fish, I was feeding an addiction. My hobby had become a compulsion, a great act of self-deception.

I had to admit to myself that there was always Something that eluded me. How did I endure the years of solitude, heavy with longing for Eden? Where could I dare to keep my solitude, heavy with awkward thoughts, sadness, and hopes? With whom could I share my solitude without embarrassment and shame?

Scraps of Paper

When I was a child, I would write down the number of fish I caught on each day. I would write my name and date the paper because I wanted to hang onto the memory. It was my feeble attempt to preserve time. Do fish journals, photo albums, and thousands of digital pictures really preserve such moments?

I added other things, maybe a line of poetry, a psalm, or a scripture. "And surely I am with you always" (Matthew 28:20) is one I remember. These elevated the event for me. I would read them, alone, in secrecy, preferably in a world that briefly had become my own. I might read the words in a dark canyon or under a tree, hoping the words would sustain me.

Even now I want to return to these places, in hope of returning to the Eden of my youth? I want to cast across a pool in the hope that I might bring Something back to me. Does the river remember me? I feel God's love in the way the sweet blue serpentine river embraces me. Can I trust that the meandering river is reaching for me in a display of love? The desires of my heart are endless. They stretch across vast meadows. They are bottomless, like the deep pools of Cheesman Canyon. I am unable to see its depth. I hope for the day when the source of all sensation will fully enclose me in the Eden of my heart?

Until then, rather than finding God's loving embrace, I often find myself utterly defeated, stripped bare, standing alone on the bank, shaking from trying to bring home the big fish that just overwhelmed me. It was indifferent to my well-being and my place among the creation. This too, I must endure.

XII

Definitively Defeated

❧❧

Admitting Defeat

Particularly in my younger days, I dared to live as a self-described accomplished angler. I kept a record of fish I caught. Of course, I hardly remember any of these petty victories.

However, I do remember those occasions when I fought fish of leviathan proportions. There was the great bass by the fallen tree that hung me up with a surge down into submerged branches. There was the huge brown that disappeared under an undercut bank and left me with a dangling leader stripped bare. There was the fish that stripped me of my fly line and all my backing. There was the giant rainbow that cut me off on the submerged boulder.

There have been days when nothing goes well. Once, my hat blew off, and I looked like a fool chasing it down river. The hat was a mask, worn to make me look like an accomplished angler. Other times, a fish beat me, but I pretended I was still in the game. It would have been far better to admit that I was decisively defeated. So I have lost a fish—and my false identity. Why can't I just admit defeat?

This is the way it is with God. I cannot have my way with God any more than I can have my way with a powerful fish. If I want to wrestle with God as Jacob wrestled with the angel, I will have to step up to an edge. In my wrestling days, I had to step on the mat and up to a line. Once I stepped up to the line, I could not retreat. There was no hiding behind hats, fishing vests, waders, long hair, suit jackets, team uniforms, or masks.

As wrestlers, we had to stand toe-to-toe, almost naked in our singlets. We shook hands and silently went to battle. This was not wrestling with God, but it was frightening. We stood there; we were vulnerable.

It is another kind of contest to step up and challenge God. Yet, in my arrogance and naivete, I have longed to shake hands and wrestle with my Creator. Didn't I want to ask God questions? Did I have the courage to ask where He has been? Did I dare to ask Him how I was supposed to live in his absence? Did I dare to admit to Him how alone I have felt and how I did not belong? Did I, like Jacob, dare to hold Him until he told me what happened to Eden?

It was terrifying to step up to this edge. Perhaps it ought to be. In a way, it was similar to wrestling with a big fish so long I did not know who had who. Emily Dickinson in her own wrestling with God, felt as though God had grasped her. Rilke, my favorite poet, also implied that as we move through life Something grabs us but we do not who it is, where it comes from, or how to find it. It is like reaching with my net or hands for a fish that I cannot quite grasp. Did I ever dare to exchange words with the presence that so easily grasped me?

In the old tale, "The Maiden King," a young man named Ivan goes out to sea to fish. On the water, he meets a loving presence. She tells Ivan that she has come from far away and that she loves him. She has known Ivan for a long time. What does Ivan do in the midst of this brilliant presence? He falls asleep.

It has been difficult to stand in an angelic presence. Such an encounter with God required all of my mind, body, and soul—even when I knew I would be defeated. It was like casting to a huge rainbow that I knew, if it took the fly, would entangle me in a logjam. Nevertheless, I made the cast. While it was highly probable that I would be decisively defeated, I had a small hope that I could win. I hoped that I might be able to turn the fish or that the fish would make a mistake. The likely defeat just validated the challenge. This makes me think that God might delight in my irreverent challenges. However, as I age, I seem less willing to approach this edge, make the cast, and bow to the surging storm that will follow.

Petty Battles and So-Called Victories

There is a Rilke poem about a man watching an immense storm approach. He knows he cannot endure the storm by himself. The poet suggests that sometimes it is better to surrender.

My battles are often petty. I choose small fights, knowing I can win. In fly-fishing, this is like always going to the same fishing hole, where I know how to catch small fish. The problem is that small victories tend to make me petty.

I often think about this poem when I spot a huge fish. There was one fish in particular, a huge rainbow that lay deep between two large submerged boulders on the Taylor River. On the Taylor tailwater, fish grow so large from feeding on mysis shrimp that it is difficult to give a fair estimation of the fish's size. As I made the cast, I said to myself, "Over thirty-two inches and over fifteen pounds." In looking back, I think the fish was every bit as big, perhaps even larger than I thought. This fish still haunts me.

I first hooked this fish on an RS2 nymph trailing behind a mysis shrimp on 4x fluorocarbon tippet. The fish shook his head several times as it twisted and arched out of the water. Then it fell downstream on the leader and broke the tippet. The second time I survived the initial headshake and downstream leap. I fought the fish for several minutes before it suddenly decided it had enough. It bolted across river and then surged back upstream alongside a boulder and broke away. I was powerless. Strategy and tactics didn't matter. Both times my line came back stripped. My flies were gone. I was decisively defeated.

It is odd how keenly I remember the fish that got away. Then again, maybe it is not odd at all. I vividly and reverently remember other defeats in my life. The Rilke poem suggests that I should be able to grow from such defeats. I only need to handle them properly. I am not very good at this, though I get a lot of practice, especially in fly fishing.

Why does defeat, especially losing a big fish, stay with me. Now that I think about it, I experience some elation when a fish overpowers me. Maybe I long to be defeated. Maybe it is refreshing to experience not being in control. Such awareness takes some of the pressure off. I can relax my neurotic, foolish, grip on life.

I do not remember my so-called victories as well as my defeats. I have caught thousands of fish over the years. Few stick out. Similarly, I do not remember my victories in human relations. Oh, but I remember the massive fish that had my number. I can still see them moving out into the deep, dark waters. They are the fish that got away, the elusive ones that I could not grasp. Yet I can still feel them between my hands and within my heart.

God Lonely in His Inner Circle

Perhaps God stands lonely within his inner circle, waiting for a challenge. When I think of God being lonely, a bit similar to how I feel, I am encouraged to step up to the edge of his circle. I linger briefly there and consider accepting the challenge.

I once peered into a deep run and caught sight of a thirty-inch fish above a cataract that plunged between high and narrow walls. I was quite certain that if I made a cast and hooked the fish, it would surge down river into the raging chute where I could not follow. I was tempted to accept the challenge anyway, cross the edge, make the cast, and take the plunge.

Another time, during a blazing sunset, I was walking a narrow trail that followed a ridgeline above the river during a colorful, blazing sunset. A breeze stirred. Beams of light shot across the sky. I felt I should respond somehow, but I was unable. My feelings in the face of such beauty were so intense that I had to turn away. I retreated from the magnificent sunset and went home. Somehow, it was easier to watch television, pay my bills, and lose myself in the practicalities of life then to open up to what nature's circle was offering me. While the experience was not physically threatening, it was a threat to my spirit.

However, there were times when I felt the courage to step up to the line and enter the circle. It reminded me of a wrestling match in my distant past. I had gone into strategic mode, begun to maneuver and look for an opening. I felt the same discomfort—the fear and anxiety—as other times, but this time I was more aware of what I would lose if I never stepped up, crossed that edge, and entered the circle. I never would have won the state championship. I never would have hooked that special fish. I would have missed the chance to glimpse the lonely heart of God. Edges are liminal spaces between life and death. Sometimes I know that if I hold back, I will lose my own life and something of the depth of God.

As I tried to write this book, I faced an edge. I felt compelled to cross this edge in order to stay true to myself. Perhaps in the end, this is all I can do. I have to admit that sometimes I have teetered on this edge. I have wanted to write some feel-good ideas that will connect me to the masses, but I knew this would have been inauthentic. At other times, I want to hurl my computer—and my manuscript— off my deck and down the cliff.

In the end, my hope is to be able to approach the edge and crossover to where God stands in the inner circle. I would like to be able to step inside and dare to remain in the circle with God. Perhaps there, we can "reason together" (Isaiah 1:18).

Undisturbed Fortified Cities

Most often I protect myself by remaining behind my masks and walls and refusing to enter sacred circles. However, I feel blessed, if I can be defeated now and then and have my walls tumble down. I have spent a good portion of my life thickening walls, trying to ensure that no one ever gets through. Rilke uses the metaphor of an undisturbed city that time and time again has held off a siege. The poet asks the profound question: Does the individual deep down want his walls to come tumbling down.

I can relate. If I have allowed my ego to construct fortified walls around me, then perhaps deep down in my loneliness I secretly desire for my walls to crumble. If I have spent a lifetime defending myself, behind strong walls, then perhaps I want something to threaten and overcome my established ego system and my set ways of sealing myself off from life.

The poem allows me to know how I have grown tired of feeling falsely secure in my fortified castles. Do I not know that there are cracks in my walls? Perhaps all along, I have known and I have secretly wished to be defeated? Deep down perhaps I want to expose myself for the coward I am and have that truth of who I am be accepted. Perhaps it is my greatest hope to have my walls come crumbling down, exposing myself, yet, having the hope that I might be fully embraced.

It is easy to become an undisturbed fortified city. Some of my strongest walls were religious. Churches and religious institutions have gladly provided me with preformed structures and, as Carl Jung, suggested a great defense against God. Sometimes I have longed for God to pick up the church building as if it were a toy dollhouse and shake it around until everything falls out. Then I could start all over again.

I constantly hold out the hope that something big lurks below the surface of the rivers I fish, beneath the church structures, and under the surface of my heart. I long for something that can defeat me. Fishing in waters where I am not in control and where I am challenged has become my greatest delight. I delight to step up to the edge of the river and cast to the biggest and strongest fish. I cast knowing I will come up empty, but I do it anyway. I need to submit.

Perhaps then, while I tie on new tippet and a new fly, I will more clearly hear his voice.

XIII

A Word Spoken In the Vast Silent Spaces

❧

Out of the Darkness: A Word

While I was fishing at dusk in the deep silence, a stranger approached and began to fish the other side of the river. There was a sense that we were divided not only by the swirling depths of the river but by fathoms of empty space. Surely I cre-ated some of that division myself. I was afraid this phantom wanted to crowd me out of *my* spot. As long as I held onto that fear, the empty space expanded. It was a strange and horrible feeling to be so petty in view of the vast beauty of the river at dusk.

We fished in silence, each one of us glancing across at the other. The stranger was sometimes present, other times vanishing. More casting, more silence. Waiting, waiting for a strike, waiting for Something. Perhaps the river itself and the empty space between us awaited a miracle. Maybe Something in our own hearts was waiting.

In that vast silent place, in that space between us, a word entered. That word was whispering from some faraway place, perhaps above the headwaters and beyond the mountains protruding out of the far off horizon, perhaps from a distant star. The word flowed down the very river that was dividing us, meandering and weaving its way to one of us—or conceivably to both of us.

Helping a Stranger Or Stay On My Side of The River

I had a fish on.

"Nice fish," the stranger said. "I have not had a strike. What did you get him on?"

"I got him on a new fly I tied. I have one more left. I can bring it across to you."

In that crossing, the river that once divided us became a place of communion. These simple words became a shared kindness.

However, such a crossing is not always so easy. On another day, the stranger on the river might not have been fishing with flies. He might have been a bait angler who threw his lead sinkers and bobber close to where I was drifting my flies. He might have edged up closer and closer until was casting over my line. Or perhaps he could have been a fly fisher, albeit one who did not know the etiquette and who crowded me at the pool where I was fishing.

On another day, the stranger across the river might have been poaching. Maybe I saw a dead fish on his stringer, and I realized he was poaching the very fish that my guiding profession depends upon. This would have taken me back to the pond and the fish I released as a child. Back then, I wondered why adults could kill fish. Now as a mature adult, I would have wondered what I should do. Should I cross the river now to talk to him? What words should I say? Should I remind the stranger of the regulations? I might have hesitated. I might have worried that the stranger was too different from me. Maybe he was from a different ethnic group. Maybe he spoke a different language. Maybe he was religious and would try to preach to me. Or maybe he was an atheist.

On another day, the stranger across the river might have been decked out in the latest clothing, flashing his $1,000 rod. I would not have been impressed. He might have needed some help, but I would have been put off by how he was posing. I might have wanted to tell him to shorten up his cast to better control his drift, but I would have assumed he didn't want my advice.

On another day, I might have seen a fellow guide. Perhaps he would have reminded me of myself, confident and arrogant when I was in my twenties and thirties. He probably would have reminded me of how, with confidence and even arrogance, I guided when I was in my twenties and thirties. I wouldn't have liked him.

On another day, the person across the river might have been a woman, an experienced fly fisher, my equal in every respect, someone who knows the river better than I do. Perhaps, on this particular evening, I have found the fly that is working, one of my own hand-tied variations. Would I have crossed the river to share it?

Is This My River and Spot of Time?

On any given day, I might have looked across the river and seen someone I didn't want to bother with. After all, this beautiful evening is *for me*, or so I think. This is my special time on the river. This is my special time with God. This is my special place, just as the pond was my Eden where I walked with God.

However, I am older and wiser now. I know that Eden, if it exists at all, is for everyone. If I exclude anyone, I exclude myself. To reject the possibility of love is to exclude myself from the kingdom. The meek and merciful are blessed and will enter the kingdom, Jesus said. How can I love only those I deem worthy?

I have a choice that is before me every day. I can walk a meadow or a canyon to fish. If I claim an angel walked with me at the pond, helped me, spoke to me, and saved me in some sense, how can I refuse to walk across the river to help a stranger?

What Does the Word Whisper in the Darkness?

It is precisely at these moments when I must consider what the word whispering down the river is saying to me. Like Norman and Paul Maclean, I, too, must listen carefully. I might have to turn over some rocks in my heart to find and hear those words. Some of the rocks in my soul are quite heavy and have settled deep in the strata of my heart. Some of the rocks have solidified and not moved in years. Yet, there are stones I can move under my feet on the bottom of the river. If I turn some of the rocks over, I might hear something. I might discover something. The stones might feel cold and smooth, ground from eons of collisions with each other and swirling sand. On the underside of the stones, my fingertips might feel some squiggling, clinging, mayfly nymphs and caddis larvae.

On this day, I looked out over the river and contemplated changing flies. I looked and listened. At first, I only heard the river bubbling, burbling, gurgling, and murmuring. But, then, what was this? It was the faintest of sounds. Was this sound here all the time, but I chose not to hear it?

It was the slightest whisper, one I could have ignored, but on this day the message came to me clearly. Jesus was the stranger I was unwilling to cross the river to help. It was him. The word did not say this stranger was *like* Jesus but the stranger *was* Jesus. This is not a simile or a poetic comparison, which I have often used throughout the writing of this book. This time, the word that came meandering down the river was different, though I sensed it had been with me all along. The timeless truth of the word was this: however I treat this stranger, whatever I do or do not do to him, I do or do not do to God.

Contemplating My Steps

At this point, I considered carefully whether I should cross the river, what my footing should be, and what I should say when I got there. I waited, hoping that I would take the first step. It was strange. I had stood so long on the bank, on my side of the river, that I was afraid my feet might have gotten stuck in the mud, or, worse, my heart had become encrusted.

Nevertheless, I had hope. If I could take that first step, it would be a leap of faith. It occurred to me that this is what Jesus meant when he said he was the way, the truth, and the life. Time and time again, Jesus taught me I must love others or my faith would be useless.

> "No one has ever seen God; but if we love one another, God lives in us, and his love is made complete in us."—1 John 4:12

> "Whoever claims to love God yet hates a brother or sister is a liar."—1 John 4:20

I realized Something. This is how I am to deal with others, be they my neighbor, my enemy, my brother and sister, or a stranger on the river. It surely does not matter whether we share a common faith. I am to love the strangers of the earth. God manifests Himself through concrete acts of love, within the creation, which includes not only human inhabitants but the lilies of the field, the birds of the air, and the fish of the rivers. As Romans 12:1 suggests, love and service to others must be my worship. And:

> " By this everyone will know that you are my
> disciples, if you love one another."—John 13:35

As long as I am able to fish on this Earth, this is how I can enter abundant life in the kingdom of God.

I recognized that this is a choice. I can stand on "my" side of the river and fish for the rest of my life. I can claim to be contemplating the beauty of God as I catch fish after fish. I can remain there, solid as a stone, never taking that step. If I do that, I will remain solidified in stone; a hellish state where no raindrops can soften the stone layers of my heart.

My First Step

Or, as I did on this evening, I wiggled one foot out of the mud. As I lifted my foot, I remembered that boy at the pond. Or, was it two boys I remembered? One was catching all those fish and smiling. The other one was sad and appeared lost. I considered them both. Then I lifted the other foot and slowly, one-step at a time, waded across the river.

I never know who exactly is across the river. On this evening, I thought the stranger might be Something of everybody I know, have loved, or have failed to love. It might be Something of my lover, brother, sister, neighbor, father, mother, angel, and all those with whom, in one form or another, I am connected. On this evening, I was not certain of my footing. I felt the tension of the waters pressing around my legs. I struggled to keep my balance.

Looking across, I recognized something in his face. What was it? A certain sadness? I wondered if I was sensing a "bruised reed" in his heart or a "smoldering wick" in his eyes? (Isaiah 42:3).

Was he lost? Was he just following the river? Did he have longings too? What was he looking for and where did he belong? Was he drenched in exile, forever glimpsing Eden? Who was he? Were my childhood longings now in him?

The Angel Speaks

As I crossed the river, I got lost in my own memories. I considered what I needed back at the pond. I thought about that sweeping cast I could never achieve as a child. I thought about the angel who I wasn't sure was ever there but who I wanted to hear and to speak to me. It seemed foolish to think such things, because I did not know if angels can talk. And if they could, would not their voices be lost in the vast empty spaces that surrounded me? But it occurred to me: on this night, all was still and quiet. Perhaps, if I listened.

When I reached the other side of the river and stood in still waters, I was still trying to remember what the angel could have said back at the pond and what I needed to hear. Then I stopped, wondering if I was hearing an angel speak:

> "I have been watching you a long time and I know
> you. I know your name. You are the kid with the
> golden fingertips who ties his own flies and I see
> catching all those fish. Do you remember us walking
> the path together to the pond?

"I know that as a kid you struggled to let time pass. I know what you were trying to do by writing those little notes to yourself; the ones you buried in the ground. I watched you bury one along the Susquehanna River where your father grew up and played baseball as a boy on a field along the banks of the river. Decades later, I watched you and your father playing catch on that field. He was coaching you to catch ground balls and pop flies. The both of you really practiced a long time and wore that glove out. He taught you how to practice and that helped you in life.

"But there was more in you, in him, and beyond than baseball; more happened on that field than you can ever know. It was more than catching balls. And, likewise, from the beginning, fly-fishing was always about more than just catching fish. Why else would you fish all day to release the fish you caught? Perhaps in the act of releasing fish and in writing yourself notes, you were trying to preserve it all in Eden.

"You wanted everything: ponds and rivers and ball fields; father, mother, brother, sister, man, woman, child; You wanted green hills, trees, valleys with flowing waters, and the girl with golden flowing hair. You wanted everything enclosed in a moment, one place in time, preserved in Eden, for all eternity. And you wanted to know the angel who knows you and has loved you forevermore.

"You tried to keep in Eden, the eternal new morning, forever rising with the sun each new day as fish rose to your fly. You would woo fish. At the pond, you found comfort from the shade of an overhanging tree and a rising fish. You hoped for one returning sweeping cast that would enclose all of it, but you could not achieve it. You tried to grasp it all, even as you grasped at the fish you caught with your small child-like hands and even now with hands weathered and aged. The fish you held, you learned to let go but not completely.

"I saw you bury a note in the bottom of a box with all the Christmas tree decorations that was stored in the attic. That was the Christmas you got your 5-weight Browning fly rod and the Plueiger reel. You buried that note as a memorial to yourself so you would remember that gift, even though you probably already knew of the significance and meaning of that fly rod. You were excited about that rod, and, oh, how you used it! How you loved to fish. You wore that rod out. The top guide still has that groove in it from all that casting you did at the pond.

"You were trying to hold onto those moments you were enjoying, and somehow you knew you could not. You tried to preserve eternity in those moments by writing down what you were feeling. You were

trying to capture time by holding onto those
moments when you had a glimpse of beauty. You
did not want those moments to slip away, but there
was no stopping it and that is frightening and sad.
Your soul was inconsolable. I want you to know that
I understand your ache for permanence is very real.
You could not preserve eternity in those moments.
No one can. But I want to tell you something else.

"You are an amazing and most interesting young
man. I admire your depth of feeling and your ability
to fish all day while pondering the deep questions of
life. What is difficult for you to understand is that
the questions and longings that are inside you, and
have been with you as early as you can remember,
are not meant to find their true place and home in
this world.

"The questions you wrestle with have been
pondered by lonely souls for thousands of years. I
see what you long and ache for, as I, too, embrace
that yearning. I am that longing. The longing you
felt, and still feel, is more real than you can ever
understand.

"I am the one who led you to the pond and gave
you eyes to see. I helped you feel the rhythm of
casting and the pause between each cast. I am the
one whom you sometimes felt in those in-between

places. I am the rest and the peace you felt deep inside your soul, when you were alone, while all around you everything was noisy and frantic.

"I was the one who put it upon your heart to release the fish you caught. I remember watching you hold those fish in your hands, loosening your grip upon each fish, as I bent low and ever so quietly suggested that you let them live. And, oh, how you complied, even without understanding or knowing me.

"I stood with you on the banks of the pond and on the banks of the meandering Dream Stream. Some times as you bent down on the water's edge and released a fish, I saw you glance up looking behind yourself as though you heard a voice, glimpsed a phantom, and yet did not know from where it came or what it was.

"While you may not remember and would be prone to forget, I am the one who would forever remember you and the devotion of your youth. I remember how as a child you loved me, without knowing me, and how you followed me into unknown lands, ponds, and rivers, where I would speak tenderly to you and you would try to listen. (Hosea 2:14; Jeremiah 2:2) I was the one who from the beginning put in your heart the longing for Eden. In small ways, you felt Eden at the pond you fished and every

place you would later fish, hoping each place would
last forever and be home.

"You ached for the Dream Stream in South Park
to remain as you once remember, but it too would
change. You wished for Cheesman Canyon to
remain empty, but the crowds came. You tried to
hold on to Eden in these places, but you could never
fully achieve or claim these places as your own. Not
yet. However, what you feel as Eden is bigger than
these places you love and fish.

"This is hard for you to understand. Even though
you became a fly-fishing guide and counselor, and
a writer telling your story; you are more. There is
more. The story you are trying to tell is not just your
story. It is the story of stories. You are part of the
story, just as the stranger is a part of the story, along
with the fish, trees, and rocks.

"You are more than a guide, a teacher, a counselor,
an athlete, a husband, a father, and writer. You
are incredibly more; more than you can ever
understand. Has anyone ever told you that before?

"For now, you remain hidden in some in-between
place that is not quite home. As a child, you found
that in-between place on the edge of the pond. You

found that place by gazing into the currents of the meandering Dream Stream and deep canyon pools. I know what it is like to be hidden, not recognized, or esteemed.

"And, even now, you exist in some in-between place when you visit man-made church structures, but you are lost somewhere between river and stone. Your voice is often lost in lonely canyons and sweeping meadows. But, it's okay. Maybe it was just the way it had to be, and will be for a little while longer. I hear you in that place and I know your lonely tears of not belonging, but you can still speak."

The Sweeping, Looping Cast

There I was standing in the river. While I was crossing the sun had proceeded to set down upon the earth, slowly and gently touching the trees on the far hillside. The last rays of light angled across the valley over a pool and revealed rainbows rising. I took my rod and started casting a white marabou streamer into the approaching darkness and under an overhanging tree that I recognized.

I turned to the angel I had been listening to, but the angel was gone. Or, perhaps the angel was the stranger all along. I looked back over the expanse of the pool and I made the cast. The line shot out and swept in a great arc over the surface. It flew farther and farther out, and I saw a shooting star break the darkness just above it. It crossed the vast distance that had touched me so deeply for so many years. Perhaps, I had made this cast long, long ago and had already brought into myself all that belonged to me. The loop had come back with all that was of me and of God, and it was how it was supposed to be.

I continued to cast into the darkness. It was not long before I felt several tremendous pulls. On that evening, I landed and released several large rainbows and a huge brown. The white streamer still had a little bit of Something in it. Perhaps even the fish remembered the fly and experienced a profound connection. At least I did.

I then climbed the ridge and followed a little path. It was nightfall, but I knew the way. I put down my rod, opened my sleeping bag and slept deeply through the night. I dreamed of a river and the tenderness of God I once knew—and still know.

> "Then the angel showed me the river of the water
> of life, as clear as crystal, flowing from the throne of
> God ... . On each side of the river stood the tree of
> life ... ."—Revelation 22:1-2

As I dreamed, I remembered my longing for a lost love and a place. I projected this tender love toward the God that I may have glimpsed in the paradise I once knew and perhaps still know.

Come back to me, God. Come back to me, Eden. I remember.

The next morning, I awakened; emerging at last.

XIV

Finally Emerging

❧❧

Someday, emerging at last from the violent insight,
let me sing out jubilation and praise to assenting angels.
Let not even one of the clearly-struck hammers of my heart
fail to sound because of a slack, a doubtful
or a broken string. Let my joyfully streaming face
make me more radiant; Let my hidden weeping arise
and blossom. How dear you will be to me then, you nights
of anguish. Why didn't I kneel more deeply to accept you,
inconsolable sisters, and surrendering, lose myself
in your loosened hair. How we squander our hours of pain.
How we gaze beyond them into the bitter duration
to see if they have an end. Though they are really
our winter-enduring foliage, our dark evergreen,
one season in our inner year—, not only a season
in time—. But are place and settlement, foundation and soil and
home

—"The Tenth Elegy," first stanza, first 15 lines, page 205
from *Selected Poetry of Rainer Maria Rilke*

Waiting for the Emergence:
A Fall Day on the Dream Stream

On a cold fall morning, I was roll casting my line through the rising mist above the Dream Stream. I was waiting for the emergence of a late season mayfly hatch. After fishing this particular run for three decades, I knew big fish were hiding in the seam lines below the mist.

This was the kind of fall morning in which I sensed winter arriving as a sweeping white wall that would drive me off the river. However, I was holding my ground, hoping for one last burst of warmth from a summer day just past. I felt the slanting rays of sunlight on my face, but they were weakening.

I was standing in the river, shivering while I looked for signs of the hatch. I was half-heartedly drifting weighted nymphs below the surface. I waited in that cold, deep place of endless time. It was a place where the currents mixed sorrow and joy, winter and summer, child and man, death and life. I kept casting my hand-tied nymphs and let them drift among whatever naturals might be stirring among the rocks. Time itself seemed to slow in these cooler waters and the approaching storm. I turned within, contemplating the mystery of God, my life, the season just past, and my place in this world. I was vaguely aware of a some deep deposit made in my soul long ago. It was rising to the surface in a powerful intuition, like a large fish rising to my fly.

It could have been five minutes or two hours, the summer past or the winter to come, when I saw the first swirl of a rainbow taking an emerging mayfly from the surface. Finally, it was what I was waiting for. The mayflies emerged and floated on the surface like tiny sailboats. They lingered in the dull warmth of the sun, drying their wings before ascending off the river. Perhaps it was the increasing cold. Perhaps it was my aging body. In any case, I identified with those mayflies so thoroughly soaked in exile, inwardly moaning and groaning, awaiting some greater transformation.

I watched the first mayflies flutter off in the morning mist. More mayflies emerged. Another fish rose and then another. What a strange complex array of feelings I experienced while watching this. I felt pain, sadness, and joy—not to mention my cold hands and feet—in this place where I did not quite belong. Then I felt a connection, however brief, as I hooked a rising sixteen-inch rainbow. I felt its life pulsating in the flex of the rod. I rose to greet the fish, lifting the rod and taking a few awkward steps—and anticipated the fish's surge down river.

Rising, Falling, Emerging

More and more of the tiny mayflies, angelic-like, emerged in the morning light. I felt they were singing out in praise; certainly not for me, but somehow affirming my presence. I marveled at their courage. They emerged, rising from the depths, mating, and dying on the surface of the water only moments later. It was happening so quickly; their brief moment of glory on Earth, one day in the year. And yet it was the story of a complete life cycle. When I cast to them, I could barely see them. Yet I sensed a great reality at work, enough to sustain me.

I too finally emerged with insight, singing out to angels who approved of my feeble attempts to live in the brevity of a morning already past and to await a morning yet to be born. Life was forever greeting me and forever taking leave. In this in-between place of death and life, future and past, memory and desire, I emerged into the light, life, and eternal nature of God. That moment touched eternity and enclosed me in life and death.

Along with the mayflies, I shed the last drops of moisture that weighed me down and ascended, knowing I would fall back to earth. I died on the outside but was reborn within, remembering, be-coming known, and belonging. I fell back to the earth, remembering a place of communion; remembering an Eden behind me, in front of me, within me, and beyond. I knew that my descent was only a foreshadowing, that I would emerge again, that I would rise again, even now.

The Brightness of One Angel

Finally, I was able to believe that the angel, who helped me find the way to the pond, still speaks to me on the South Platte River. The angel never left, confirming my choice to hold to truths I discovered as a child. This angel was the one who would not allow me to please others for a superficial sense of belonging. The angel confirmed, perhaps even ensured, I did not belong in mainstream culture. At the same time, the angel kept reminding me of some oth-er far-off place that was always in my mind: Eden. This angel, along with a mayfly shimmering in the morning light, could burn through the masks I wore to church on Sunday mornings. Sometimes, the words I heard there could have come from those pull-string dolls. At other time, my masks were hardened, and couldn't see the seeds of faith trying to grow deep within my heart. All of these masks will become more and more brittle from the drying sun until they crack open and fall off, permitting the seedlings of faith to reach out toward the light.

It isn't easy. The masks I wear tease me, hanging on for dear life, dangling like nymphal shucks, and barely covering my face. I keep going onto the stage of life, pretending to be what I am not. Those who step back might see something like a bad play; the acting is poor and the costumes are deficient. Everyone knows how bad it is, but no one objects and the show goes on. Sometimes I recognize myself, just for a moment. In my mind, I yell, "Oh no. It is me. I cannot even act! What am I doing on that stage?" I feel deep shame, but this too is part of my transformation.

I am among the actors posing on a poorly structured stage that threatens to collapse with each step I take. Sometimes, I am unable to see the instability of the stage, unable to see how ridiculous I look, reciting the same old scripts that give me the slightest sense of belonging. At other times, I am reciting the same scripts, which makes me feel I belong but in a hideous way. No one seems to care who wrote the scripts. No one asks, "Who wrote this?" I keep on acting. Meanwhile, Rilke implies that the angels are confused and cannot tell if they are moving among the living or the dead, as the director comes out, stepping over and around the broken masks scattered on the teetering stage. I can't believe no one wants to leave the stage.

From time to time, I have had to step off the stage. This was not easy. This acting a part has been my life since a child. I have usually found it difficult and sometimes almost lost my balance. Then I asked myself, "Who am I without a costume? What do I do? Where can I go?"

This morning, I was able to step off the stage into the river. I grounded my feet in the river bottom while I watched the emerging mayflies and the rising fish, all living without pretense. Finally,

I experienced a show more worthy of my attention. I watched the winged adults emerge, transformed into creatures that can no longer feed on the former things of this world. The mayflies, took to the wind, leaving behind the stage, hoping only to perpetuate life.

Battling the Champion: Stepping Back in Time

As I sensed my true need, I emerged in praise to the Creator of angels, fish, and the earth. I observed the mayflies, struggling to break free of the surface and move into the world of light. As I watched, I was almost envious. Here I was, attached to this stone-bottomed river. I was cold, tired, and sore. However, I identified with those mayflies. They were a tiny reflection of the greater story, which I was only beginning to recognize. They brought joy and passion deep into my soul.

Just as God's laws are written on my heart, so is my true spiritual predicament.

> "… what may be known about God is plain to them, because God has made it plain to them." —Romans 1:19

What became evident on this morning is that deep down in my heart, I was aware that without God, I was utterly alone, in despair.

Within my soul, I became aware of my desperation, my compromising poses, and the frightening abyss all around me. The angel confirmed that I needed this deep awareness of my human condition. I was poor, blind, and naked before God—and yet I had no idea of my true need (Revelation 3:17). It seemed that God allows, perhaps even creates, the void in me; only He can fill this void and transform me. There is no other way. I realized I must start on the other end of joy. I must embrace the pain, alienation, and meaningless of the void to understand how I do not belong. Jesus blessed those "who mourn" and are "poor in spirit"(Matthew 5:3-4). Only then, can God fill my void and lead me home.

With my new-found clarity, I gazed into a pool and cast to the champion of the river— a deep bodied ten-pound-plus rainbow. Barely visible, the fish took the fly, a tiny-sized 24-blue winged olive parachute, and here I was, participating in a sacred connection once again. The pulsations of Something beautiful, heavy, and pure overwhelmed me. The fish possessed a peculiar purity in its indifference to me; it wanted nothing from me; except to escape my presence. It shook its head, trying to free the hook. It was I who had the complex desire to unite with this fish, with everything around me, and with the precarious act of taking in the line, shortening the distance between the fish and me—all with the hope of eventually holding the fish in my hands.

I was like a child again, desiring to land this trophy fish, stake my claim, and perhaps even take a photo of it. Yet there was more. There was the familiar longing to possess the fish, to become a part of its world and the beauty that is all around me. In this longing there was the hope that this other world, which I had just entered, would not shut me out. Once again, I found myself standing on the edge of this beauty, the connection sustained and maintained in a delicate balance by the tension held in a 3-pound test leader. What a precarious position I was in; connected to the earth, the creation itself, the incarnations of God, the bugs, and the fish. I stood there with feet firmly planted on the bottom of the river, holding my ground, yet aware the real battle was yet to begin. I recognized this fish as an overwhelming challenge. It was already bending the rod and straining the leader to a breaking point, which reminded me of a battle long ago. I surfaced from memories and dreams as clear as the pools I fish, from a time long before I knew this river. I found myself making slight changes in my body, maneuvering myself for a better angle on the surging fish by slightly adjusting the direction and angle of the rod. As I jockeyed for position, ready for a series of explosive surges from the fish, I clearly remembered a similar sequence from long ago. I remembered a quiet place of struggle and tension and a great hope of connection.

The fish countered the pressure of the rod by plunging deep to the bottom, then shuddering its massive head as it tried to shake the hook free. Then, just as quickly it changed strategy and leaped out of the water, displaying its massive size. Complex instincts took over as I countered and the fish countered in a rapid exchange of moves that I clearly remembered from another time. I found myself reliving Something.

My body was now older than it was then. I felt the aches and groans, even deep in my soul, as I tried to maneuver around boulders and push through swirling currents in pursuit of the fish. As I moved, I realized it had been forty years since I made that one, powerful, sweeping wrestling move late in the biggest wrestling match of my life. That's what I was reliving. As I thought back, I emerged then in thankfulness for the sheer beauty and terror of both the most significant event in my athletic career and wrestling this rainbow. The fish catapulted its muscular body out of the water while, miraculously, the hook held to the corner of its jaw.

Entering Deep Silent Pools

As I battled the fish, memories of other times spent in darkness came back to me. I used to run alone at night. I worked with my weights in poorly lit basements. I tied my flies in shadowed corners. I walked in darkness on the path to the pond. I cast thousands of time in lonely dark canyons.

From the beginning, the angel approved of my repeated retreats from the world of noise and bright lights to experience the purity of silent pools. I remembered how as a child I stood at the edge of the pond, gazing within and allowing that pond to become a vast inner pool and a refuge. It prepared me to understand God's call; often I needed to enter a place of pause, silence, and depth, free from the restraints, motives and demands of society and even of important people in my life. The retreats I took into nature allowed my inner world to grow and stay with me, even in the midst of crowds. I learned how to drink from the waters of my inner pool, even when I found myself trapped in the constructs of society. In my imagination I can go to the quiet place along the water's edge, where I can observe images of God's faithfulness.

Here I was, rising again from a deep pool onto the higher ground of the bank, my rod held high, lifting slack out of the line, still in pursuit of a leviathan. It was a sacred moment. Inconsolable tears shed off me and ran down my waders. The angel had confirmed that the times I spent living in sadness were holy obedience to a pursuit of real rather than superficial happiness. The angel confirmed that the path to deep joy goes through deep sorrow. "Blessed are you who weep now" (Luke 6:21). I *have* discovered joy in the pain of the waiting. I have begun to emerge by surrendering to the pain and sadness of life.

The angel confirmed the familiar path *we* once walked to the pond, a path that has merged with the meandering Dream Stream in the vast meadow of South Park. I have realized that I still walk that path, by choice, and that I am not alone. With the mayflies all around me, covering the water, transforming, emerging, and flying off like little angels, how could I be alone?

In a great paradox, I often still feel God's absence and still cry out, "God where are you? Who are you? Are you here?" I have accepted that I do not know God or nature as well as I would like. I may not even know the blue-winged olive mayflies. Yet God and nature know me and remember me; therefore, I feel I am not alone.

Yes, the world could forget me or consider me lost. Yet, who, other than God, knew how secure I was gazing into my own inner pool and the true life that was set before me. I was protected by angels wooing, guarding, leading, and enclosing me within the sacred womb of the forest; a forest of no shame, allowing me to freely choose. How could I view myself with shame or disgrace, when God enclosed my soul and "leads me beside quiet waters" (Psalm 23).

I emerged at last, knowing God stands by the spiritual aliens of the world "Do not oppress the widow or the fatherless, the foreigner or the poor." (Zechariah 7:10). I came to believe that to be a sojourner, a resident alien, a stranger on this Earth, and to never quite belong, is my highest honor. I have learned to seek my place among the fish in natural landscapes and receive glimpses, tugs, and touches of divinity. I have learned to wander and slowly settle my feet into the bottom of the river. When I cast to the elusive forms, sometimes I am able to hold the fish in my hands. However, I have also come to understand and accept that I can never quite *hold* what upholds me and what I seek.

The angel, who walked with me to the pond, confirmed my place, reminding me of this position of honor. How could I ask for a more pure and honorable escort, standing with me, willing to defend me, whispering so tenderly? The breath of God moves out over the world whispering over landscapes, then pauses gently to breathe tenderly over my inconsolable heart. I feel God's breath.

I have also learned that I cannot judge those who did not follow me to the pond (or any path), because, perhaps, it was I who did not allow them to follow. In my selfishness, I may have wanted whatever I was able to sense was at the end of the trail to myself. Or perhaps, I thought it was too troublesome to try to explain all that I was feeling, and received, even in part. And besides, how many people could walk the same path before there is a crowd and then an unconscious mob.

However, I hope I can now share whatever was given to me at the pond, along the meanders of life, and within the enclosed inner forest of my heart. I emerged from the forest knowing that whatever of God came to me at the pond, perhaps mysteries uttered from the foundations of the world, it was and is out of the sheer love and grace of God, available to all.

Yes, God affirmed my choice, but my choice was never quite my own. How could I ignore an angelic escort into Eden? I had no place else to go. The angel and God within me, joining at last, are now allowing me to sing out in jubilation and praise for the path we once walked. I am, once again, beginning to believe.

Violent Insights

The angel confirmed on the way to and at the pond the passionate insights that formed in my heart. They were too heavy for a child to carry. Now that I am older, I can bear them. These insights found a way to merge into my being, even without my full consent. They have become a part of me.

Throughout my life and my meandering along the river, new insights formed. The angel confirmed my struggle to treasure these insights, even as I would often fail to understand and value what was growing inside me. I slowly learned that those insights themselves— along with the person I had become—could not find a comfortable place in this world.

The angel confirmed my struggle to share the insights with those around me. It was hard. How could I share revelations that were like the pure, snowmelt flowing from the mountains? They could only be compromised, diluted, polluted, countered, rationalized, and exploited—by me and by the many people who could not understand. These insights barely survived just below the surface of my heart. Even now, I can barely explain or even begin to understand what the angel revealed to me at the pond, within the forest, or on a meadow stream. The whispers can be misinterpreted, deconstructed, and muted by those who could not believe. Nevertheless, the question remains: Can I now believe? Can I choose to emerge in faith, remember what I heard, and share in love?

When Jesus spoke violent truths about his own life and the cost of following him, his own disciples could not accept it. They tried to interpret his life in terms of personal interests and the ways of the world. When Jesus announced that he must suffer many things, be rejected by the elders, and be killed (Luke 9:22), Peter protested. Like Peter, I am not very good at handling violent truths and the numerous "deaths" I have to face. I have tried to gloss over these truths and balance them with interpretations and negotiations, until there was nothing of purity left to hear or see. All that remained was my own selfish agenda.

> "You are a stumbling block to me; you do not have
> in mind the concerns of God, but merely human
> concerns."—Matthew 16:2)

Perhaps it sounds strange for me to say that deep spiritual insights can be violent. This is a harsh truth all its own. Some spiritual insights have shaken the very foundations of my cultural and religious identity. While these insights may have had no dwelling place in the world system, I was able to bring them into my own vision. I made a place for them on the edge of my heart and the edge of the wild places. These are places where I can hold them for whoever will meet me. I can ask others to observe what I have captured. What I have to offer is sometimes no more than that elusive fish who gets away. I seem to have nothing in my hands. I have only held out my arms and said, "It was this big." But this nothing is really Something, a mystery of incredible vastness. In that space of nothing, living streams and vast meadows, I have been able to grow my own soul. Perhaps you can too.

Met by Grace

I emerged at last, knowing the blessedness of my awkward and clumsy attempts at belonging. I was able to come forward, knowing I was among the broken, the poor in spirit, and those who mourn. I was one who casts his flies out of tune, without poetry, while often ignoring God's handiwork, the *Poiema*, the true poem of who I am and what is written in my heart (Ephesians 2:10). I was still without a "home," but I felt even more blessed because of that truth. Do I possess more by coming to God in endless poverty rather than via a self-professed religion and a superficial identity.

I finally understood the blessing of not catching every fish I saw and cast to. Jesus took only a few fish and fed the multitudes. I had to understand that his "food" was different from the fish I was seeking. I had to learn that where I was lacking, God could provide. I saw clearly that my clients would not catch all the fish they hoped for. There is not enough fish in the world to satisfy our hunger, certainly not in the rivers of Colorado where fish populations always seem to be in jeopardy.

I emerged at last, praising the fish that escape my grasp, a grasp that most often clutches too tightly. The angel praised all the times I secretly hoped for a fish to escape. How could I not desire to witness the fish swim free and find its way back to its place of belonging. I longed for the same thing.

However, as enlightened (or delusional) as I came to be, I found myself wanting to land this particular massive fish with an intensity I have not felt since I was a child. I wondered why this desire was different. How had I changed over the decades? Had I matured—or was I reverting to my childhood when landing a fish defined my existence? To be honest, I felt a bit foolish and childish facing the old fear that I would come so close to landing this fish, only to lose it just beyond my grasp.

I thought back to my wrestling days and remembered how critical the last seconds of a match could be. If I had lost the state championship in the last split second, my life might have been completely different.

I instinctively continued to face the fish, moving cautiously forward, wary of a sudden move. I was adhering to an old habit carried over from my wrestling days. Countless competitions played in my head:

"There can be no mistakes."

"Be careful."

"Stay alert!"

"Alert, alert, alert! "

I lifted the rod and carefully tracked the fish by following where the leader entered the surface current. I saw boils of water rise from the propulsions made of the fish's muscular body. I was alert with a focus that had become an instinct, a state of mind acquired from years of competition and decades of fishing. I felt the tension of a fish of great weight. I worried that I'd have to carry the weight of disappointment, half-expecting the fish to throw the hook in the last moments.

The fish surged again. I responded by moving down river, trying to bridge the gap between the fish and myself.

As I battled, I sang out in thankfulness to the angel, who urged me as a child to release the fish I caught at the pond. This is the angel, who without my awareness, very gently placed his hands upon mine and loosened the grip of my small hands upon the fish. I was able, in joy, to watch the fish swim free. Sometimes, as an adult, I am able to let go of the tenacious grip I place on life, the expectations I place upon others; even God.

In this moment, I could sense the angel urging me to let go of my clutch on life. I realized I was not in control and let go of the reel handle, allowing the gigantic fish to run and have its way to the far bank. I continued to move with the fish and seemingly into life itself, remembering the words: "Whoever finds their life will lose it, and whoever loses their life for my sake will find it" (Matthew 10:39).

I stand in the tension, uncertain of how this story would end. I tried to maintain contact without clutch. I held my ground in a delicate balance. I flowed into a familiar give and take. It was Something I recognized from the wrestling match of long ago.

Sometimes the fish escapes. Sometime my clients and I are disappointed. That's the way it is. I had to learn to let go of not only of all losses but of my self-perceived and self-declared failures, along with my grandiose expectations. I had to let go of the delusion that I can always be successful as a guide, teacher, counselor, husband, father, and friend. Sometimes I choose the wrong fly, the wrong hole to fish, or the wrong technique to use. Sometimes I fail to love. But I must let go of this perception. I must let it flow on down the river. In this battle, I accepted that this monster fish might break free and enter the flow of the river. Someday, I thought, I myself might be able to break free, enter that infinite flow, and lose who I think I am.

In spite of my short comings, I have been able to recognize

that Grace has often met me (and meets me even now). While guiding a client, I was sometimes surprised by Grace. More than once, a client and I have turned away from the river after a day of failure, only to find a fish on the line, tugging and seemingly asking for our attention. At times, I have sensed that a client has received more from the experience than I could ever know, even far more than the fish caught in the net. I still clearly remember that wrestling match, I have never been able to explain how I ended up perfectly shooting under my opponent and locking him in an embrace that I knew I would not release. I was merely flowing with the greater river of life.

Meeting Grace in the flow of life is far more wonderful than whatever I could achieve on my own. Those moments remain with me. The great fish continued to pull out line and became more and more frantic, still displaying no signs of fatigue. As I battled this fish, I slipped on the river bottom, which delayed my ability to reposition myself and rod. Too late; the slip allowed the fish to run deep along the backside of a submerged boulder; the leader caught on the bottom corner of the boulder. I was afraid it would cut through the tippet, but then, just as quickly the fish changed direction again, a mistake on its part (or was this destiny?). The leader cleared, and I was free of the boulder, straight and tight to the fish.

I became faintly aware of the times when I somehow eluded a mishap. Sometimes, as was the case in my wrestling match, the outcome changed the direction of my life. I realized there was a fine line between what we call "success" and "failure." There is seldom a rational explanation for how I avoided a particular downfall.

Emerging in Love

At last, I was standing alone in the river. I was one with the flow of the river, understanding that not every relationship would result in transformation, neither for myself nor for those fishing along-side me. At times, I had failed to love. Simple as that. I was weighed down by my own lack of faith. I was unable to live in the transform-ing love of God. However, I *was* able to drop my persistent disillu-sionment in others. I came into the light of knowing that loneliness and disconnection were not *their* fault, nor were they mine. For a brief moment, I basked in the freedom of not blaming anyone, not even myself. In that moment, I was able to move upward, reaching out into a broad sky—expanding in love.

The angel conveyed to me that the walls I erect around my-self had to be in place when I was younger but do need to be there now. This too is part of my story. Perhaps it is the story of all of us. Even though I was inside those walls, I hoped for an inner blooming. While fishing with others, I often felt Something shared with them. Something in each one of our hearts rose up. Something would move among us without our knowing; Something would appear, vanish, move toward the other, and perhaps be taken in. Together, we blos-somed in love and grace while we cast to rising fish in a vast meadow that forever expands or in a canyon that never ends.

The angel approved of those times when I threw common sense away and walked where I normally would not. Sometimes I was willing to be lost to the river, trying to love someone I had judged as unworthy. There were times when someone fell in the river and I lunged to catch them. We were at the mercy of the river, perhaps only saved by Grace.

The angel affirmed the value of the stranger on the far bank of the river, even if that stranger was completely different from me or only wanted to fish my hole. I had to learn that I never knew in ad-vance who a person really was or what that person could give to me or others. While helping someone who had fallen in the river, I also had to fall, along with the dying mayflies and other fallen men and women, never knowing if we would rise again. On that morning I pursued my giant fish into a deep meander, a hole I knew all too well. I threw common sense away and took the plunge, trying to tippy toe along the bottom, cold water spilling over my waders. My attempt to stay with the fish was an act of pure and utter foolishness. The hole deepened until I entered a quiet flow. All was calm. Once again, this did not seem to be a choice on my part. Nor did I feel in danger. I was simply surrendering to a flow outside me—yet within me. Still in the flow of this tiny act of faith, I pulled myself up again, emerged from the hole, and stepped up onto the bank. I was drenched but still in pursuit of the fish downriver.

Life Is Not About Me

One of my violent insights is that life is not about me. Even my own life is not about me. My book is not about me, even though I have written extensively about my life. When I fell, someone rose to pick me up. When someone else fell, I was able—sometimes—to rise to the occasion and help them up. Sometimes I lost a fish, only to see someone else catch it. A mayfly trapped on the surface draws the attention of feeding trout. In its life and death, it allows other mayflies to emerge safely. One hooked fish scares other fish to hide in an undercut bank and avoid capture. Some of the tiny mayflies escaped hungry trout, thanks to my sloppy casts that frightened fish away; without my knowing, those sloppy casts extended the life of both fish and mayflies. One man's glory can be another's pain. One man's painful death can be the glory of creation and rebirth. Mayflies lay their eggs in the river, then die, having given life to the next generation. Fish escape my grasp and run up the river to spawn. It's all part of a bigger story, which I often miss and wind up outside. Fly-fishing allows me the chance to stand on the firm Earth, and cast inside that bigger story. As I contemplate the bigger story of my life, and remain connected to the large downward plunging fish, I more clearly see the stranger across the river and let him enter my life.

Divine Reflections on the River

I emerged at last with the clear insight that the places I have fished reflect the divine story. However, I began to understand the bigger story only when I engaged with the concrete world that lies before me and under my feet. Therefore, I pressed on, trying to become the larger story by meandering along rivers and casting for fish. The habitus of fly-fishing has always offered me a way to become intimate with the natural world. It is fly-fishing that enables me to consider the lily, the bugs of the air, and the stranger across the river. As I follow the serpentine river and its flowing waters, I have a better chance to match the natural world with my inner landscape—and God's own eternal and invisible attributes. It makes sense to first understand the visible, earthly things before spiritual things (John 3: 12). When I emerged, I realized that asking the earth to teach me (Job 12:8), with the expectation that God will speak through the creation, is a spiritual practice. For example, if a fish waited for me to notice it, and I caught and released it, I thought the spirit of creation had been urging me to return the fish to its watery home. On the other hand, if the fish refused to take my fly, the Creator might be trying to teach me about my own insignificance within the creation.

In some ways, I was better at this as a child. In the Eden of my youth, the fish seemed to speak to me—and perhaps I tried to speak to them. Even now, I wish I could feel that childlike delight of catching a fish and then letting it swim out of my hands back into the silent pond. That act of granting freedom sustained life for both the fish and Something inside my soul. In that fateful evening, the giant rainbow finally tired. Yet even in its fatigue, its contortions expelled large volumes of water to the surface in swirling wakes. My rod continued to bend over as I walked with the fish, my long handled net drawn. I still could not drag her against the current to a place close enough to my net. I moved toward the fish, but the river pushed the fish away. She made her last, lazy surges downstream. I was in a stalemate with the fish, neither able to move her nor able to approach her with my net. I was unable to enclose what I desired. Did I dare to put more pressure on the fish and frayed leader?

During this stalemate, in this pause, the stranger spoke from across the river, "Do you need help?" He pulled out his own long-handled net and walked toward me.

"Yes, please." I accepted, aware that I typically refuse such help.

He skillfully slipped his net under the massive fish, careful to keep the net in the water so the fish could still breathe. We shook hands. I looked in his eyes, failing to recognize him as someone I might know. Still, we shared Something, although there were no words to describe or name our connection. Perhaps we only shared the river with the large fish that inhabits its waters.

We admired the fish before I released it and watched her swim back to her place among the rocks and currents. In that moment, I definitely felt Something—a fish and a man of flesh and blood, together with me on a river we call the Dream Stream.

I watched the stranger walk away, downriver.

The Invisible Incarnated

The invisible angel confirmed to me that I was to find my path and my habitus in this visible, incarnated world of rock canyons, leaping fish, flowing waters, blooming meadows, swarming bugs, and strangers (who can sometimes be angels). The assenting angel confirmed that as I walked the path to the pond, each step touched the firm earth and perhaps left a slight depression. At other times, my hurried steps pushed away dirt to a place it had not been before. I might have been too eager to make my first casts in the morning light. However, I can tell you that no angel carried me, and some of this dirt disturbed by my footprints surely remains.

I confirm that the groundskeeper, the guardian of the pond, who forty-five years ago gave permission to me, a mere boy, to fish, was a real man whom I could hear and see. He had a life, with heartache and joys I knew nothing about. His exterior was frightening, and he yelled across the pond, but I could understand his words. In the end, he and I made a bargain. He granted me access to a sacred place where I could fish, and I agreed to honor this place. That bargain changed my life in this real world, and perhaps bound me to things in the world to come.

I confirm that the strangers I often see across the river are flesh and blood. At times, we approach each other and shake hands. I can feel life and warmth in their hands. I sometimes might drop one of my tiny flies in the palm of the stranger's hands. I might notice cracks and wrinkles, the marks of a life spent fly-fishing on this Earth. My clients are flesh-and-blood real people. While guiding and teaching someone to cast, I might place my hand over a client's casting hand and feel his or her arm movements, most often out of tune with my own as I try to have this client feel the cadence of the casting motion. With a little practice, we together can feel the expanding loops reaching across the river to real, feeding, pulsating, leaping fish. I have felt those connections to both fish and people in this world.

Sometimes these casts, without my awareness, have gone out

like prayers into a realm that I did not know but that allowed me to
see myself and others differently. In this other place, I sometimes
saw another boy at the pond, a boy who is now a man. I sometimes
have the sense that I am emerging into my true identity and place
of belonging. Sometimes, too, I glimpsed a loved one who was fully
alive, complete, and not worn down by the struggle of living outside
of Eden.

I have emerged with the understanding that I must begin,
and perhaps end, with physical casts to the fish that I can, at least
sometimes, feel in my hands. I have emerged feeling both sadness
and joy, trickling over wounds of having lived most of the time in
exile. Today I am in Eden, but at the same time I have not quite
arrived. I still long for what eludes me. However, I know that it is
a blessing to spot living fish in living waters or to grasp the hand of
another while gazing into another realm and longing for a kingdom
yet to come.

Turning Within

Finally, I understood that I was among those who possess
a sensitivity to the cycles of the earth and have been able to experience God revealing Himself through nature. Every spring, I feel
emboldened to walk farther up river, into the widening meadows or
narrowing canyons, in search of the headwaters. There is something
about this that takes me back to looking for the source of the little
creek that fed the pond I fished as a child. In the late fall, I feel a
turning within, a slowing down that corresponds to the decreased
flows in the river and the waning hunger of the fish. In this season
of slowing down is when I feel my inner cadence most in tune to the
Creator.

As I move from fall into the quiet of winter, I have the sense that being in touch with the earth is a blessed path. Winter is a sacred place, allowing me time to slip away from society, if even for a few moments, into the quiet. I move inward in sync with the earth and with all creation itself, gathering whatever intuition God might allow me to experience. Through winter, the fish also turn inward and rest, barely stirring on the bottom of the deep pools of the meandering river. The internal rhythms of fish slow down. They eat less, in harmony with the diminishing cycles of insect hatches. I hear the whir of dragonflies less often and then not at all. The tricos and blue-winged olive mayflies cease to shimmer in the morning light. I myself slowly slip away and flow into deep inner pools in the quiet of God.

I understand now that being in tune with the mysterious Earth, which God made for his purposes and glory, is a blessing beyond belief. Those who wish only to be happy, defined as being well connected to the best clubs of the world, will find it difficult to enter my world. My response can only be that it is a holy act of obedience to move slowly into the sacred place and season of winter. Doing so, however slowly, enables me to experience the glorious emergence into the new season of spring. How magnificent it is to emerge again with the mayflies and the fish in the meandering river who respond to them.

Having emerged at last, I know how difficult it is to share these insights with you. It is not easy to see these divine reflections just as it is often difficult to see a large trout hiding among boulders in a deep run. Such intuitions have their place within the heart of God, the earth, and the deep places of my soul. I must speak of them. I must write. I must try. I must bear witness to the wonders I have experienced.

Having emerged at last, I am still a fly-fisher. I best understand such divine insights by casting a fly and hooking a pulsing, leaping fish. This is my task, role, and life. However, I retain the hope that I might occasionally bring to the net more than a fish.

Not Just a Season in Time

I spent long periods of time experiencing disconnection from fish and people. I emerged from this dark place knowing that those periods of disconnection were of great spiritual significance, more than the mere passing of a season. Rilke explains that such periods amount to more than "one season in our inner year."

I emerged from darkness knowing that I often filled the sacred void inside of my soul with distractions, rationalizations, consolations—some borrowed from religion. I had to learn that only God can fill this sacred void and grant me true belonging. Sometimes, I thought I was successful in alleviating my pain, but in the end I only separated myself from my own soul.

It was difficult to come to God with inner poverty instead of so-called accomplishments. It took some courage. It took brutal honesty to admit that my feelings of not belonging were not simply a matter of getting caught between seasons. I was not stuck briefly in a valley. It was more than that, Something beyond time itself. Rilke said that pain is "our place and settlement, foundation and soil and home." For me, certainly, these periods of darkness were where I lived. It was comforting to realize that these times—and places—are the very foundation of life, God's life and my life. My pain is deepest in my soul, within the heart of God.

I learned not to waste my hours of pain but to make the most of them. I can grow and transform if I do not waste my hours of pain, instead allowing those hours to fuel my inner growth. I found that by acknowledging my alienated condition, the pain would no longer fester inside of me. The disconnection I felt would be transformed by my own heart and soul. Then I could find my true place. In so doing, I entered the reality of the true human spiritual condition and no longer posed among others as if on a stage. I entered a holy and quiet place, finding my true identity hidden in God. In that holy place of beauty and pain, I began to see with great clarity, perhaps even glimpsing Something of the depths of the heart of God.

The Pain and Joy of Life

Having emerged at last, I now understand that embracing the disconnection and the suffering that is part of life is the only way to fully live. Suffering and death are unavoidable. Without pain and death, I can have no true joy. To live in the passion of Christ is to embrace my own suffering, pain, sadness, and alienation. This is a difficult path for me to follow.

The angel confirmed that the path of Jesus, which was love, could only occur in the midst of hate and misunderstanding. As he walked through the ridicule, mockery, interrogation, and the judgment of others, he continued teaching, ministering, and loving. Sometimes, he had to disappear from their midst (Luke 4:30, John 8:59), only to emerge again. As a fly fisher, I too disappear. I retreat to a river, only to revive and emerge again with a new vitality and sense of belonging.

When Jesus spoke the truth, he was accused not of having an angel but a demon. However, during his trial in the wilderness (Matthew 4:11) and his torment in the garden, he was alone and abandoned—until angels came to comfort him (Luke 22:43). When his own community exasperated him, he went alone to the wilderness and the mountain. As a fly fisher, it is typical for me to spend time alone and pray in my own manner. I may climb a mountain, walk a meadow, or follow a river. Then I can listen to the angel. Others

may pray and fast, in the public square, which is their reward in full
(Matthew 6:5).

Having emerged at last, I understand that the world could
not accept the One who loves so freely and completely. I understand
fully well that the crowds eventually concluded that Jesus would not
give them the new social order they demanded, so they abandoned
him. They hung him on a tree. Yet, he too has emerged again. I can
emerge with him—at least sometimes. Then I can sing out in thankfulness and praise.

Having finally emerged, I understand that I must participate
in his suffering and sense of not belonging to this world system in
order to experience the power and joy of my own resurrection and
rebirth on Earth.

> "I want to know Christ—yes, to know the power of
> his resurrection and participation in his sufferings,
> becoming like him in his death ..." —Philippians 3:10

The power of joy comes from my "participation in his suf-
ferings," which frees me from this world system and enables me to
enter the kingdom of light. A path that avoids the pain and suffering of Christ avoids life itself. It is a form of petrified religion, still
entombed; crusty like the dried out and lifeless, nymphal shucks of
the mayflies. I carry an image of myself as a small, insignificant child,
walking to a pond alone and teaching himself to fly-fish. The pain
and the joy captured in this image work together. Joy fills my soul
and enlarges my heart, when I see myself fly-fishing on the banks
of the pond and catching the occasional fish while I wonder why
I do not quite belong to the culture around me. Nevertheless, as I
remember this picture, I have to ask myself again. What is my pain?
Am I alone, and if so, why?

Perhaps, beyond and within the image of a child, an angel emerges.

Angels Overhead

I have had glimpses of Eden. I know it exists, even now, even here. In this, I am like the ugly duckling looking up at the strange but beautiful swans flying overhead. I hear them calling down to me in voice familiar and so tender that it breaks my heart and, at the same time, fills me with hope. The possibility of truly belonging to Something causes me to be beside myself, filled with uncontrollable hope. I think of Jesus, ridiculed, lost, wandering, trying to find his voice and place in a world that would not have him.

Having emerged at last, I can sing out in jubilation and praise. The angels—and the mayflies—remind me that there is bigger life around me. I can emerge at last, with the creation, and sing out in jubilation and praise to assenting angels. Life is bigger than my pains, my joys, my own existence, and certainly my struggle to find my place in the world. Ironically, my lack of belonging in the world *is* my belonging; in the pain of not belonging, I find my place.

I am among those wandering orphans, aliens, and strangers of the earth who finally emerge in nakedness and without shame. Like the mayflies, I can shed the shuck that weighs me down. I emerged and cried out, aching for my "true adoption as sons and daughters" (Romans 8:23). Today my soul surrounds me, comforts me, contains me, and gently caresses me, like the surrounding forest wrapped around me as a child at the pond.

I do not accept the pain of my alienation as a passing phase in life. I do not look ahead to the end because the pain of alienation is, as Rilke says, so much more.

If pain is not only a season that will pass, then what else

could it be? "Not only" implies that there is something else. There is, but it is both beyond this world and a part of this world. By refusing to waste my hours of painful alienation, I gain far more than endurance. The pain of my alienation is *more than* a season in time and more than character development. The pain of not belonging gets transformed into a peculiar sense of belonging. In this realm of living on Earth, the pain of my alienation is a permanent condition. It is who I am. At the same time, I emerged from the pain of my alienation in a way that transcends time and life itself.

Transcending Time

My heart and the angel confirmed that the pain of alienation transcends time and life itself by becoming inside of me the very things I long for—Eden and home. When I experience everyday pain, I am fond of saying, "This too shall not pass." However, the aching in my soul for a home is quite different. This pain is a spiritual paradox. This pain does not end, but it is not permanent; it is both and neither in a process that transcends time, death, and life itself. My feeling of disconnection somehow has become the place where I connect with God, the place I can call home.

When I was a child, I walked the solitary trail to the pond. I stepped into "another place." In a strange paradox, the pain of being alone transformed me to a person who could connect to the natural world and find a type of Eden. Every moment of loneliness gets integrated into my soul and brings me closer to home. It still works that way. Every ache and moan in my spirit reminds me that I belong somewhere else. That place lies both here and beyond, at the same time and beyond time.

I have choices. I can choose to forget. I can ignore the angel who comes to me in the night and reminds me to remember my true place. On the other hand, I can choose to share my own story with you. I can choose to embrace the child who remembers and who, as an adult, refuses to ignore, to forget, or to be easily consoled. I have emerged again and again with assenting angels. I remember both the pain and the comfort of God within my heart that has grown inside me.

The Path to Eden

My path to the world beyond lies on the earth, particularly on the banks of the rivers I fish. It is in my midst and yet beyond. It is in my heart and all around me as I make connections, be they on purpose or by accident. I live in a world of both alienation and connection. It is a glimpse of Eden. The path to Eden can be lonely, dark, and confusing with many twisting turns. However, this path leads to life and true connection with others who understand loneliness.

Saint John of the Cross spoke of finding his own secret ladder or hidden path to God that defied the conventions and the so-called lights of his culture.

For me, and perhaps for others who fly-fish, the secret path follows the river from high in the mountains, down to the vast green meadows. Here the river meanders. And here lies, for me and some of my fellow fly fishers, the edge of Eden.

At last Eden is my home, even if it is off in the distance and unexplored meanders remain with Something lingering on the far bank.

If you would like to discuss any of the issues
presented in this book, contact me at
Suragea1@aol.com

Made in the USA
Middletown, DE
14 October 2023

40532615R00159